Feminism an   D1634786

VERSITY
COLLEGE

Gender and Psychology
Feminist and Critical Perspectives
Series editor: Sue Wilkinson

This international series provides a forum for research focused on gender issues in – and beyond – psychology, with a particular emphasis on feminist and critical analyses. It encourages contributions which explore psychological topics where gender is central; which critically interrogate psychology as a discipline and as a professional base; and which develop feminist interventions in theory and practice. The series objective is to present innovative research on gender in the context of the broader implications for developing both critical psychology and feminism.

Sue Wilkinson teaches social psychology and women's studies at Loughborough University. She is also Editor of *Feminism & Psychology: An International Journal*.

Also in this series

Subjectivity and Method in Psychology
Wendy Hollway

Feminists and Psychological Practice
edited by Erica Burman

Feminist Groupwork
Sandra Butler and Claire Wintram

Motherhood: Meanings, Practices and Ideologies
edited by Ann Phoenix, Anne Woollett and Eva Lloyd

Emotion and Gender: Constructing Meaning from Memory
June Crawford, Susan Kippax, Jenny Onyx, Una Gault and Pam Benton

Women and AIDS: Psychological Perspectives
edited by Corinne Squire

Attitudes toward Rape: Feminist and Social Psychological Perspectives
Colleen A. Ward

Talking Difference: On Gender and Language
Mary Crawford

Feminism and Discourse

Psychological Perspectives

edited by
Sue Wilkinson
and
Celia Kitzinger

SAGE Publications
London · Thousand Oaks · New Delhi

Introduction, selection and editorial matter
© Sue Wilkinson and Celia Kitzinger 1995
Chapter 1 © Kathryn Matthews Lovering 1995
Chapter 2 © Celia Kitzinger and Alison Thomas 1995
Chapter 3 © Erica Burman 1995
Chapter 4 © Julie Hepworth and Christine Griffin 1995
Chapter 5 © Wendy Hollway 1995
Chapter 6 © Sue Widdicombe 1995
Chapter 7 © Margaret Wetherell 1995
Chapter 8 © Corinne Squire 1995
Chapter 9 © Rosalind Gill 1995

First published 1995

SAGE Publications Ltd
6 Bonhill Street
London EC2A 4PU

SAGE Publications Inc
2455 Teller Road
Thousand Oaks, California 91320

SAGE Publications India Pvt Ltd
32, M-Block Market
Greater Kailash – I
New Delhi 110 048

British Library Cataloguing in Publication data

A catalogue record for this book is available from
the British Library.

   ISBN 0–8039–7801–4
   ISBN 0–8039–7802–2 (pbk)

Library of Congress catalog card number 95–074610

Typeset by Type Study, Scarborough
Printed in Great Britain by Biddles Ltd, Guildford

Contents

Notes on the Contributors

Erica Burman teaches developmental and educational psychology, psychology of women and women's studies at the Manchester Metropolitan University. She is co-director of the Discourse Unit based in the Department of Psychology and Speech Pathology. Her publications include *Psychological Theory and Feminist Practice* (edited, Sage, 1990), *Discourse Analytic Research* (co-edited), *Deconstructing Developmental Psychology* (Routledge, 1994), *Qualitative Methods in Psychology* (co-authored, Open University Press, 1994), *Challenging Women: Psychology's Exclusions, Feminist Possibilities* (co-authored, Open University Press, 1995), and *Deconstructing Feminist Psychology* (edited, Sage, 1996).

Rosalind Gill is a lecturer in sociology at Goldsmiths College, University of London. She is editor (with Keith Grint) of *The Gender–Technology Relation: Contemporary Theory and Research* (Taylor & Francis), and author of *Gender and the Media* (Polity Press, forthcoming).

Christine Griffin lectures in social psychology at the University of Birmingham. Her research interests include the transition to adulthood, especially for young women; uses of qualitative methods in social psychology; and feminist perspectives on issues of gender and power. She is one of the founding members of the journal *Feminism & Psychology*, and is a member of the independent UK-based Alliance of Women in Psychology. Her main publications include *Typical Girls?* (Routledge & Kegan Paul, 1985) and *Representations of Youth* (Polity Press, 1993).

Julie Hepworth is a research associate at the Centre for Cultural Studies, University of South Australia, Adelaide. She completed her doctoral thesis on poststructuralism and eating disorders at the University of Birmingham, which she is currently preparing for publication as *The Discovery of Anorexia Nervosa: Discourses of Science, Medicine and the Body* in Sage's Inquiries in Social Construction series. Her research interests include postmodernism and psychology, qualitative methodology and public health, social representations of the body, the construction of medical discourse and psychopathology, and narrative therapy.

Wendy Hollway is a reader in gender relations in the Department of Applied Social Studies, University of Bradford. She has researched and published on questions to do with subjectivity, gender, sexuality, the history of work psychology and gender relations in organizations. Her published books are *Work Psychology and Organizational Behaviour* (1991), *Subjectivity and Method in Psychology* (1989) and *Changing the Subject*, with Henriques, Urwin, Venn and Walkerdine (1984).

Celia Kitzinger is director of women's studies at Loughborough University and the author of *The Social Construction of Lesbianism* (Sage, 1987) and *Changing Our Minds: Lesbian Feminism and Psychology* (with Rachel Perkins, New York University Press, 1993). Her edited books include *Heterosexuality: A 'Feminism & Psychology' Reader* (with Sue Wilkinson, Sage, 1993).

Kathryn Matthews Lovering is a senior lecturer in psychology and co-ordinator of the Women's Studies Programme at the University of Plymouth. Her current research interests are in the psychology and history of the female body and menstruation, especially in relation to adolescence. Having been a youth worker, teacher and educational psychologist, she completed her doctorate on 'Discourses of Menstruation: Girls, Menarche and Psychology' in 1994.

Corinne Squire is with the Women's Studies Program at Trenton State College, New Jersey. She researches and writes on HIV/AIDS and on popular culture. Her publications include *Women and AIDS: Psychological Perspectives* (edited, Sage, 1993) and *Morality USA: Representations of Morality in Contemporary Culture* (with Ellen Friedman, Minnesota University Press, 1996).

Alison Thomas is a senior lecturer in the Department of Applied Psycho-social Studies at the University of East London. Her research interests include gender and identity; gender relations and the social construction of sexual harassment; and she is currently engaged in a comparative study of the development and implementation of university sexual harassment policies in Canada and the UK. She is joint editor (with Celia Kitzinger) of *Sexual Harassment: Contemporary Feminist Perspectives* (Open University, 1996).

Margaret Wetherell is a senior lecturer in social sciences at the Open University. She is the author of *Discourse and Social Psychology* (with Jonathan Potter, Sage) and *Mapping the Language of Racism* (with Jonathan Potter, Harvester Wheatsheaf). Her main research interests lie in the development and application of theories and methods of discourse analysis to the fields of gender and 'race'. She is currently working (with Nigel Edley) on a project on the discourses of masculinity and has recently published a text reviewing the major theoretical perspectives in work on masculinity, *Men in Perspective* (with Nigel Edley, Harvester Wheatsheaf).

Sue Widdicombe is a lecturer in social psychology at the University of Edinburgh. Her research interests include the current debates surrounding the concept of self, identities and subjectivity; language; youth subcultures; and the relationship between culture and self, especially in Arab societies. She is author of *The Language of Youth Subcultures: Social Identity in Action* (with Robin Wooffitt, Harvester Wheatsheaf, 1995).

Sue Wilkinson teaches social psychology and women's studies at Loughborough University. She is founding – and current – editor of *Feminism & Psychology: An International Journal*, and her books include *Feminist Social Psychology* (Open University Press, 1986) and *Heterosexuality* (with Celia Kitzinger, Sage, 1993).

Introduction

Sue Wilkinson and Celia Kitzinger

The 'turn to language' is a defining feature of contemporary social science; and central to it is 'the emergence of a discourse framework' (Parker, 1992: xi). Discourse analysis has been described as 'a new wave of research sweeping across social psychology', and one which is currently 'almost synonymous with "critical" and in some cases "feminist" research' (Burman and Parker, 1993: 1, 9). Given the long history of feminist concern with language, from the nineteenth century on (see Cameron, 1990, for an excellent review; also the 'landmark' texts by, for example, Lakoff, 1975; Thorne and Henley, 1975; Spender, 1980; McConnell-Ginet et al. 1980; Kramarae and Treichler, 1985; and Cameron, 1985), it is perhaps not surprising that discourse analysis has become so popular among feminist psychologists (as witnessed, for example, by the numerous discourse analytic papers published in the international journal *Feminism & Psychology*, such as Burman, 1992; Gavey, 1992; Gilfoyle et al., 1992; Chesters, 1994; Crawford et al., 1994). What is surprising is the curious absence of any text dealing specifically with discourse analysis from a feminist psychological perspective.

Forms of discourse analytic work range widely, from the primarily linguistic (such as Stubbs, 1983), through conversation analysis and ethnomethodology (such as Atkinson and Heritage, 1984), to semiotic, psychoanalytic and poststructuralist/postmodernist variants (such as Henriques et al., 1984). Across these forms, however, non-feminist writing on discourse analysis routinely ignores the contribution made by feminists, while feminist writing on discourse analysis often excludes psychology altogether. So, for example, 'feminism' is not indexed in such key mainstream discourse analytic texts as Norman Fairclough's (1990) *Discourse Analysis*; Teun van Dijk's (1985) *Handbook of Discourse Analysis*; Deborah Schiffrin's (1994) *Approaches to Discourse*; Jonathan Potter and Margaret Wetherell's (1987) *Discourse and Social Psychology* or Derek Edwards and Jonathan Potter's (1992) *Discursive Psychology*. Even Ian Parker's (1992) *Discourse Dynamics* has only two references in the index to 'feminism and discourse analysis' (131, 140): these pages briefly mention the work of Walkerdine, Hollway, Squire, Gavey and Haraway as contributing to the development of poststructuralist discourse analysis – and that's all. Similarly, the omission of work by psychologists in interdisciplinary feminist work on discourse is apparent from volumes such as the *Discourse & Society* Special Issue on 'Women Speaking from Silence' (Houston and Kramarae, 1991) which includes contributions from researchers based in sociology, speech and communications studies, women's studies, English literature, linguistics, and adult education, but not one contributor who identifies herself as a psychologist; and the volume in the Advances in Discourse Processes series on *Gender and Discourse* (Todd and Fisher, 1988) which includes only one contribution from a psychologist (Kathy Davis). The omission of psychological perspectives in feminist discourse analytic writing is clear, too, when well-known feminist writers on – and popularizers of – discourse analysis, such as Deborah Tannen (1994), make virtually no reference to contributions from psychologists. There has been no attempt to pull together the diverse strands of feminist psychological discourse analytic research in a single collection; nor to consider in any sustained way the value of discourse analysis for the project of feminist psychology.

This book fills that gap, offering an edited collection of discourse analytic work which is specifically feminist in content – constituting both a 'showcase' for a major strand of contemporary feminist social psychology in Britain, and a critical evaluation of discourse analysis in relation to feminism. This book brings together, for the first time, a collection of original chapters by feminist psychologists exploring the contributions and contradictions of discourse analysis.

The first part of the book, entitled 'Empirical Work', consists of four chapters not primarily concerned with arguing the merits of a discourse analytic perspective, but which – on the whole – simply assume these as self-evident and get on with the work of 'doing' discourse analyses in a feminist context. These four chapters present discourse analytic work on key feminist issues of particular interest to feminist psychologists: adolescent knowledge about menstruation (Lovering, Chapter 1), sexual harassment (Kitzinger and Thomas, Chapter 2), gendered representations of childhood (Burman, Chapter 3), and anorexia nervosa (Hepworth and Griffin, Chapter 4). They include very different kinds of data, analysed at very different levels: data from group discussions with school children, textually analysed with the help of the computer program ETHNOGRAPH (Lovering); data from interviews with adult men and women, thematically analysed with reference to social context (Kitzinger and Thomas); and data based on broader socio-cultural representations, analysed by deconstructing the discursive imperialism of mainstream institutions, including film, advertising, and developmental psychology (Burman), and therapy, psychiatry, and medicine (Hepworth and Griffin).

It could be argued that it is the *topic* of these chapters that makes them feminist – they function primarily as illustrations of what can be *done* with discourse analysis, in contrast to other theoretical or methodological frameworks. They are united by their shared view of language as an interactive activity, mediating linguistic and socio-cultural knowledge, and constituting a site for the construction of identities and subjectivities – and they also see language as a key site for feminist resistance.

From a discourse analytic perspective, the language within which experience is framed is seen not simply as describing the social world, but also as, in some sense, constructing it. So, as Hepworth and Griffin (Chapter 4) and Kitzinger and Thomas (Chapter 2) show, respectively, 'anorexia' and 'sexual harassment' are, in part, created by the language that is used to describe them. Such phenomena do not have their origins inside the individual (indeed, the concept of 'the individual' is itself a product of Western discursive practices: Kitzinger, 1992), but, rather, they are constitutive of individuals as social products. In discourse analytic psychology, '[i]nstead of studying the mind as if it were outside language, we study the spoken and written texts . . . – the conversations, debates, discussions where images of the mind are reproduced and transformed' (Burman and Parker, 1993: 2).

In this way, the discursive location of the individual frames his/her 'personal' experience of self and subjectivity: 'What it means to be an individual person in the "modern" world involves taking on *as our own* the very discursive practices through which we are constituted' (Davies, 1990: 506, italics in original). So, Lovering's (Chapter 1) analysis of 'the transformation of the girl-child into the bleeding woman' rests centrally on the ways in which girls' subjectivity is shaped by the available discourses, practices and meanings surrounding menstruation. (The theorization of subjectivity is taken further by Hollway (Chapter 5), in the second part of the book.)

An attention to discourse facilitates a historical account of psychological (and other similarly hegemonic) knowledges, and mounts a critique of practice derived from such knowledges by challenging their truth claims. So, Burman (Chapter 3) shows how prevailing Western discourses of childhood (in both popular and psychological texts) are deeply gendered, while Hepworth and Griffin (Chapter 4) examine the discursive continuities and disjunctures between nineteenth-century texts about anorexia and feminist analyses over one hundred years later, and the inter-relationship of such discourses in interviews with British health care workers. Indeed, it has been argued that the current popularity of discourse analysis owes much to the ways its analytic tools can be used to inform political practice and struggles (Burman and Parker, 1993): the chapters in Part 1 *demonstrate* its utility in the pursuit of feminist goals (while chapters later in the book *debate* its utility for feminism).

In the first two chapters, the authors (Lovering; Kitzinger and Thomas) document moves from positivist agendas (exposing negative attitudes and ignorance about menstruation, and developing a 'watertight' definition of sexual harassment, respectively) to discourse analytic ones. However, the authors' subsequent analyses lead them to very different political ends. While Lovering is critical of existing sex education practices in schools, which pay little attention to the meanings of menstruation for young women, Kitzinger and Thomas regard the development of institutional policies on sexual harassment as largely futile. They argue, rather, that the assertion of one view of reality over another is a common technique employed by a dominant group in order to maintain its position of power – and that what is needed instead is a more sophisticated understanding of the ways in which sexual harassment is rendered insignificant or invisible (in other words, how it is discursively defined and managed).

The second part of the book, entitled 'Theoretical Advances', consists of five chapters which offer reflections upon the utility of discourse analysis (both as theory and as method) for feminists. The authors of three of these chapters (Hollway, Chapter 5; Wetherell, Chapter 7; Squire, Chapter 8) provide broadly favourable evaluations of discourse analysis; while the remaining two (Widdicombe, Chapter 6; Gill, Chapter 9) express serious reservations.

Key among the issues addressed by these chapters is the status afforded to the 'extra-discursive' – that is, material beyond the discourse analytic text, whether this is primarily characterized in terms of an 'exterior' world of social practices and their material effects, or in terms of an 'interior' world of subjectivity and intersubjectivity. While Wetherell (Chapter 7) worries about the extra-discursive, she clearly privileges the linguistic over the social or the psychological, arguing that '[h]ow social objects . . . are constituted in talk is pivotal to the nature of those objects. Talk about these things does not play a reflective or after-the-event role; it is the medium of the formation of social objects and social practices' (140). By contrast, Hollway (Chapter 5) assumes experience which is extra-discursive: the experience of egalitarian heterosex, for which feminist discourse offers no words (as do Kitzinger and Thomas, Chapter 2, in their discussion of 'unrecognized' sexual harassment).

Hollway argues that the dominance of discursive approaches in social science has led to 'a remarkable avoidance of the extra-discursive'. Further, she contends that 'a recognition of the fact that all understanding of the world is mediated through language has been falsely reduced to a premise that the world can be understood as discursive' (91). Hollway's remedy for this alleged reductionism is to add a psychodynamic dimension to the theorization of subjectivity.

A very different solution is advocated by Gill (Chapter 9), whose conception of the extra-discursive is located firmly in the social world. As part of her indictment of postmodernist discourse analysis as hopelessly relativistic, Gill identifies feminists' need for a vocabulary of value, 'without which we will be left theoretically and politically paralysed in the face of enduring inequalities, injustice and oppression' (165).

Contributors to Part 2 also seek to document the range of different forms of discourse analysis (see, for example, Squire, Chapter 8; Gill, Chapter 9), and sometimes to differentiate between them in terms of their particular advantages or disadvantages for the feminist project. So Gill argues, in relation to the rampant relativism of much postmodernist discourse analysis, that 'the way in which relativists theorize the relationships between politics, personal life and academic research is antithetical to feminism. They explicitly proscribe political commitments in their research . . .' (173). Widdicombe (Chapter 6) is also critical of poststructuralist/postmodernist discourse analysis: specifically of the way in which it is typically used *by feminists*. She takes issue with 'the analytic rush to identify discourses in order to get on to the more serious business of accounting for their political significance' (108), asserting that 'by elevating their own political agendas as the pre-established analytic frame [feminist] researchers may actually undermine the practical and political utility of the analyses they undertake' (111). For Widdicombe, the solution is to favour the 'unfashionable' ethnomethodological variety of discourse analysis, to focus on 'the mundane contexts of interaction [where] institutional power is exercised, social inequalities are experienced, and resistance accomplished' (111).

More generally, there is detailed consideration within these chapters of the implications of discourse analysis for developing feminist theory and politics. While there is, of course, no *necessary* coincidence between the interests of feminists and discourse analysts (as Squire points out in Chapter 8: 145), the potential for fruitful engagement is clear. Wetherell says: 'Together discourse analysis and feminism produce a radical and liberating scepticism' (Chapter 7: 135); while Gill's view is that 'discourse analysis has an enormous amount to offer feminists. It offers a principled and coherent means by which feminists can study talk and texts of all kinds – shedding light on old questions and provoking new ones. It has the potential to revitalise feminist studies of language . . .' (Chapter 9: 167). Squire presents the benefits of doing discourse analysis for feminist psychologists as (at least) threefold: as instrumentalist (it provides 'a respectable institutional front'); as pragmatic (it offers 'some help in answering questions about method and theory that block their work', together with a 'qualitative yet systematized method'); and as political (it offers 'hope for a radicalization of the discipline') (Chapter 8: 146–7). However, there is considerable debate as to whether there is a *necessary* connection between discourse analysis (as theory or method) and a critical politics (as Burman and Parker, 1993, and Parker, 1992, sometimes seem to suggest); and whether discourse analysis is necessarily of value for *feminist* political purposes.

There is a growing feminist literature (for example, Lovibond, 1992; Soper, 1990; Jackson, 1992; Wilkinson and Kitzinger, 1995; see also Gill, above) arguing that discourse analysis/postmodernism is antithetical to feminism; indeed, although using discourse analysis here in pursuit of feminist goals, Burman is elsewhere (1990; 1991; 1992) quite sceptical about its value for feminists. Many contributors to this volume remain optimistic, however: those who demonstrate discourse analysis in action in Part 1 and, in Part 2, Wetherell, who proposes 'a feminist politics of articulation' (141), and Squire, who exhorts feminist psychologists consistently to conjoin 'narratives of pragmatism' and 'narratives of extravagance' in their discourse analyses (146).

Gill (Chapter 9) is more equivocal. Although, as noted above, she sees great potential for the use of discourse analysis by feminists, she follows Burman (1992) in distinguishing between the *applications* of discourse analysis and the theory itself, and goes on to suggest that it is precisely those features of discourse analysis's *theoretical* commitments making it so productive for feminists, that also make it deeply problematic. The stress laid by discourse analysis on simple 'diversity' masks *power* differences; its notion of multiple, fragmented subject positions can lead to the denial of any single identity around which to organize; its emphasis on the micro-politics of power downplays macro-structural inequalities; and – most importantly – its commitment to relativism disavows the grounds for feminist politics. Ultimately, as a feminist, Gill rejects the postmodernist discourse analytic position on relativism as offering 'no principled alternative to realism by means of which we might make *political interventions*' (171, emphasis in original). She argues, instead for a type of 'passionately interested inquiry' (175);

'a relativism which is unashamedly political, in which we, as feminists, can make social transformation an explicit concern of our work' (182).

In sum, then, this volume highlights the uses of discourse analysis by feminist psychologists and illustrates its applications to a range of feminist topics (Part 1); it also provides a critical evaluation of the theory/method for the feminist project of intellectual, social and political change (Part 2). It is difficult to identify foundational premises or techniques which are specific to discourse analysis, not only because of the breadth and conceptual/methodological 'fuzziness' of the term, but also because of the common ground it shares with other critical approaches in social science (for example, social constructionism, the study of rhetoric, ideology, textuality, critical ethnography – and qualitative methods more generally). Nonetheless, this volume addresses many of the key issues raised by discourse analysis for feminists.

Many feminist social scientists have argued that there is no single feminist method, no one approach to data collection or analysis which is distinctively and inherently 'feminist' (Wilkinson, 1986; Peplau and Conrad, 1989). Thus there is nothing distinctively feminist about the theory or method of discourse analysis. Although not all of the contributors to this book would call themselves discourse analysts, all are feminists and/or are engaged in feminist research – and all have found some aspects of discourse analysis of value in their work. As editors of this volume, we have brought together leading British feminist psychologists working in discourse analysis, and have raised for debate and discussion some of the key issues in the relationship between feminism and discourse. We consider this book to be an essential resource for all feminists, psychologists, and discourse analysts seeking to explore and make sense of the complexities and contradictions of doing feminist psychological discourse analytic research.

References

Atkinson, J.M. and Heritage, J.C. (eds) (1984) *Structures of Social Action: Studies in Conversation Analysis*. Cambridge: Cambridge University Press.

Burman, Erica (1990) Differing with deconstruction: a feminist critique. In Ian Parker and John Shotter (eds), *Deconstructing Social Psychology*. London: Routledge.

Burman, Erica (1991) What discourse is not. *Philosophical Psychology* 4(3), 325–42.

Burman, Erica (1992) Feminism and discourse in developmental psychology: power, subjectivity and interpretation. *Feminism and Psychology* 2(1), 45–60.

Burman, Erica and Parker, Ian (1993) Introduction – discourse analysis: the turn to the text. In Erica Burman and Ian Parker (eds), *Discourse Analytic Research: Repertoires and Readings of Texts in Action*. London: Routledge.

Cameron, Deborah (1985) *Feminism and Linguistic Theory*. London: Macmillan.

Cameron, Deborah (ed.) (1990) *The Feminist Critique of Language: A Reader.* London: Routledge.

Chesters, Liz (1994) Women's talk: food, weight and body image. In Sue Wilkinson (ed.), Doing it by degrees: feminist undergraduate dissertations (special feature). *Feminism & Psychology* 4(3), 449–57.

Crawford, June, Kippax, Susan and Waldby, Catherine (1994) Women's sex talk and men's sex talk: different worlds. *Feminism & Psychology* 4(4), 571–87.

Davies, Bronwyn (1990) The problem of desire. *Social Problems* 37(4), 501–16.

Edwards, Derek and Potter, Jonathan (1992) *Discursive Psychology.* London: Sage.

Fairclough, Norman (1990) *Discourse Analysis.* Cambridge: Polity Press.

Gavey, Nicola (1992) Technologies and effects of heterosexual coercion. *Feminism & Psychology* 2(3), 353–66.

Gilfoyle, Jackie, Wilson, Jonathan and Brown (1992) Sex, organs and audiotape: a discourse analytic approach to talking about heterosexual sex and relationships. *Feminism & Psychology* 2(2), 209–30.

Henriques, Julian, Hollway, Wendy, Urwin, Cathy, Venn, Couze and Walkerdine, Valerie (1984) *Changing the Subject: Psychology, Social Relations and Subjectivity.* London: Methuen.

Houston, Marsha and Kramarae, Cheris (eds) (1991) Women speaking from silence. Special Issue of *Discourse & Society* 2(4).

Jackson, Stevi (1992) The amazing deconstructing woman. *Trouble and Strife*, 25, 25–31.

Kitzinger, Celia (1992) The individuated self: a critical analysis of social constructionist writing on individualism. In Glynis Breakwell (ed.), *The Social Psychology of Identity and the Self Concept.* London: Academic Press/Surrey University Press.

Kramarae, Cheris and Treichler, Paula A. (eds) (1985) *A Feminist Dictionary.* London: Pandora Press.

Lakoff, Robin (1975) *Language and Woman's Place.* New York: Harper and Row.

Lovibond, Samantha (1992) Feminism and postmodernism. *New Left Review* 178, 5–28.

McConnell-Ginet, Sally, Borker, Ruth and Furman, Nelly (eds) (1980) *Women and Language in Literature and Society.* New York: Praeger.

Parker, Ian (1992) *Discourse Dynamics: Critical Analysis for Social and Individual Psychology.* London: Routledge.

Peplau, Letitia Anne and Conrad, Eva (1989) Beyond nonsexist research: the perils of feminist methods in psychology. *Psychology of Women Quarterly* 13, 379–400.

Potter, Jonathan and Wetherell, Margaret (1987) *Discourse and Social Psychology: Beyond Attitudes and Behaviour.* London: Sage.

Schiffrin, Deborah (1994) *Approaches to Discourse.* Oxford: Basil Blackwell.

Soper, Kate (1990) Feminism, humanism and postmodernism. *Radical Philosophy* 55, 11–17.

Spender, Dale (1980) *Man Made Language.* London: Routledge.

Stubbs, Michael (1983) *Discourse Analysis.* Oxford: Blackwell.

Tannen, Deborah (1994) *Gender and Discourse.* New York: Oxford University Press.

Thorne, Barrie and Henley, Nancy (eds) (1975) *Language and Sex: Difference and Dominance.* Rowley, MA: Newbury House.

Todd, Alexandra Dundas and Fisher, Sue (eds) (1988) *Gender and Discourse: The Power of Talk.* Volume 30 in the series *Advances in Discourse Processes* (ed. Roy O. Freedle). Norwood, NJ: Ablex Publishing Corporation.

Van Dijk, Teun (ed.) (1985) *Handbook of Discourse Analysis.* New York: Academic Press.

Wilkinson, Sue (1986) Sighting possibilities: diversity and commonality in feminist research. In Sue Wilkinson (ed.), *Feminist Social Psychology: Developing Theory and Practice*. Milton Keynes: Open University Press.

Wilkinson, Sue and Kitzinger, Celia (1995) The queer backlash. In Diane Bell and Renate Klein (eds), *Radically Speaking: Feminism Reclaimed*. Melbourne: Spinifex Press.

Part 1

EMPIRICAL WORK

1

The Bleeding Body: Adolescents Talk about Menstruation

Kathryn Matthews Lovering

The transformation of the girl-child into the bleeding woman is, and has been, for me a problematic and fascinating subject for research. In 1989 I began what was to have been a feminist but otherwise conventional psychological study into 'The effects of menarche on aspects of girls' self-concept'. Over the next three years I made the difficult but liberating move to a feminist poststructuralist discourse analysis of menstrual discursive practices and girls' subjectivity. It is this move and its results that I want to discuss in this chapter.

Background – making the move

When I began my original research into the effects of menstruation on girls, I learned from contemporary psychological research (see Ruble and Brooks-Gunn, 1982; Scott et al., 1989; McGrory, 1990; Rierdan and Koff, 1990) that adolescents have largely negative attitudes to, and a lack of knowledge about, menstruation. However, this literature does not address the questions of *why* adolescents have such negative attitudes, nor of *how* they remain so ignorant of such a common event. The social and political aspects of menstruation never feature in these accounts of girls' experiences of menarche, nor are feminist issues debated. I became increasingly intrigued by this psychological silence on these aspects of menarche, the source of adolescents' negativity, and what menstruation might mean for girls and boys.

There did not seem to be a place for my questions, values and desires within the conventional psychology of menarche. As Nicolas

Rose (1985:3) comments, psychology has emerged as an 'individuated scientific discourse' which seeks to produce rational and objective explanations of a unified subject that are 'true'. This scientific psychology bases its claims to truth on formalized methods of experimentation and data collection with an emphasis on reliability and validity, and it assumes

> that ignoring the constitution of science within political desires, values and interests will somehow increase the reliability of accounts of nature and social life. (Harding, 1991:148)

As a feminist, I found this standpoint increasingly incompatible with my commitment to the improvement of women's position in science and society, and with my experience as a menstruating woman and female researcher. The separation of the means of doing research from its ends, the removal of the researcher from the research process, and the assumption that 'facts' can be collected about the social world can place the researcher in the position of simply reflecting and perpetuating the 'unequal power relations which already exist in the society' (May, 1993:41). I found myself in just this position with a paper I gave early in my research – entitled 'The Experience of Menarche: Misconceptions and Miseries'. Here I inadvertently pathologized the female body (as a source of miseries), labelled girls as 'ignorant' (they don't or won't understand the biology of menstruation), and placed the fault with either the mother or the teacher (they should tell girls about 'it'). It was never my intention *just* to reflect existing power relations, or to 'blame' women for their own oppression, or to detach myself from my research

> . . . in such a way that we strip 'ourselves' from descriptions, or describe our involvements in particular kinds of ways – as somehow 'removed' rather than full-blown members of the events and processes we describe. (Stanley and Wise, 1983:155)

Slowly I realized I needed a different theory and methodology. Conventional psychology does not address the production of knowledge, the issue of power, or questions of meaning: it does not account for the patriarchal nature of menstrual attitudes or for the scientific production of knowledge/ignorance about menstruation. Even women psychologists researching menarche have focused on the quantification of menstrual attitudes and knowledge rather than questioning their nature or source. Their research is based on the 'taken-for-granted, common-sense facts' (Henriques et al., 1984:2) of the female body and of menstruation which is always everywhere 'tabooed' and the symbol of 'womanhood' (see Laws, 1990, for a critique of these essentialist ideas).

Neither is the more explicitly feminist qualitative methodology in psychology – which aims to 'give a voice' to women – necessarily a 'valid one' (Bhavnani, 1990: 141); in part because such an approach does not theorize the social aspects of women's subjective experience, and in part because it does not consider the production or meaning of silence. Too often, this research neglects the issue of social and power relations in the formation of women's experience and 'voice' as well as neglecting questions of who is being empowered, and in whose interests this empowerment is being enacted.

I required an analysis that would enable me to get behind the assumptions of the present psychology of menarche so that I could analyse menstrual conceptions and practices, their meanings for boys and girls, and girls' subjectivity. The psychological approach concerned with these questions is associated with what is called poststructuralist psychology and discourse analysis as influenced by the work of Michel Foucault, and 'already has a history in psychology' (Parker, 1992: 1). It was to this approach that I decided to move.

Unfortunately for those of us new to this area, there are major difficulties in such a move. The first is that the category 'discourse' within the social sciences is, as Cousins and Hussain (1984: 77) pointed out more than a decade ago, 'becoming embarrassingly overloaded and more likely to induce confusion than any clarity it might originally have been set to produce'. Discourse has been put to various uses, from extending the theory of ideology to informing philosophical debate about knowledge and reality. In psycholinguistics it has focused on structural linguistics with an 'emphasis on structural analysis and its relative neglect of content' (Henriques et al., 1984: 105). In contrast, poststructuralist discourse analysis as influenced by Foucault has a central concern with content and therefore is a 'step away from language' (Parker, 1992: xi). In part it is this paradoxical move to discourse but away from language, as well as its break with many of the major assumptions of modern psychology (Kvale, 1992), that make this analysis problematic as well as 'curious, useful, dangerous and liberating' (Parker, 1992: xi).

So what does this move to discourse mean for my analysis? It means that by using the term 'discourse' I am establishing a critical distance from concepts of language and internal mental states which ignore how our subjectivity is constituted by history, culture, and power relations. Rather than assuming, as do attitude tests or inductive content analysis, that language reflects some individual internal state, I assume instead that discourses 'do not simply describe the social world, but categorise it, they bring phenomena into sight' (Parker, 1992: 4–5). As my additional research into the present history of the psychology of menarche revealed, the 'pre- and post-menarcheal' girl of psychological research did not exist as an object of study before 1937: she was a historical and cultural construction of psychological practice. In the same way, we could question whether menstrual attitudes tests and questionnaires simply report individuals' beliefs or whether they actively produce them.

This move to a poststructuralist discourse analysis does not come easily. We have to give up ingrained habits of thought and practice. Not only must we think of discourse as bringing 'phenomena into sight', but we must not distinguish between theory and practice. Knowledge must always be conceived of as practice. In this way we can consider how knowledge comes into being rather than assuming it just stands for some 'real' thing; and how knowledge(s) regulate and discipline bodies. For example, when I first began my research into menarche and girls, I just took it for granted that the female body and male body are completely different, have always been completely different, and will always be completely different. This seems just 'common sense' as well as scientific 'fact', and it underwrites much research into the menstrual cycle. *But* this has not always been the case: there have been and are different ways of seeing the human body. Early sixteenth-century British anatomy and medicine viewed the female and male body as essentially the same, although some differences were recognized (Laqueur, 1990). Even in the scientific Victorian era, a prizewinning feminist scientist and physician argued for the similarities between the female and male body, stating that between the 'two sexes, is a difference not of kind, but of degree' (Jacobi, 1878: 101). Importantly, she was arguing against such biological sex differences because in practice these scientific 'truths' were being produced to deny women equal access to education, professions, and politics.

A feminist poststructuralist discourse analysis allows us to see the female body as a 'medium of culture' and, as Foucault has argued, 'a *practical*, direct locus of social control' (Bordo, 1989: 13), as well as a material, biological body. Far from being the pre-given object about which psychologists make 'discoveries', the body is 'trained, shaped, and impressed with the stamp of prevailing historical forms of selfhood, desire, masculinity, femininity' (Bordo, 1989: 14). And if, as Chris Weedon (1987: 2) argues, 'patriarchal power rests on the social meanings given to biological sexual difference', then it is fundamental to a feminist psychology of menarche that we tackle questions of how and where knowledge is produced, and by whom.

These questions about knowledge are especially important if we accept that the production of psychological knowledge is always open to the effects of politics. There is always the danger of psychology re-producing rather than challenging, resisting, or transforming existing relations of power. We can become enmeshed by the practices of institutional psychology so that we are drawn into collusion with the forces that sustain our subordination as women. We see this happen in the history of menstrual research with women researchers (see Helene Deutsch, 1944; Phyllis Greenacre, 1950; and Therese Benedek, 1952), re-producing the arguments of anti-feminist male biologists that women's emotions and social behaviour are controlled by their 'sexual cycle', arguments that have been used repeatedly to restrict women's participation in public life. These women psychologists re-produced the very arguments which were used to subordinate their own, and other women's, interests and ambitions.

In the research on menarche, it has been anti-feminist (and male-dominated) discursive practices that have constructed the onset of menstruation as a 'critical' period marking the menstruating girl both as vulnerable to trauma and as fundamentally different (biologically different) from the adolescent boy. This construction of menarche as a 'significant' developmental event – with no male equivalent – signalling 'womanhood' and 'femininity' remains unexamined by many women research psychologists. Menarche is treated as a pre-given object of biology: not as the historical creation of a particular kind of twentieth-century science. So that even as women in psychology are seeking to redress the gender imbalance in psychological practice with more research by women on topics of interest to women, they re-produce patriarchal conceptions of the female body by ignoring the historical and cultural construction of their subject. With a psychology ignorant of history and devoid of power relations, we risk mistaking man-made objects for nature-given realities, thereby inadvertently supporting the *status quo*.

In contrast, when a poststructuralist discourse analysis is applied to the psychology of menarche, knowledges of the female body and menstruation are treated as historical and cultural productions involving the participation of wider social practices. The psychology of menarche and adolescents' experiences are seen as produced by particular discursive practices located in history and society; not by the 'truth' of an independent, materially given object which psychologists 'discover'. It is these patriarchal, cultural and scientific discourses and practices of the female body and sexuality which constitute girls' understanding and experience of their body, femininity, and menstruation.

This, then, was the framework which I brought to my analysis of adolescents talking about menstruation. Although it is through an analysis of their conversations that I make sense of the girls' and boys' knowledge and experience, these conversations must be interpreted. Knowledge and meaning are not directly reflected in words because as Wendy Hollway (1989: 42) says:

> . . . a theory of meaning incorporating personal history, culture, unconscious processes and social differences is required to make good sense of them.

As a consequence of my move to a 'new' analysis the aims of my research changed from investigating the 'effects' of menstruation to questions about the discourses and practices available to young adolescent girls and boys in relation to menstruation, the meanings menstruation has for them, and the ways in which these discourses, practices, and meanings constitute girls' subjectivity.

Methodology

Having discussions and having problems

I held a series of discussions with young adolescents on 'Growing up', the purpose being to encourage them to talk about different aspects of being a girl or boy 'growing up', including puberty and menstruation. The discussions were in semi-structured, single sex groups in order to encourage a 'diversity of participants' accounting practices' (Potter and Wetherell, 1987: 164). I thought informal groups would produce a wider range of material than the more traditional one-to-one formal interview with a set of specific questions.

Although problems and 'mistakes' in research are often written out of accounts, I want to point out that these group discussions were done before I had adopted my present theoretical position. When I planned them I thought of them either as focus groups or as a pilot study, but as soon as they started I realized they would be invaluable as a study in themselves. Even though I was undecided on my exact approach, I knew I was not attempting to test attitudes or beliefs, nor trying to obtain representative or normative data or statistically significant 'results'.

Participants – recruiting girls and boys

I recruited the participants from a state school in a large town in the South West of Britain. The school had boys and girls from all abilities and socio-economic classes but few from ethnic minorities. The participants were all eleven to twelve years old. As the pupils in this school were placed in one of three academic ability bands, I decided to have a girls' and boys' discussion group from each band. I visited three classes to tell the pupils about my research, and to request volunteers for the following week. The pupils who volunteered were

Table 1.1   *Constitution of the discussion groups*

Ability band	Girls	Boys
Low	Group 1, 5 girls	Group 2, 9 boys
Middle	Group 6, 7 girls	Group 5, 4 boys
High	Group 3, 6 girls	Group 4, 2 boys
	TOTAL 18 girls	TOTAL 15 boys

The groups are numbered in the order in which I saw them.

given a letter to parents informing them about the research. In the event the discussion groups were constituted as in Table 1.1.

Data collection – having and recording discussions
For the discussions, I used the semi-structured guide illustrated in Box 1.1. Although I wanted the adolescents to 'elaborate on their views in a relatively naturalistic conversational exchange' (Potter and Wetherell, 1987: 165), I needed the discussions to cover the same topics more or less systematically. I used the guide as a prompt sheet for myself, referring to it more or less depending on how the discussions developed. The groups met in empty offices or class-rooms. I audiotape-recorded them using a standard portable cassette recorder with a small high quality microphone.

Data processing – notes, transcriptions, THE ETHNOGRAPH
As soon as possible after each discussion group, I took structured process notes under the headings in Box 1.2. These notes proved invaluable to me in two ways: first, doing them made me reflect on and record my own reactions to and handling of the discussions – in a sense a form of supervision; second, I now have a reflective record to use as part of any subsequent analysis (see last section of this chapter).

I personally transcribed the discussion groups on to a word processor using a consistent orthographic system which I developed. Although at the time of the original transcription I still did not have an exact method of analysis, I did know it would be more content-oriented than language-oriented. I was interested in ado-lescents' comments on puberty, bodies, and menstruation: what they would actually say and *not* say.

Later I decided to use THE ETHNOGRAPH (Seidel et al., 1985, 1988), a programme for computer-assisted analysis of text-based data. At the same time I adopted the more standardized form of notation developed by Gail Jefferson (Potter and Wetherell, 1987: 188–9); see the Appendix at the end of the chapter.

Box 1.1 Guide for semi-structured discussion group

1 General introduction to topic of growing up and physical development.

2 Feelings about growing up.
How does it feel?
What is good about it?
What is bad about it?

3 Knowledge about the physical development of boys and girls.
What have you been taught about growing up?
What happens to boys?
What happens to girls?
Is it easier/better for boys/girls?

4 Sources of information.
Where have you got your information from?

5 Menstruation.
Have you heard of menstruation?
What have you been told about it?
What do you think happens when a woman menstruates?
Why does it happen?
Who has told you?

6 Adequacy of information.
Do you think you know enough about growing up? physical development? menstruation?
Who teaches you: Where? When? With whom?
Do you have any questions?

7 *For girls only*. Feelings and attitudes about menstruation and menarche.
What is it like for girls to reach menarche? the first period?
What are you worried about?
What will be good about it? What will be bad about it?
What do you think menstruation will be like?
How will it affect you?
How do you feel about it?

Box 1.2 Group discussion process notes: headings

1 How I felt
2 General emotional tone and reactions
3 Non-verbal behaviour
4 Content – recalled
5 Implications and thoughts

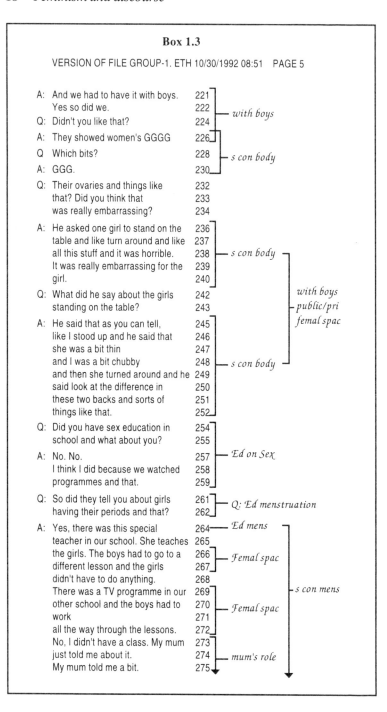

Box 1.3

VERSION OF FILE GROUP-1. ETH 10/30/1992 08:51   PAGE 5

A:	And we had to have it with boys.	221
	Yes so did we.	222
Q:	Didn't you like that?	224

— *with boys*

A:	They showed women's GGGG	226
Q	Which bits?	228
A:	GGG.	230

s con body

Q:	Their ovaries and things like	232
	that? Did you think that	233
	was really embarrassing?	234

A:	He asked one girl to stand on the	236
	table and like turn around and like	237
	all this stuff and it was horrible.	238
	It was really embarrassing for the	239
	girl.	240

s con body

Q:	What did he say about the girls	242
	standing on the table?	243

with boys
public/pri
femal spac

A:	He said that as you can tell,	245
	like I stood up and he said that	246
	she was a bit thin	247
	and I was a bit chubby	248
	and then she turned around and he	249
	said look at the difference in	250
	these two backs and sorts of	251
	things like that.	252

s con body

Q:	Did you have sex education in	254
	school and what about you?	255
A:	No. No.	257
	I think I did because we watched	258
	programmes and that.	259

— *Ed on Sex*

Q:	So did they tell you about girls	261
	having their periods and that?	262

— *Q: Ed menstruation*

A:	Yes, there was this special	264
	teacher in our school. She teaches	265
	the girls. The boys had to go to a	266
	different lesson and the girls	267
	didn't have to do anything.	268
	There was a TV programme in our	269
	other school and the boys had to	270
	work	271
	all the way through the lessons.	272
	No, I didn't have a class. My mum	273
	just told me about it.	274
	My mum told me a bit.	275

— *Ed mens*

Femal spac

Femal spac

s con mens

— *mum's role*

My use of THE ETHNOGRAPH in the data analysis was useful for what could be called the mechanical part of qualitative data analysis. It does not take over the interpretive or 'thinking' part of the work, but it does take over the cutting-and-pasting activities. It enabled me to code, recode, and sort my data files into analytic categories and discourses. In Box 1.3, the print-out from Group 1 shows both how THE ETHNOGRAPH prints text, and how I coded and recoded segments. As illustrated, text can be put into more than one category; for example, in the case of lines 238 to 248 below, four different categories are used: sex education with boys (labelled 'with boys'), discourses of public and private (labelled 'public/pri'), female space (labelled 'femal spac'), and constructions of the body (labelled 's con body').

With THE ETHNOGRAPH, I could review text, mark segments, and then display, sort, and print segments in any order or sequence I desired and identify as well as cross-reference text. Furthermore, I could revise my coding scheme as I went along. I found it particularly useful to print out all the text in a particular category, for example 'constructing the body' (s con body) as shown in Box 1.4. Then, using these print-outs, I could cross-reference segments with complete transcripts for analysis.

Initial content analysis – becoming intimately familiar
After completing the transcription, I read (and re-read) the transcripts in order to do an initial content analysis as well as to familiarize myself thoroughly with the text. It is important to emphasize that this analysis was not an inductive context analysis in which I assumed that if I read the girls' 'authentic voices' carefully enough that I would begin to discern the 'unheard' and 'unimagined'. My analysis was done in the light of my discursive history of the cultural and psychological construction of the female body, sexuality, and menstruation. It was this research that gave me a position outside present dominant discourses from which to identify present discursive practices. Without this critical position, I could only reproduce the dominant discourses because my subjectivity has been produced within the same culture and by the same power relations as the girls I am researching.

Having become intimately familiar with the content of the transcripts, I sorted the text into categories using THE ETHNOGRAPH, and printed the sorted output (an example of which is shown in Box 1.4). This generated an enormous amount of information and paper: I had created over fifty categories, and I ended up with literally about two inches of printed sheets, about 250 pages of categorized data. I realized that THE ETHNOGRAPH program could only *assist* my analysis,

Box 1.4 Constructing the female body

SORTED OUTPUT FOR FILE GROUP-1 12/3/1992 15:14   Page 1
SORT CODE: S CON BODY

GROUP-1   KL   + Content I Recalled.

E. #-FEMAL SPAC #-PUBLIC/PRI

SC: S CON BODY

$-S CON BODY
  : because the girls felt as if the 61 | -$
  : boys laughed and looked at them. 62 -# -$

GROUP-1   A   + discussion about growing up

E. %-WITH GIRLS

SC: S CON BODY

#-S CON BODY
  : A: They showed women's GGGG 226 -# -%
  :   #
  : Q: Which bits? 228 #
  :   #
  : A: GGG. 230 -#

GROUP-1   A   + discussion about growing up

SC: S CON BODY

#-S CON BODY
  : A: He asked one girl to stand on the 236 -#
  :   table and like turn around and like 237 #
$-PUBLIC/PRI $-FEMAL SPAC $-WITH GIRLS
  :   all this stuff and it was horrible. 238 # -$
  :   It was really embarrassing for the 239 #
  :   girl. 240 #
  :   #
  : Q: What did he say about the girls 242 #
  :   standing on the table? 243 #
  :   #
  : A: He said that as you can tell, 245 #
  :   like I stood up and he said that 246 #
  :   she was a bit thin 247 #
  :   and I was a bit chubby 248 # -$
  :   and then she turned around and he 249 #
  :   said look at the difference in 250 #
  :   these two backs and sorts of 251 #
  :   things like that. 252 -#

not do it, and that I needed a focus for the research if I was not to be overwhelmed by data.

At this point, I returned to the aims of my research to structure my analysis. Under each aim, I printed the relevant sorted categories, cross-referencing them with the complete transcripts. Using these categories and transcripts, the knowledge gained from my historical and cultural analysis, my own experiences as an adolescent and as a woman, my own experiences of conducting the research, and my own intuition (see Hollway, 1989), I prepared the following analysis.

Results and discussion: Adolescents talk about menstruation

Discourses and practices available to young adolescents in relation to menstruation

As young adolescents, none of the boys and few of the girls would have had personal or direct experience of menstruation; therefore, both the content and context of their learning about menstruation would constitute its meaning for them. I begin here with the adolescents' discussions of 'growing up', the starting topic for each discussion.

There were similarities in the boys' and girls' conversations about growing up; they all looked forward to leaving school and having girl/boy friends, but the differences between them were more marked. Although these adolescents seemed to inhabit the same physical and cultural world, their social and subjective world was, and is, different. The girls talked about their desire for more independence from adult surveillance and social regulation. There was an eagerness to escape the confines of the female adolescent 'moment' in which people 'worry' about them; yet their futures appeared both vague – unplanned and unknown – and full of responsibilities:

A: When you get older then you have to think about what you are going to do with your future and that's worrying.

A: I don't know. I want to grow up quicker. At the moment we have to stay at home and if you want to go out then you have to get your parents to take you out whereas when you get older then you just do what ever you want.

A: = Be more independent.

A: = yes = yes = yes.

A: I don't know. I'm looking forward to it but it's not going to be any better than now because there is still going to be trouble but they will just be different. It won't be childish trouble but grown-up trouble.

In marked contrast to the girls, the boys did not appear constrained
or confined by adult concern; rather their difficulties were about their
misbehaviour, 'getting into trouble'. When they talked about their
growing up, they talked about a 'male' future of freedom from school
and having jobs (and a wife); not freedom from parental control and
concern.

In these adolescents' conversations, the more difficult aspects of
adult responsibilities and 'grown-up trouble' feature in the futures of
girls rather than boys, and they are based on the body. Although
adolescents know from their own lives that women can work and men
can stay at home, it is the female body which 'bleeds', 'births', and
has 'breasts'. As the boys said:

> A: I think it is easier to be a boy because you don't have to go through
> periods and things like that.
> A: And you don't have to have children.
> A: And you get to get out of the house.
> A: We have to do the jobs more.

It was the bodily aspect of growing up that girls found the most
problematic. In the group discussions they would allude to the body
by talking about 'When you are growing and EVERYTHING [pause] well
getting taller, I don't like it'; or when I asked a group of girls, 'What is
it that you don't like about growing up, then?', there was a long pause
with an evasive description of getting 'moody'.

Their difficulty and embarrassment was in part the result of British
culture's regulation of talk about the body and sexuality between
adults and adolescents: such matters are not openly or easily
discussed in public or across age or gender. They belong within what I
have called a 'private' discursive practice, not so much unseen and
unspoken as covered up and hushed up. At best they are confined to
talk in the toilets, 'we talked about it in our loo'; and at worst not
spoken about even between mothers and daughters: as one girl said:
'My mom isn't [able to talk about it]'.

But more than this, the female body is culturally constructed as
embarrassing and somehow shameful whereas the male body is not.
Consider these three lines from the girls' discussion. We had been
talking about their 'sex' education in school. They commented that it
had been taught with both boys and girls present. So I asked them:

> Q: Didn't you like that?
> A: They showed women's GGGG
> Q: Which bits?
> A: GGG

They could not openly discuss the female body, they just giggled.

It would be possible to argue that the girls were ignorant of the names for 'women's bits'; that their giggling was caused by the programme they were shown or by the teaching – perhaps a joke or funny event. But from my own experience, I would argue that the female body was experienced by these girls as embarrassing and somehow shameful. Here it is what is absent from the text rather than what is present which identifies the implicit theme (Billig et al., 1988) of shamefulness. The girls cannot bring themselves to name the parts of a woman's body.

Not only is the female body shameful, it is extra-ordinary, whereas the male body is ordinary – the focus neither of attention nor of oppression to the same extent as the female body. The girls in their discussion did not mention 'show[ing] men's GGGG'. In contrast, when I discussed boys' physical development with the boys, they said: 'In science we did some measuring the boys and girls like that [   ]'. There were no giggles. When asked about boys' bodies, the boys mentioned 'science', but when the same group of boys were asked about girls' physical development they responded:

A: GGGG
A: They separate the girls in primary school to talk to them.
A: But we don't know what it is about.

Again there was giggling about the embarrassing and somehow shameful female body. And, most strikingly, there was the separation of girls' bodies from science: they became something that boys 'don't know' about.

In Western culture since the nineteenth century, patriarchal science has constructed the female and male body as essentially different. The female body has become the reproductive and sexual body, and the object of fascination and regulation. This fascination with women's (not men's or girls') reproductive organs has resulted in a focus on what is seen as girls' sudden and problematic physical development into women – sexual, menstruating women. In contrast, boys' development is seen as a gradual growing up marked by largely unproblematic changes in size. The girls' comments demonstrated their acute awareness of this:

A: They [school teachers] don't talk about the boys very much, only the girls = yes = yes.
A: It doesn't seem fair. They are laughing at us. Not much seems to happen to the boys.
A: Girls all go funny shapes = yes = like that = yes.
A: Because the boys, they don't really . . . change very much. They just get a little bit bigger. [   ]

> A: It feels like the girls go through all the changes because we are not
>   taught anything about the boys REALLY. [   ]

These constructions of the female and male body as essentially
different, always already sexed, and private, regulate the knowledge
that children (and adults) have of the body and menstrual cycle. With
the dominant practice of women concealing their menstruation, this
means that children are rarely aware of it. The girls and boys in this
study gave few indications of seeing or hearing about it in public or
private before around ten years old. Even as they did learn about
menstruation, through educational lessons or books, it was hard for
them to comprehend. For the boys it seemed like some kind of
amazing but 'far-fetched' female science fiction. For the girls it was
more like a fascinating but frightening gothic horror story:

> A: we didn't really understand it and thought it was funny
> A: = about getting pains and suddenly start bleeding
> A: = so that we got really worried [   ]
> A: so you make jokes about it and things.

Of course as girls grow older, they are exposed to more information
about the menstrual cycle, both through education at home and
school, and through other women sharing their menstrual experiences. However, for the girls in this study, such exposure was rarely
progressive. Often it appeared so minimal and vague that it did not
allay the girls' fears or answer their questions. Even worse, much
adult talk was of menstrual miseries, pains, and inconvenience.
There was no discourse of menstrual pleasures and desires:

> Q: Is there anything that you need to know more about?
> A: No = no =
> A: = yes, about what sort of towel you use =
> A: AND HOW IT WORKS, it is too embarrassing. [   ]
> A: [   ] I knew a girl who had started and she said that it was like a RED
>   HOT POKER STUCK IN HER SIDE and that made me REALLY WORRIED [   ]
> A: You hear some really funny stories and then you REALLY WORRY [   ]
> Q: So you don't hear many good things about it do you?
> A: No NO NO!!

With these discourses and practices of the female body and menstruation, what does menstruation come to mean for young adolescents?

Meanings of menstruation for young adolescents

As a product of the female body connected with fertility, and
sexuality, as well as private bodily functions, menstruation remains
an extremely problematic subject for young adolescents. Their ability
to articulate its place in their lives and psyches is limited. In this

study, the adolescents only alluded to menstruation indirectly as 'it', and did not raise the subject unless I explicitly asked. But this limitation does not signify that menstruation was without meaning or significance for them: rather, its meanings were not straightforwardly revealed in their conversations. In order to understand what menstruation might mean to these adolescents, it was necessary to consider: the social practices of menstruation; what is *not* said as well as what is said; and signification (Hollway, 1989).

Adolescents usually learn about menstruation from other people. In schools, it was often taught outside the normal classroom curriculum and/or routine. Sometimes it appeared not to have been taught at all, or so minimally that the pupils either missed it or didn't remember it (see Prendergast, 1989). Girls and boys were separated, with women having responsibility for the teaching of both. At home, mothers or, less often, other female relatives were the sources of knowledge for girls and for boys. But even here within the domestic sphere, the influence of dominant discursive practices could be seen. Mothers would tell the girls 'a bit about it but not much' or they would be 'embarrassed', with some mothers finding it so problematic that they did not discuss it at all. It becomes a family secret, in that everyone eventually 'knows' about 'it' but no one talks about 'it':

Q: So did they tell you about girls having their periods and that?
A: Yes, there was this special teacher in our school. She teaches the girls. The boys had to go to a different lesson [   ].
A: There was a TV programme in our other school and the boys had to work all the way through the lessons [indicating they were separated from the girls].
A: No, I didn't have a class. My mom just told me about it.
A: My mom told me a bit.
A: My mom's told me a bit about it but not much. [   ]
A: My mom doesn't she is embarrassed. [   ]

Another aspect of menstrual education was more painful and problematic. Once boys learned about menstruation they often used it as a means to ridicule and oppress girls, even more so if the girls and boys were taught together. These girls were talking about their co-educational 'sex' education:

A: In our school, it was done in front of the boys, and it was really embarrassing.
   [several girls at once]
A: They don't talk about the boys very much, only the girls.
A: Yes. Yes.

A: It doesn't seem fair. They are laughing at us. Not much seems to happen to the boys.

A: Girls all go funny shapes, yes, like that yes.

A: And it gets really embarrassing and she said things like [pause] I've started.

Not only was menstruation embarrassing, but it was frightening, and this was not only because of its association with menstrual discomfort. In the absence of experience of either their own or another's menstruation, and not having graphic, specific information about starting their periods, pre-menarcheal girls can be frightened of this unknown but unavoidable event entailing blood from 'down there'. In Western society, blood signifies injury and/or attack, and is not connected with health or safety. Western society also highly regulates and disciplines talk about sex and excretion. So when young adolescents are told about a process in which the female body bleeds from 'down there', these statements carry numerous cultural and personal meanings – including technicoloured media images of ritualized violence, forbidden sexuality, and childhood accidents. It is difficult for adolescents and adults clearly to articulate the connections between menstruation, blood, genitals, sex, injury and danger. The dominant educational and scientific teaching about menstruation emphasizes its normality as part of 'growing up' and 'having babies'; therefore its association with danger and sexuality is suppressed. In my discussions, boys never mentioned it and girls only talked about it indirectly or fleetingly, although the links were clear: 'About getting pains and suddenly start bleeding so that we got really worried.'

For these adolescents, menstruation came to signify the intimate, private, and always sexual female body. With its links both to sexuality and to blood, it was fascinating and horrifying, an ever-present potential but largely unseen and unspoken practice. For boys, its essential femaleness and circumscribed practice constituted it as a subject which males might exploit to construct masculinity and power, but not understanding or empathy. For girls, menstruation brought undesirable attention and male oppression, and an undesired 'bleeding' associated with pains, injuries, and accidents. The promised sign of 'growing up' and 'having babies' offered few advantages to young adolescent girls in the absence of menstrual pleasures or privileges. Finally, how did these discursive practices and meanings constitute girls' subjectivities?

Constituting girls' subjectivities
In order to discuss the ways in which discursive practices and meanings constituted these girls' subjectivities, I begin with an example from a

girls' group. The girls had been discussing their 'sex' education, which led one girl to describe an incident in school with a male teacher when she was about nine or ten years old. This particular incident illustrates how the discursive practices of the female body and gendered power relations constitute female subjectivity, and how male power can be exercised in such a way as to re-produce the dominant discursive practice of subjecting the female body to the male and public gaze.

Q: [   ] Did you think that was really embarrassing?
A: He asked one girl to stand on the table and like turn around and like all this stuff and it was horrible. It was really embarrassing for the girl. [This girl was in fact her.]
Q: What did he say about the girls standing on the table?
A: He said that as you can tell, like I stood up and he said that she was a bit thin and I was a bit chubby and then she turned around and he said look at the difference in these two backs and sorts of things like that.

This is a painful scene to imagine. At this age (nine to ten years old), children can be very silly and prone to crude jokes: some girls are developing into young women, while most boys and many girls are still childlike. In a classroom of perhaps twenty-five to thirty children, a girl finds herself instructed by a male authority to stand on a table in front of all the class so that class members can examine her body. The result for this girl was 'horrible'.

It is not that this practice 'affected' her 'attitude' to herself or her body – as if her attitude were some stable, pre-given, unified object to be 'influenced' by external events. Rather, her identity and subjectivity are continuously in the process of constitution by the social. The event described above comes to constitute a part of her subjective experience of her body, which is transformed by power relations into something 'horrible'. Another text from the group discussion illustrates this transformation of girls' bodies into a source of oppression and distress. Girls from another group were talking about 'sex' education.

A: [   ] I just can't stand it when the boys laugh.
A: You don't just try to think about it but you just laugh it off or try to pretend that it doesn't bother you. [   ]
A: (Boys) shouldn't laugh at it.
A: Because it puts us off and makes us hide it all inside.

The girls talked of their distress when the female body and menstruation were the subject of laughter by boys, and their words captured how their subjectivity was constituted. It made these girls 'really self-conscious', 'puts us off', and 'makes us hide it all inside'.

Girls did get angry with boys. At times they tried to deny or resist this discourse by 'laugh[ing] it off' or not 'think[ing] about it'. But the pervasiveness of this 'patriarchal sexist discourse' (Walkerdine, 1990: 5) was evidenced in a reflective analysis of my own experience as a female researcher while doing this research. The following extracts are from a discussion with nine adolescent boys. The text in italics is from my process notes.

> Q: Do any of you know why girls have those (periods)?
> [*The discussion quickly becomes chaotic and for me difficult.*]
> A: I don't know.
> A: GGGG (not clear) [   ]
> A: What did he say?
> A: Tell us (not clear) come on tell us.
> A: I'll tell it (not clear)
> A: Come on tell me
> [Several boys start talking loudly all at once.]
> [*A disjointed discussion about menstruation and sex education followed during which I asked the boys:*]
> Q: What do you think is good about being a boy as opposed to being a girl.
> A: [Loud exaggerated COUGH COUGH loud talking]
> A: You don't have to have billiards [breasts]
> A: GGGG
> A: You don't have to have tits
> A: GGGG [loud talking]
> A: They call them bosoms [they are called bosoms (unclear)
> A: Mam, mam, they knock you out
> A: GGGG
> A: Well you say that (not clear)
> A: No [no
> [*The boys' behaviour was smutty, sexist, and oppressive. My next intervention was intended to shame them into better behaviour but only encouraged them to exploit the power of this patriarchal discourse further.*]
> A: I can see why the girls wouldn't want to have sex education with the boys.
> A: GGGG HaHaHa [loud laughing] [loud talking]
> A: Oh don't be so disgusting
> A: [loud talking] GGGG
> A: The boys don't have to have fannies
> [*All I wanted to do was get out of the room as fast as possible!*]

It could be argued that this event was an empirical problem in that I did not handle the discussion correctly. However, I was an experienced forty-year-old secondary school teacher, youth worker, and educational psychologist when this discussion took place. I argue that it was not my inexperience or mismanagement that led to this event, but rather that in this context I became a woman in the company of a group of young men using a patriarchal sexist discourse – and I experienced it as oppressive and distressing. It is these sexist discursive practices and gendered power relations which constitute girls' and women's subjectivities and give the female body and menstruation its particular meanings.

In conclusion, I argue that this analysis, a feminist poststructuralist discourse analysis, is particularly powerful as a means of investigating the discursive practices of the female body and the ways in which women's subjectivities are constituted by their experiences in the social world. And with the revealing example from my own experience of the operation of patriarchal sexist discourse, I rest my case for the usefulness of this approach for feminist psychological research.

Appendix: Transcription notation

Developed by Gail Jefferson (Potter and Wetherell, 1987: 188–9)

Extended square brackets mark overlap between utterances, e.g.:

    A: Right [so you
    B: [I'm not sure

An equals sign at the end of a speaker's utterance and at the start of the next utterance indicates the absence of a discernible gap, e.g.:

    A: Anyway Brian=
    B: =Okay

One or more colons indicate an extension of the preceding vowel sound, e.g.:

    A: Yea::h, I see::

Italic indicates that words are uttered with added emphasis; words in capitals are uttered louder than the surrounding talk, e.g.:

    A: It's not *right*, not right AT ALL

A full stop before a word or sound indicates an audible intake of breath, e.g.:

    A: I think .umm I need more

Round brackets indicate that either the material in the brackets is inaudible or there is doubt about its accuracy, e.g.:

    A: I (couldn't tell you) that

Empty square brackets indicate that some transcript has been deliberately omitted. Material within square brackets is clarificatory information, e.g.:

    A: Judy [the speaker's sister] said [   ] it's fine

30 *Feminism and discourse*

Note

I wish to express my appreciation to Valerie Walkerdine of Goldsmiths' College, Michelle Cohen of Richmond College, and Carla Willig of Middlesex University for their conversation and constructive criticisms. They made possible my difficult and always fascinating move to poststructuralist psychology and discourse analysis.

References

Benedek, Therese (1952) *Psychosexual Functions in Women*. New York: Ronald Press.

Bhavnani, Kum-Kum (1990) What's power got to do with it? Empowerment and social research. In Ian Parker and John Shotter (eds), *Deconstructing Social Psychology*. London: Routledge. pp. 141–53.

Billig, M., Condor, S., Edwards, D., Gane, M., Middleton, D. and Radley, A. (1988) *Ideological Dilemmas: A Social Psychology of Everyday Thinking*. London: Sage.

Bordo, Susan R. (1989) The body and the reproduction of femininity: a feminist appropriation of Foucault. In Alison M. Jaggar and Susan R. Bordo (eds), *Gender/Body/Knowledge*. New Brunswick and London: Rutgers University Press. pp. 13–33.

Cousins, Mark and Hussain, Athar (1984) *Michel Foucault*. London: Macmillan Education.

Deutsch, Helene (1944) *The Psychology of Women: A Psychoanalytic Interpretation*. Vol. 1: *Girlhood*. London: Research Books.

Foucault, Michel (1976) *The History of Sexuality*. Harmondsworth: Penguin.

Greenacre, Phyllis (1950) The prepuberty trauma in girls. *Psychoanalytic Quarterly* 19, 298–317.

Harding, Sandra (1991) *Whose Science: Whose Knowledge? Thinking from Women's Lives*. Milton Keynes: Open University Press.

Henriques, Julian, Hollway, Wendy, Urwin, Cathy, Venn, Couze and Walkerdine, Valerie (1984) *Changing the Subject: Psychology, Social Regulation and Subjectivity*. London: Methuen.

Hollway, Wendy (1989) *Subjectivity and Method in Psychology*. London: Sage.

Jacobi, Mary Putnam (1878) *The Question of Rest for Women during Menstruation*. New York: Putnam.

Kvale, Steinar (ed.) (1992) *Psychology and Postmodernism*. London: Sage.

Laqueur, Thomas (1990) *Making Sex: Body and Gender from the Greeks to Freud*. London: Harvard University Press.

Laws, Sophie (1990) *Issues of Blood: The Politics of Menstruation*. London: Macmillan.

May, Tim (1993) *Social Research: Issues, Methods, and Process*. Milton Keynes: Open University Press.

McGrory, Arlene (1990) Menarche: responses of early adolescent females. *Adolescence* 25, 265–70.

Parker, Ian (1992) *Discourse Dynamics*. London: Routledge.

Potter, Jonathan and Wetherell, Margaret (1987) *Discourse and Social Psychology*. London: Sage.

Prendergast, Shirley (1989) Girls' experience of menstruation in school. In Lesley Holly (ed.), *Girls and Sexuality*. Milton Keynes: Open University Press. pp. 85–108.

Rierdan, Jill and Koff, Elissa (1990) Premenarcheal predictors of the experience of menarche: a prospective study. *Journal of Adolescent Health Care* 11(5), 404–7.

Rose, Nicolas (1985) *The Psychological Complex: Psychology, Politics, and Society in England 1869–1939*. London: Routledge and Kegan Paul.

Ruble, Diane and Brooks-Gunn, Jeanne (1982) The experience of menarche. *Child Development* 53, 1557–66.

Scott, C., Authur, D., Owen, R. and Panizo, M. (1989) Black adolescents' emotional response to menarche. *Journal of the National Medical Association* 81, 285–90.

Seidel, J.V., Kjolseth, R. and Seymour, E. (1985, 1988) *THE ETHNOGRAPH: A Program for the Computer Assisted Analysis of Text Based Data*. Qualis Research Associates, P.O. Box 3129, Littleton, Colorado, 80161, USA.

Stanley, L. and Wise, S. (1983) *Breaking Out: Feminist Consciousness and Feminist Research*. London: Routledge and Kegan Paul.

Walkerdine, Valerie (1990) *Schoolgirl Fictions*. London: Verso.

Weedon, Chris (1987) *Feminist Practice and Poststructuralist Theory*. Cambridge, MA: Blackwell.

2

Sexual Harassment: A Discursive Approach

Celia Kitzinger and Alison Thomas

The term 'sexual harassment' is both a triumph and a problem for feminism. A triumph because the phrase, invented in the mid-1970s by North American feminists (Farley, 1978; MacKinnon, 1979), seems to describe and label an experience common to most women, and so enables us to identify and organize against this form of male violence. One of the earliest to use and publicize the term was Lin Farley (1978) in *Sexual Shakedown*: she identified a form of male behaviour in the workplace which, she said, 'required a name and sexual harassment seemed to come about as close to symbolizing the problem as the language would permit'. Before the 1970s, then, the label didn't exist and the behaviour it identified was 'just part of life' – a problem without a name. The term 'sexual harassment' is a word invented as part of women's renaming of the world, reflecting and constructing *women's* experience and labelling a form of behaviour newly recognized as something which women need not passively endure, but can actively protest against, and resist.

Since the 1970s, there has been a wide range of surveys documenting the incidence of sexual harassment and testifying to its frequency and pervasiveness. Many public bodies and institutions world-wide now regard 'sexual harassment' as a serious cause for concern, and have formulated specific codes of practice and grievance procedures to deal with it. 'Sexual harassment' is now deemed illegal in British law, in so far as it can be construed as an act of sexual discrimination under the provisions of the 1975 Sex Discrimination Act (the first successful case, Porcelli *v.* Strathclyde Regional Council, reached the Employment Appeal Tribunal in 1986); and in 1991, following a report by Rubenstein (1987), the European Economic Community issued a Recommendation and Code of Conduct on Sexual Harassment (Lester, 1993). The 'triumph' lies, then, in the extent to which organizations have been forced to take on board, and to incorporate into their policies and codes of conduct, concerns initially raised by feminists.

(Dziech and Weiner, 1984: 18), sexual harassment 'is not, in the vast majority of cases, ambiguous behaviour': some men simply 'find it convenient to make sexual harassment a confusing topic' and the confusion is often 'transparent pretence'. In parallel manner, women who resist using the term 'sexual harassment', or who hesitate in applying it to their own experiences, have sometimes been treated with exasperation by feminists – as dupes of patriarchy, unable to recognize their own oppression and in dire need of having their consciousnesses raised. According to this type of positivist feminist argument, questions about definitions are seen as diversionary tactics, distracting attention away from male abuses on to abstract philosophical concerns or trivial issues, undermining feminist and trade union campaigns to stop sexual harassment.

Whereas the positivist approach sees differing definitions of sexual harassment as a problem for research design and policy implementation (how, after all, do you assess the incidence and frequency of sexual harassment if people can't agree on what sexual harassment is?), the discourse analytic approach, by contrast, sees the failure to establish universally accepted definitions of sexual harassment not (purely) as a Machiavellian male plot, nor simply as a technical problem for research design, but rather as a research topic in its own right. A discourse analytic approach to sexual harassment enables us to address precisely that which is assumed and that which is obscured in positivist research: that is, questions about the social construction of sexual harassment, and the ways in which it is discursively defined and maintained, ignored or minimized. Language does not simply reflect a pre-existing reality; it is not a transparent medium through which unchanging 'facts' or 'accurate' definitions are conveyed. Rather, through language, we actively construct our experience – a simple claim that lies at the basis of discourse analytic research. Sexual harassment is socially constructed and discursively negotiated. This is not to say that it is not 'real'. It *is* to say that its reality is in large part constituted by language, and by the symbolic meanings we attach to parts of our bodies and to male/female interactions, and by the ways in which we interpret social reality.

The research reported here explores the way in which 'sexual harassment' is constructed through discourse, and, in particular, the mechanisms through which the erasure of sexual harassment (by both women and men) is accomplished. We conducted semi-structured tape-recorded interviews with six men and fifteen women. Since the specific purpose of these interviews was to elicit discourse about ambiguities in the very concept of sexual harassment, and we were not concerned with reporting its incidence, we did not seek a 'random sample' but rather recruited participants primarily on the basis of their willingness to spent time discussing this topic. Interviewees ranged in age from twenty to sixty-five, and included middle-class and working-class, white, Asian and Afro-Caribbean participants. Interviewees were given a written version of the key questions several days before the interview. These questions read as follows:

1 Please describe a *typical* example of sexual harassment from your own experience. What made it typical? What does the term 'sexual harassment' mean to you?
2 Can you think of an incident which you didn't think was sexual harassment at the time, but now, looking back, you think that's what it was?
3 Can you think of an incident which you thought was sexual harassment at the time, but now, looking back, you realize it wasn't?
4 Can you think of an incident which, at the time, you weren't sure whether or not it was sexual harassment, and now, looking back, you're still not sure about?
5 Can you think of a time when something happened and you thought it was sexual harassment, but someone else didn't?
6 Can you think of a time when something happened and you didn't think it was sexual harassment, but someone else did?

Interviews were transcribed orthographically by the authors and we have reported various aspects of our findings elsewhere (Thomas and Kitzinger, 1994). In this chapter we focus on the denial of sexual harassment, that is, on discourses which explain why the label 'sexual harassment' is (or was) an inappropriate label for a particular incident. Our interest is not whether a particular incident is, or is not, 'really' sexual harassment, but rather the discursive mechanisms through which incidents and experiences are actively excluded from the category of 'sexual harassment'. We draw attention to the different ways in which our male and female participants construct these denials, and relate our findings to contemporary writing on sexual harassment in the media and in popular books.

Victimhood

Most women we interviewed were able to describe events which they had labelled 'sexual harassment' only in retrospect, and a common reason given for initially refusing the label was a rejection of victim status. In striking contrast with these women's accounts, none of the men we interviewed explicitly rejected the 'victim' label in describing experiences of sexual harassment. Men, whether describing being accused of sexual harassment, or whether describing their experience on the receiving end of sexual harassment, tended to emphasize their own 'victim' role.

One woman participant describes experiences which took place at her boarding school when she was in her late teens:

> Boys will be boys, you know. There were times when they put broomsticks between their legs and made holes in my study unit with the broomstick handles, and there was sexual innuendo about 'invading Wendy's hole'. I don't think I would have called it sexual harassment. I see now that it was sexual harassment, but when you're in a situation in which nobody else labels it that way, you get persuaded into their way of thinking, that it's 'only a bit of fun'. When we went sailing, they took Anna's bra off and hoisted it up the mast, and there was no one else would've called that sexual harassment. I'd've been looked at really strangely and they'd've thought I was off the rails if I'd've called it that. Sexual harassment meant someone wanting to go to bed with you, and they'd've said, 'Ha ha, there's no way we'd want to go to bed with you, Wendy.'

Another woman describes working as a barmaid, pawed and leered at by 'lecherous men':

> I just felt that it couldn't really be bad enough to be sexual harassment, because everyone else put up with it. I think I saw it as something in me that I must be oversensitive to it. And now I don't think *I'm* oversensitive: I think *they're* overintrusive. (Laura)

It is hard to see what either of these women had to gain by labelling their experiences as sexual harassment at the time, in situations in which no one would have supported their perceptions. In fact, both were quite explicit about having decided to avoid defining their experience as sexual harassment:

> If I imagined that it was sexual, it made me feel nasty. If they weren't just putting their arms around me in a friendly way, if there was more to it than that, it made me feel horrible. So I tried to dismiss it from my mind. It was mainly for my own benefit that I didn't label it. It would've made me feel horrible if I'd carried on doing the job and letting myself stay in a situation where that was happening. So I told myself it wasn't happening to make it easier to stay in the job. (Laura)

> I couldn't have got away from them. I was stuck at the school. So I didn't want to see it as sexual harassment because if you're in a situation you can't get away from you'd rather defuse the situation, and you do that by labelling it in personal terms – like 'this is just Bloggs having fun'. If I'd labelled it sexual harassment I'd have had to feel really angry and hurt

and upset and distressed, and those were all the feelings I was trying *not* to have. (Wendy)

Both Wendy and Laura, then, seem to have been making a rational choice *not* to label their experiences as sexual harassment: they were coping with their situations by refusing to acknowledge what was happening. While the label 'sexual harassment' obviously offers survival strategies for some women in some situations, in other circumstances it labels too clearly, and too painfully, the extent of their oppression. As Laura said, 'It's labelling yourself a victim'.

Other women expressed similar views:

> I think I sometimes don't label it because you have more emotional freedom that way. I feel more liberated if I *don't* think of someone else as harassing me. You're defining your own oppression. The word 'harassment' is sort of setting yourself up as an object. (Dipti)

> I have this idea that if I refuse to acknowledge it as sexual harassment, then it's *not* sexual harassment, because I'm refusing to relate on those terms. And by ignoring it, that means he's not going to get the benefit of knowing that I'm scared. (Rita)

> I just refused to see what was happening because I wanted to insist on my own rights as an academic. I wanted to see our conversation as an academic discussion, so I insisted to myself that's what was happening – which, at one level, it was. But by refusing to acknowledge the other level until it was too late, I nearly got myself raped. (Barbara)

> I know this is going to sound daft, but I'm the sort of person who is known to stand up for herself and her rights. If I was sexually harassed, I would be expected to . . . I would expect *myself* to direct complaints down all the appropriate channels and bring my harasser to justice. I know I would have to do that – I couldn't allow myself to be harassed and not kick up a fuss about it. I've never occupied the passive victim role! Now, when I think of what is involved in taking a sexual harassment case to an industrial tribunal – the hours it would take, the commitment and energy it would need – I just know I don't want to do that. So I have a huge vested interest in *not* seeing myself as having been sexually harassed. If I'm honest, I think there's a sense in which I can't afford to notice that I'm being sexually harassed, because the consequences would be too horrific. (Eve)

The term 'sexual harassment' describes female subordination. When women say, to themselves or to other people, 'I am *not* being sexually harassed', one of the things they are saying is, 'I am *not* a victim. I am *not* a subordinated person'. Unable to change the situation they are in, women gain what little power they can by insisting on defining that situation in their own terms. Women who 'make a joke of it' or 'play along' succeed in avoiding the blatant demonstration of their own victimhood: they are 'choosing' what would otherwise be forced upon them. They, like women who simply try to ignore sexual harassment, can also, of course, be accused of encouraging it. There are costs attached to rejecting the 'sexual harassment' label – costs potentially as severe as the costs of accepting it. All women can do is decide in any given situation whether the label is likely to be in their own interests or not – and decisions made on the basis of personal interest may or may not be in the interests of women as a group.

The whole concept of so-called 'victim feminism' has been criticized in the media and in popular books which suggest that in its concern about rape, sexual harassment, and male violence against women, feminism has positioned women as victims. Reflecting on the Supreme Court case between Judge Clarence Thomas and Professor Anita Hill, journalist Chrissy Iley (1991) complains that 'Hill has turned every woman into a victim incapable of fighting her own corner', and writer Naomi Wolf (1993: 205) has said that 'we must be wary of new definitions of sexual harassment that leave no mental space to imagine girls and women as sexual explorers and renegades'. Women's unwillingness to present themselves as victims is clearly a feature of their refusal to use the 'sexual harassment' label.

Pervasiveness

The question of definition is closely tied in with the issue of the pervasiveness of sexual harassment: obviously, the more inclusive the definition, the greater the frequency of incidents which can be logged. One man described how very rare sexual harassment was in his experience.

> *Robert*: In more than thirty years in higher education I've only ever come across one case.
> *Celia*: Does that surprise you?
> *Robert*: No. No, it doesn't surprise me. I've only ever managed universities or international organizations, and I suppose both are more civilized than some institutions, and people are more considerate, and possibly more controlled, than in some other places.
> *Celia*: What sort of other places?
> *Robert*: Oh, I don't know. . . . Places like cotton mills. . . . The university sent round some piece of paper about sexual harassment, but I didn't read it. I didn't think it was needed in our organization.
> *Celia*: Other people say they've seen lots of sexual harassment: why do you think that is?
> *Robert*: Well, people of your generation seem to complain of it more than people of my generation. I think manners have got worse. Some of us were brought up to be polite to people and to think there are

things you do, and things you don't do. So I think it's partly a
generation problem, and partly a class problem.
Celia: A class problem?
Robert: Well, a working-class problem.
Celia: You think there's more sexual harassment in the working classes?
Robert: Must be. I mean, there's a lot of talk about sexual harassment,
and I don't see it amongst my own class, so it must be happening in
other classes.

In a survey conducted by the National Union of Students (NUS)
amongst students at the elite academic institution to which this male
interviewee is referring, 61 per cent of female students claimed to
have experienced sexual harassment, and a college Women's Officer
is quoted as saying:

My main anxiety is that what I call sexual harassment is just an accepted
part of the social life in college. When I try to define it, people say, 'that's
ridiculous – it goes on all the time!' *Well exactly!* (Watts, 1990)

In contrast to the male interviewees, many of the women who spoke
to us described sexual harassment as a pervasive feature of social
interaction between men and women:

Retrospectively I understand that *all* of my sexual interactions with boys
and young men as a child and as a teenager . . . *all* of those I define, in
retrospect, as sexual harassment. It was the pressure to go further than you
wanted to go – the assumption of access. I remember the first time my
boyfriend kissed me, and really disliking it, and thinking I was going to
choke . . . And just thinking . . . It really did come into my head . . . 'I
asked for this . . . this was what I wanted.' And he didn't have to say
anything. It was just scripted in my head that made me not go 'ugh!' You
know, I actually got used to it, and liked it afterwards, but this first
experience I felt to be very intrusive and very insensitive and, you know
. . . yuk. (Jackie)

Some feminist theorists have suggested that *all* social and sexual
interactions between female and male are forms of sexual harassment, and that the term 'sexual harassment' itself is politically
problematic, because the concept of sexual harassment (coercive and
power-maintaining sexual behaviour) relies upon the possibility of
non-coercive and egalitarian heterosexual relationships. It implicitly
assumes that there are conditions under which women can volun-
tarily assent, of our own free will, to sexual activity with men, and
that this sexual activity will not establish or perpetuate power
differentials (see Hollway, this volume). In a world in which women
are controlled by 'the institution of compulsory heterosexuality'
(Rich, 1980), these conditions for voluntary and non-coercive

heterosex are hard to imagine (but see the contributors to Wilkinson and Kitzinger, 1993).

Discursive moves like these which make sexual harassment very pervasive – an almost inevitable part of social relationships between women and men – were firmly resisted by most of our male interviewees. As one man said:

> Some women have such a broad notion of sexual harassment that even talking to a woman, or holding a door open for her, is sexual harassment. Well, that's just silly. You can't define everything that happens between men and women as sexual harassment. Sexual harassment has got to be sort of at the far end of a continuum of coercion – well, rape's at the far end and sexual harassment is somewhere in the middle. Things that happen all the time between men and women, those can't be called sexual harassment. (James)

In much of the discourse we collected from men (and from some heterosexual women), sexual harassment, because it is seen as a problem, was defined as clearly separable from 'normal', ordinary, taken-for-granted social relationships between men and women – and, in particular, as clearly distinguishable from 'consensual' heterosexual relationships. The logic of this discourse demands that if anything is pervasive in Western culture, if it is a taken-for-granted aspect of social life, then it cannot, by definition, be a problem. Therefore, it cannot be sexual harassment ('You can't define everything that happens between men and women as sexual harassment') – because, in this discourse, everyday life is not problematized. What in (some) women's discourse is seen as 'everyday dripping tap sexual harassment' (Wise and Stanley, 1987) is, in this discourse, not sexual harassment at all. It has to be 'at the far end of a continuum of coercion' to be sexual harassment. It is a logical extension of this line of reasoning for a judge to rule that sexually explicit language and pornographic posters displayed in an office do not amount to sexual harassment 'when considered in the context of a society that condones and publicly features and commercially exploits open displays of written and pictorial erotica' (cited in the *Guardian*, 15 March 1988). Thus the very same feature of sexual harassment, its sheer pervasiveness, can be used both (by, for example, feminists) to stress the importance of acting to stop it, *and* (by for example, the male interviewee and judge cited above) to discount its existence.

The final twist in this discourse about sexual harassment comes with the claim that, if sexual harassment is not very common, then there is no need to act. A male business administration dean says:

If it's an 80–90 per cent problem, then we have to do something, but if it's say, only a 7 per cent problem, I would give it less priority. (Quoted in Dziech and Weiner, 1984: 15)

Given that many men discount any definition of sexual harassment which makes it a '90 per cent problem', the double bind is this: if it's commonplace, it isn't really sexual harassment; if it's rare, then it isn't really a problem. It has to be rare to be real; but if it's rare, then there's no need to worry about it.

In sum, then, feminist discourse on sexual harassment has drawn attention to its pervasiveness ('it happens all the time'), and this is reflected in the discourse offered by many women who spoke to us. The discursive move which then functions to annihilate sexual harassment goes something like this: if it happens all the time, if it's a regular feature of social relations between men and women, if it is inherent in heterosexual relationships, if it's utterly pervasive in society, then it *isn't* sexual harassment: it can't be, because sexual harassment is – by definition – a problem, and we can't render problematic the whole of our society. Sexual harassment, according to this discourse, is a discrete, clearly definable, manageable and separable part of social life which can be eradicated by means of institutional policies and procedures while leaving the social structure otherwise intact.

Sexualizing

One explanation that has been offered for the apparent intractability of sexual harassment is differences in social perception. According to this theory, men perceive more 'sexiness' in the social behaviour of women than do women: women are (without knowing it) behaving in ways men interpret as provocative (Abbey, 1982). Implicit in this theory is the idea that sexual harassment is caused by, or related to, a man's sexual attraction to the woman he is harassing. It would, of course, be possible to define sexual harassment in such a way that it could only be said to have taken place if the male harasser was, in fact, sexually attracted to his victim, and some of our male interviewees did just this. Sexual harassment was identified by most of the men we interviewed in terms of some underlying sexual interest on the part of the harasser:

Sexual harassment is trying to get a woman into bed with you after she's made it clear she doesn't want to. It's not taking no for an answer. (Fred)

My definition of sexual harassment would be people pressing unwanted attentions on someone else with a view to carnal collaboration when it has been made clear that these are unwelcome. (Robert)

Some men explained that this sexual interest may be unconscious:

Chris: Well, it might be something to do with hormones but . . . well, like it or not, I think that . . . whether you, I mean I, like it or not, I'd like to put forward a belief that . . . that adolescents, because of pubertal changes, are much more prone to that sort of thing, particularly when they're sexually naive, as in this case.

Alison: You're not going to say that men have a sort of drive to sexually harass women – or are you?

Chris: On an unconscious level, yes. If you go through puberty not knowing about sexual relationships (which most people do) and then you find yourself attracted to women, yet unable to recognize that as an attraction, then you're more likely in those circumstances to channel your sexual attraction through ways which are potentially pathological but defensive.

Alison: Like?

Chris: Well, I always used to tease women or girls . . . I'm talking about when I was thirteen now . . . I always teased the girls that I fancied, but I'd never admit to myself that I fancied them and that was what I was doing . . . I was immature, as I think most boys are at that age.

When sexual harassment is defined in terms of sexual interest, it opens the way for men to talk, not just about their hormones, their sexual drives and their uncontrollable urges, but also about the difficulty of knowing whether or not a woman is willing, and how to tell in a culture in which men are supposed to take the initiative.

It's a big problem, because quite often, if I haven't taken the initiative, nothing happens. I've found it quite equal between men and women at a friendship level, but when the relationship changes from friendly to sexual, it's been mainly up to me. (Andrew)

Sometimes women give out sexual messages non-verbally, but then when you make it explicit they claim that's not what they wanted. I don't think that's sexual harassment – it's just mixed messages. (James)

Many women, by contrast, were explicit in stating that the events they were describing as sexual harassment were not sexual *per se*. One woman responded to the interviewer's question about her experiences 'What made it sexual harassment?' like this:

It was sexual harassment although there was no sexual thing, because he was employing his masculinity against me because I wasn't male. It wasn't sexual in the sense that, you know, if I'd dropped my knickers that would have solved it. That wasn't what he was after. (Teresa)

Another participant used, as illustration of the fact that sexual harassment 'isn't always about sex', her experience of sexual harassment from a gay man:

> I was with Dave and Tony, who are both gay, and Tony went out saying 'I'll leave you two alone together'. Dave raised his eyebrows and said archly to Tony, 'Well, there's an offer I can't refuse.' I saw that as sexual harassment, and of course it was nothing to do with his sexual attraction to me: it was male bonding, with me used as glue. (Carol)

Women's complaints of sexual harassment are seen as being off-target (or even self-congratulatory) by those who construct sexual harassment as rooted in sexual attraction. The man who is not sexually attracted protests his innocence:

> I didn't intend any sexual invitation. I thought it was a friendly compliment. So I don't see how it can have been sexual harassment. (Fred)

More indignant males, subject to accusations of sexual harassment which they read as allegations of their sexual attraction to the woman concerned, respond with phrases like 'Fancy yourself, don't you?' or 'You should be so lucky!' But from some women's point of view:

> Most situations of sexual harassment are nothing to do with sex. I mean, that suggests that if women said, 'Take me, I'm yours', the problem would be dealt with. I don't think that's true. I think most men would be horrified if the woman they were sexually harassing turned round and said, 'Okay, let's go to bed'. The whole point of what he's doing is that he knows she doesn't want sex with him. (Mary)

In sum, the question of whether or not 'sexual harassment' is, by definition, 'sexual' – and what we mean by 'sexual' – is contested. For many people (especially, it seems, for men) sexual harassment without sexual attraction doesn't count as the real thing.

Power

As some of the quotes from women in the preceding section illustrate, sexual harassment is often discussed primarily in terms of power, *and this is part of the definition of sexual harassment*. It is not just that sexual harassment happens because men have power and women don't: more fundamentally, sexual harassment is itself a way of 'doing' power:

> I think they do it . . . for power over somebody, to show their mates that they're somebody, they're one of the lads. I think sex is one way you get power over somebody else if you're a man. (John)

> Sexual harassment seems to me to be about ownership and control. It's a man saying, 'Your body belongs to me. I have the right to ogle and grope

you, and you have to put up with it.' And it's a way of saying to other men, 'Look what I possess.' It's to do with power. (Tina)

Campaigns against sexual harassment have also stated very clearly that sexual harassment is to do with establishing and maintaining male power.

> As with rape, sexual harassment is not a sexually motivated act. It is an assertion of hostility and/or power expressed in a sexual manner. (Alliance Against Sexual Coercion, 1981: 17)

Lesbian sociologists Sue Wise and Liz Stanley (1987: 64) make the same point: sexual harassment, they say 'may sometimes involve "sexual" behaviours of one kind or another, but this "sexual" is the means to an end and not an end in itself. Power is the desired element involved; and females and sex are merely means of enabling them to "do power".'

There is a central irony here. Women say: it was about power, it was sexual harassment. Men say: it was about power, therefore it *wasn't* sexual harassment. In many men's discourse, sexual harassment is about sex, and sex has nothing to do with power. Several men explained that women misunderstand the situation:

> I think women often don't realize that it's not basically sexual; it's to do with power and status. A young attractive woman has a very high status among men – they know that this cute young thing is the sort of thing movie stars are willing to risk their fortunes over. Her status is way above that of the balding forty-five year old man in our looks- and sex-based society. It isn't really sex he's after – the aim is to bring her down a peg or two, so I wouldn't call it sexual harassment. (James)

> Harriet said it was sexual harassment, but I still don't see it as sexual harassment. I would class it as being a status-related thing. It was a status thing, not a sexual thing. (Fred)

> They do it as part of the power relations between boys and girls in school or wherever. . . . I wouldn't really call it sexual harassment. (Chris)

These men, then, are explaining women's experience of sexual harassment in terms of power: 'the aim is to bring her down a peg or two'; 'it was a status thing, not a sexual thing'; 'part of the power relations between boys and girls'. It isn't to do with sex; it is to do with power. *And therefore it isn't sexual harassment.*

The advantages of a discursive perspective for feminism

To sum up, we have explored four discursive mechanisms through which the erasure of sexual harassment is achieved. The first of these is most commonly used by our female participants: the refusal of victimhood ('I can't have been sexually harassed because I'm not a victim'). The remaining three, while available as discursive moves to women, seem more often to be used by our male participants. These involve (i) the claim that frequently occurring, taken-for-granted behaviours comprising 'normal' or 'natural' social interaction between men and women cannot count as sexual harassment; (ii) the claim that only behaviours motivated by sexual desire, with the goal of sexual intercourse, can count as sexual harassment; and (iii) the claim that behaviours the primary aim of which is to assert power and dominance are not fundamentally sexual and cannot count as sexual harassment. These strategies together work a form of magic – and with the sleight of hand of a vaudeville conjurer, sexual harassment simply disappears by definitional fiat.

Positivist researchers (feminist and non-feminist alike) have expended a great deal of time and energy on the attempt to devise watertight definitions of sexual harassment. We have argued here that these are largely futile. From a discursive perspective, the assertion of one construction of reality over another is one of the techniques employed by any dominant group in order to maintain its position of power (Berger and Luckmann, 1967). In the examples cited above, everyday discourse functions to render insignificant or invisible precisely those actions which feminist discourse constructs as routine instances of sexual harassment. As Collinson and Collinson (1992) point out:

> An uncritical belief in the power of either codes of practice or employment legislation to change attitudes and practices on sexual harassment reflects a highly mechanistic, non-sociological understanding of organisations. The complex *social* relations and practices of organisations cannot be reduced to narrow, legally constructed and/or formally defined rules of conduct.

What is needed instead is an understanding and deconstruction of the discursive techniques used to render sexual harassment invisible or non-existent, and an understanding of how it is that the 'victims' of sexual harassment are themselves complicit in this process.

At a time of backlash against feminism, when feminist gains are being attacked as 'political correctness' and when students at the Massachusetts Institute of Technology, acting for 'freedom of speech', burned copies of the sixty-eight-page booklet *Dealing with Harassment at MIT*, which they described as 'a total abrogation of free expression' (Davies, 1994), we cannot, even if we wanted to, impose a single 'right-on' feminist definition of sexual harassment. Charges of exaggeration, oversimplification, inadequacy or inflexibility beset any such attempts. Nor do such definitions enable us to understand the complexities of recent widely publicized cases, such as the accusations and rebuttals of sexual harassment at Simon's Rock College in Massachusetts (Botstein, 1990), or the accusations of sexual harassment by two lesbian graduate students against feminist theorist and literary critic Jane Gallop (Talbot, 1994). As feminists striving to understand and to tackle abuses of power, we need to understand the mechanisms through which incidents and experiences are constructed as or actively excluded from the category of 'sexual harassment', and to develop a more sophisticated understanding of the complexities within which the definition and discursive management of 'sexual harassment' is enmeshed.

References

Abbey, A. (1982) Sex differences in attributions for friendly behavior: do males misperceive females' friendliness? *Journal of Personality and Social Psychology* 42: 830–8.

Adams, J., Kottke, J. and Padgitt, J. (1983) Sexual harassment of university students. *Journal of College Student Personnel* 23, 484–90.

Aggarwal, A.P. (1987) *Sexual Harassment in the Workplace*. Toronto: Butterworths.

Alfred Marks Bureau (1982) *Sex in the Office*. Borehamwood, Herts.

Alliance Against Sexual Coercion (1981) Organizing against sexual harassment. *Radical America* 15: 17–34.

Berger, P. and Luckmann, T. (1967) *The Social Construction of Reality*. London: Penguin.

Botstein, L. (1990) J'Accuse. *Lingua Franca* June, 21–4.

Canadian Human Rights Commission (1983) *Unwanted Sexual Attention and Sexual Harassment: Results of a Survey of Canadians*.

Collins, E. and Blodgett, T. (1981) Some see it . . . some won't. *Harvard Business Review* 59, 76–95.

Collinson, D.L. and Collinson, M. (1992) Mismanaging sexual harassment: protecting the perpetrator and blaming the victim. *Women in Management Review* 7(7), 11–16.

Davies, J. (1994) Codes of Mr and Miss Conduct. *Times Higher Education Supplement* 14 January, 14.

Dziech, B. and Weiner, L. (1984) *The Lecherous Professor*. Boston: Beacon Press.

Farley, L. (1978) *Sexual Shakedown: The Sexual Harassment of Women on the Job*. New York: Warner Books.

Gruber, J.E. (1992) A typology of personal and environmental sexual harassment: research and policy implications for the 1990s. *Sex Roles* 26, 447–64.

Herbert, C. (1989) *Talking of Silence: The Sexual Harassment of Schoolgirls*. London: Falmer Press.

Industrial Society (1993) *No Offence*. London: Industrial Society.

Iley, C. (1991) Blurred line between flirty and dirty. *The Sun* 18 October, 9.

Kenig, S. and Ryan, J. (1986) Sex differences in levels of tolerance and attribution of blame for sexual harassment on a university campus. *Sex Roles* 15, 535–49.

Lester, T.P. (1993) The EEC Code of Conduct on Sexual Harassment. *New Law Journal* 22 October, 1473–4.

MacKinnon, C. (1979) *Sexual Harassment of Working Women: A Case of Sex Discrimination*. New Haven, CT: Yale University Press.

Name Withheld (1992) Why women don't quit jobs when they are sexually harassed. *off our backs* January, 5.

Powell, G.N. (1986) Effects of sex role identity and sex on definitions of sexual harassment. *Sex Roles* 14, 9–19.

Rich, A. (1980) Compulsory heterosexuality and lesbian existence. *Signs: Journal of Women in Culture and Society* 5(4), 631–60.

Riger, S. (1991) Gender dilemmas in sexual harassment policies and procedures. *American Psychologist* 46(5), 497–505.

Rubenstein, M. (1987) *The Dignity of Women at Work: Report on the Problem of Sexual Harassment in the Member States of the EC.* Equal Opportunities Unit, DGV, European Commission.

Talbot, M. (1994) A most dangerous method. *Lingua Franca* February, 1 and 24–30.

Thomas, A. and Kitzinger, C. (1990) Sexual harassment: when it isn't seen that way. *British Psychological Society Psychology of Women Section Newsletter* 5, 4–7.

Thomas, A. and Kitzinger, C. (1994) 'It's just something that happens': the invisibility of sexual harassment in the workplace. *Gender, Work and Organisation* 1(3), 151–61.

Watts, J. (1990) Rape in the quad. *Observer.* 25 November.

Wilkinson, S. and Kitzinger, C. (eds) (1993) *Heterosexuality: A 'Feminism & Psychology' Reader.* London: Sage.

Wise, S. and Stanley, L. (1987) *Georgie Porgie: Sexual Harassment in Everyday Life.* London: Pandora.

Wolf, N. (1993) *Fire with Fire: The New Female Power and How it will Change the 21st Century.* London: Chatto and Windus.

3

'What is it?' Masculinity and Femininity in Cultural Representations of Childhood

Erica Burman

What is it? Well, I know it's a baby. The question, of course, is whether it's a boy or a girl, and the persistence of this question flies in the face of many a firm commitment to antisexist practices. It withstands the conviction that gender is not somehow fully emergent or functioning from birth, and even that gender demarcations are, or should be, irrelevant to the early psychological life of infants. The first, obvious reason why this question spills out of my mouth is that this is the conventional question to ask; it constitutes the 'appropriate' response to a new birth. Secondly, cultural practices for marking and constructing gender go way beyond the pink and blue, to enter into interpretations of foetal movements in the womb, or of the polaroid print-outs from the ultrasound scans, as in the declaration of mothers-to-be that 'He's waving at me'. But more than this, given the highly gender-divided and stratified nature of social practices, establishing if 'it's' a boy or a girl *is* relevant to knowing how to deal with, interpret, come to terms with this new addition to humanity. It reflects how, within current social arrangements, gender is central to our definitions of human subjectivity. To treat a baby as gender-neutral, as an 'it' rather than a 'he' or a 'she', therefore, is tantamount to denying its (or perhaps I should say his or her) humanity.

I open with this example to highlight how there is a certain ambivalence within our resistance to gendering babies, and perhaps children too. In this paper I want to explore a range of cultural representations of children, and to consider the significance of the gendered associations these hold. My emphasis will be on the varieties of, and tensions between, these differing gendered representations. I am going to evaluate something of the significance of the ways gender representations enter into contemporary discussions in the UK of children and childhood. The implications of these extend beyond how we look at and treat children. I will be suggesting that it is important to acknowledge the diversity of discourses of childhood in order to move away from analyses which treat 'childhood' as a monolithic cultural category. Admitting the fragmentary and sometimes contradictory representations of childhood that are available permits speculation on, firstly, their meanings; secondly, the roles they may be playing within the cultural–political arena; and thirdly, the wider social tensions this variety of definitions indicates.

Gendering the child

Is the child a girl?
Since the eighteenth century, with the birth of the modern notion of childhood (along with the modern state), the child has been regarded as vulnerable and in need of care and protection. Positioning children as standing outside worldly preoccupations, this romantic notion endows them with a unique, privileged perspective on daily practices – as more natural and more free from contamination by an alienated and alienating civilization. Such notions are of course embedded within colonial philosophies, such as that 'civilization' is a Western quality, while the association with nature is commonly attributed to subordinated groups, including women and black people. Carolyn Steedman (1991) has argued that, in so far as it has been gendered, the dominant European representation of the child is as feminine: in Victorian England, the quintessential child was a little girl. And from then on, it is little *girls'* writing that has been held up as a looking-glass: as offering both insight into the 'other' world of childhood, and a quaint, innocently beguiling commentary on social practices. This is so, irrespective of whether the texts were actually written by the young girls or, more interestingly, were written adopting the narrative voice of a young girl (Steedman, 1982).

Significantly, in terms of cultural associations, the category of childhood is feminine, but 'youth' is masculine. The *real* children who were the object of the social and legal gaze were primarily male, those boys and young men considered likely to be 'delinquent', who constituted a threat to the social order. Control, rather than protection, has motivated nineteenth- and twentieth-century British legislation on child welfare (Dingwall et al., 1984), and the UK is not alone in this. Further, the representation of children as passive, immature and vulnerable both required and lent credence to compulsory schooling, itself functioning to regulate the conduct of this potentially unruly group (Hendrick, 1990). A conception of children as passive and knowing nothing worked to disenfranchise their class and community knowledge and replace it with socially approved training and socialization. In this sense the notion of the educable child rendered young people economically as well as intellectually dependent, while it was the economic independence arising from their (albeit exploited) labour that constituted them as a source of social disorder.

Growing boys

If the state of childhood is rendered feminine, the developing child, the child of developmental psychology (itself a product of nineteenth-century practices of regulation and surveillance: Rose, 1990) is masculine – in a number of ways. Firstly, in a very direct way, developmental psychology exemplifies what Spender (1980) calls 'he-man language'. Until recently, accounts uniformly referred to the child as 'he'. While this was, and continues to be, defended as referring to the 'generic he', this sets up an invidious situation whereby the child is either treated as male or accorded some kind of anomalous trans-gendered or gender-free status. Those of us who are convinced of the constructive power of language must assume that this use of gendered pronouns contributes to the prototypical developing child being constituted as masculine (see also Burman, 1994a).

Secondly, the developmental model is masculine in the sense that it privileges culturally masculine qualities. Carol Gilligan (1982) has pointed out how models of moral development treat the discourse of separate and equal rights expressed by boys and men, and associated with masculinity, as developmentally superior to moral accounts expressed by girls and women that emphasize relatedness and are associated with femininity. Moreover, while gendered assumptions enter into the structures through which development is said to occur, development is portrayed as following a structural path from attachment to detachment, from concrete to abstract thinking, from dependence to autonomy. Here too we see the 'higher' levels of development associated with masculinity, with the 'less developed' stages associated with femininity. As Valerie Walkerdine (1988) elaborates, competence itself is gendered through the term 'mastery'.

The gendering of developmental accounts is overdetermined in a variety of ways, with science, itself gendered, treated as synonymous with thinking – as in Piaget's model of the child as mini-scientist (Piaget, 1957). This is taken up in toy advertisements which move from child-centred discovery to the gender-stereotyped model of scientific problem-solver, as in the text to a toy advert:

He's researching surface texture, differentiating between colours, and developing his audiosensory perception. He thinks he's playing with a rattle. (Duplo, 1984)

Other advertisements purvey a model of child as scientist, astronaut, baby pioneer and construction engineer, the last with small print that reads:

> Even the simple act of picking up one of the blocks helps a baby learn how to grip. Once he's mastered that he'll try stacking them up. This is good too – it develops his eye/hand co-ordination. And even if he knocks the whole lot down, it's still educational. (It shows a baby he's in control and gives him his first feelings of independence.) (Advertisement for Fisher Price toys, 1991)

Notice how being destructive or making a mess is sanitized ('if he knocks the whole lot down') into being 'educational', so that any protesting mother is positioned as impairing his motor ('developing eye/hand co-ordination') and emotional ('shows a baby he's in control and gives him his first feelings of independence') development.

The significance of gender associations sometimes takes on highly explicit as well as implicit forms within developmental psychological accounts, as in this extract:

> A key to the mental hygiene of early childhood lies in building up adequate self-dependence. Even in infancy this principle of self-dependence must be respected. Not only from the breast must the child be weaned. By slow gradations he must develop fortitudes which lie at the basis of detachment . . . If his mother must leave the house, he must be content to watch her through the window, even though it costs him a struggle. In time he must learn to go to bed alone, and later, to school alone. These are elementary lessons in self-reliance . . . (Gesell, 1950: 261)

The process of acquiring 'self-reliance' or 'self-dependence' is seen as a gradual achievement akin to weaning, requiring bravery, that is, a manly 'fortitude'; and an achievement which is not without cost, without a 'struggle'.

The psychic 'costs' of growing up bring about a nostalgia for the happy state of omnipotence attributed to childhood. This is capitalized upon by marketers so that the reader is invited to 'Remember that feeling of total control', with the explicit rendering of car as toy restoring that sense of mastery to 'take you from 35 years to 4 years in an instant' for a 'test drive down memory lane' (advertisement for the Peugeot 405, 1992). The text moves between addressing the sophisticated adult consumer of technology – 'Integrated Chassis Design

(ICD). A unique configuration of suspension layout, weight distribution and bodyshell rigidity' – and invoking 'the child within' by adding in parentheses, after this list of technical specifications, '(it sticks to the road like chewing gum to a school desk)', this functioning both to reiterate and to transgress the boundary between serious adult and playful child. Quite apart from the spurious romanticization of 'that feeling of control', it scarcely needs pointing out that by both image and text the 'you' who 'handled your favourite toy car' is clearly positioned as male. And if the playful activity of childhood is constructed as male mastery to sell expensive toys to wealthy adults (male or female?) in this car advertisement, in another the very ownership of a car is naturalized within the life course, through its associations with physical maturation ('All life's journeys should be unforgettable'; advertisement for the Rover 400, 1992). But the representation of development itself renders the white, middle-class male child as norm, as the boy who aspires to stand out and succeed – for whom 'life is too short for boring cars' (Rover 400, 1992).

Of course, feminist psychoanalytic accounts such as those by Dorothy Dinnerstein (1977) and Nancy Chodorow (1978) have placed great weight on the fact that most children are mother-reared, in accounting for the current structuring, not only of masculinity (wrought by the cost of surrendering the first feared and loved object), but also of gender inequalities. While such accounts focus on the significance of the primary caregiver being a woman, my current interest is in why her child has been so uniformly represented as a boy. Denise Riley (1983) noted that the childcare books emerging in the late 1940s and 1950s were so imbued with the 'desert island' abstracted and asocial approach to child development that the term 'couple' was used to refer to *mother and child*, rather than the mother and her adult partner. This couple, like the one it alludes to but differs from, is also a heterosexual one, in which the passive, containing woman is positioned as serving and facilitating the active male. Indeed there is a whole host of popular cultural texts which explicitly play on the slippages between woman/man and mother/son. In terms of the Gesell extract quoted above, we could note that the fortitude necessary for the transition from attachment to autonomy is apparently required by mothers too. As the chorus of a 1940s jazz song entitled 'Psychology' puts it:

Some day he'll leave me and I'll let him go.
Some other women will win him I know.
Till then I'm bouncing him on my knee
Because my baby is only three
And he taught me psychology. (Kay Cavendish, NBC)

Overdetermined as this mirroring of mother–child, woman–man relations may be, we should speculate on the investments that maintain it. Clearly one consequence of representing the mother–child relation as a mother–son relation is that this suppresses the homoerotic dynamic that would be present if the child were female. And speaking of investments, parallels are drawn between the maturation of the developing male child (and the mother who brings him up to leave her) with that of the maturation of financial savings in the slogan for a bank (formerly a building society) 'Growing, Growing, Gone', where capital growth is portrayed as being as 'natural' as physical development over the passage of time (Abbey National, 1992). Here the developing child, and the changing role of his (and again it is 'his') mother, function not only as a mark of the natural inevitability of the life cycle, but also as a reminder of the differing financial demands children of different ages make, with a triptych of images of mother encouraging 'his' first steps towards a toy, seeing him off to school, and finally at his wedding (Abbey National, 1992).

The child as 'other' to the man

Culturally, maturity is equated with masculinity. We seem to be returning to the same old story of women and children functioning together as the 'other' of men, with women infantilized as passive and inferior. The child, like the woman, is an object to be known, the boundaries of whose personal privacy are violated without apology, whose actions are surveyed, regulated, measured, and constructed by the omnipotent viewer, who is positioned as 'caring'. Many fears and fantasies are both conveyed and repudiated within this concept of 'care'. What this conception sets up is a version of the 'master–slave' dialectic, whereby the (male) adult surveyor of the child/woman can both identify with and refuse the passivity and helplessness which she (as object both as child and woman) exemplifies. The conception of a detached, competent (male) adulthood presupposes an attached, dependent, helpless (feminized) childhood. The point here is that the competent male model needs the incompetent female for its demonstration, just as the master needs the slave to constitute and maintain his lordly status.

But before we get too depressed by the monolithic hegemony of cultural representations, I want to stay with the variations, albeit variations on a theme, for a little longer. So far we have a situation where the developing child, the child in the state of developing, is rendered masculine, while the state from which 'he' (sic) is developing, childhood, is feminized. But are infants always passive, feminine objects of nurturance? No. I suggest that where babies and children are active in the expression of their wants, needs, frustrations, they become culturally masculine. To make a perhaps far-reaching connection, perhaps the awe with which women who actively voice their desires are regarded (that is, they are regarded as castrating) can be compared to the terror inspired by the uninhibited demands of a needy infant. My point here is that the equation between woman and child is not absolute, nor is the direction of associations necessarily one-way. So far I have presented some contrasts between one set of cultural representations of childhood and another set, those of developmental psychology. I have focused on the latter partly because it is an important resource for technical legislative regulation of contemporary forms of childhood (Rose, 1990; Hendrick, 1990). But now that we have explored some of the contrasts, I want to move beyond asserting equivalences and slippages between woman and child to address the inter-relations between these definitions.

Gender/child inter-relations

As dynamic

The first point is that adult–child relations are relational: each structures and constitutes the other. Models of childhood presuppose and give rise to prescriptions for mothering. The insecure, needy child requires the 'good enough' mother; the communicative child requires the 'sensitive' mother; the behaviourist child requires the mother who manages and structures 'his' reinforcement history; the 'progressivist' child requires the playing mother. (Owing to the exclusivity accorded to the mother–child 'couple', the responsibilities of a father figure are less specified.) Clearly these roles and relations reinscribe familial ideologies which tie women to children and take them outside the (adequately) paid labour market. But the important issue here is that definitions of mothering exist *in relation to* definitions of childhood, *and vice versa*. So, changes in women's roles give rise to changed positions for children. While it has taken many years and many academic research disputes (and research careers) to establish that children *can* be adequately cared for without the full-time participation of their mothers (for example, Hennessy et al., 1992), it is important to see the positions of mother and child as mutually dependent. Ann Solberg's (1990) study of Norwegian children of working mothers suggests that they regard themselves (and are regarded by others) as more grown up by virtue both of their greater participation in domestic labour and of spending more time at home on their own. If we treat definitions of mothering and of children as separate we could fail to appreciate existing or novel forms of contemporary childhood subjectivities, or worse still, see them only as deviant forms from the desirable norm – as is the case with the pathologization of non-Western children who violate Western conceptions of the happy, playful, innocent child by leading autonomous, responsible and far from carefree lives. If we acknowledge, then, that definitions of childhood are not fixed, and indeed may be undergoing change, then the question that follows is: what is the nature and implication of such change?

The right to choose
Firstly, this is the era of rights and charters, both internationally and, more specifically, in the UK. Along with the Parent's Charter and the Educational Reform Act (1988), the Patient's Charter and privatization of the NHS, we have the Children's Act (1990) and the rallying cry of children's rights. Children in Britain now have a 'right' to be consulted about their care and custody, and local authorities are required to seek their views (although whether they actually act according to children's wishes is another matter: Bell, 1993). Key test cases have been presented and sustained where children 'divorce' their parents. The discourse of rights employed here has a different ring from the discourse of children's 'needs' that informed, for example, custody decision-making formerly (although the discourse of needs is alive and well – if only by virtue of it being claimed by children themselves). Discussion in terms of 'needs' positions adults as having a duty to provide conditions necessary to the child's well-being (with the proviso that perceptions of what constitutes children's needs have varied according to social and historical conditions: Dingwall and Ekelaar, 1986). The current situation is one where 'choice' rules over 'need'. But the same issues of determining what children want still arise. Fineman's (1989) analysis of the implementation of child advocacy in the USA suggests that what this does is to legitimize the existence of yet another layer of professionals who draw on and recycle existing definitions of child development to inform their consultations with, and interpretation of their consultations with, children. Just as the proposal to lower the age of consent for girls in the name of children's rights is a thinly disguised attempt to reduce state responsibility for 'teenage mothers', the lesson for us in the UK is that the rhetoric of choice is likely to be more illusory than real.

Consumption as participation
Secondly, corresponding with the liberal discourse of choice and rights, children are positioned as consumers. Rather than (or as well

as) engaging in moral panics over what children see on TV, we have children treated as mature, discerning viewers (Messenger Davies, 1989). Child psychologists can then set themselves up in business to develop the child market, arguing that 'today's children are more sophisticated than ever before and have a right to information about goods that are available' ('The man who loves to sell candy to babies', *Observer*, 29 July 1990). A more subtle variety of this argument marks the departure from a 'care and protect' model of childhood to one of participation and understanding. As psychologist Brian Young puts it: 'Advertising is part of life. Kids must learn to deal with it' (in 'Plaything of the Advertisers?', *Independent on Sunday*, 1 December 1991). The Britain of the 1980s has been portrayed as hard and money-grabbing. Within this material and psychic economy children have functioned as signifiers of their parents' occupational and material status, exemplified by the 1990 Children's World slogan 'Fashion for the Upwardly Mobile'. An article from the September 1989 issue of *Parents* magazine – incidentally the only article in the issue which has anything to do with men – is a fashion feature where father and children have been whisked off to department stores and dressed up for display. There is little to suggest that this set of significations is changing.

Hence it is important to notice the maintenance of particular models of childhood within these novel forms. The autonomous nature of the child is emphasized within the recent discourse of child choice in clothing by juxtaposition with the parents' (usually the mothers') reactions. An article which discusses the clothes some pre-schoolers 'opted' for explains the preference for comfort with the comment 'Children are sensual by nature and like things that feel as well as look good' ('Left to their own devices', *Guardian*, 27 May 1991). The article reports a mother asserting children's rights to full participation in the fashion world:

> I think kids should have as much spent on them as adults. Good clothes give them confidence. I get satisfaction from them looking good, and they do too. They hate clothes from Marks and Spencer. They want to look different. (*Guardian*, 27 May 1991)

It should be recalled that the liberal discourse of rights treats all rights as equal and equivalent, and consequently flattens out relations of power and inequality. While feminists have recognized the ways this has dogged debates (for example, over pornography: Cameron and Frazer, 1984), the gender-free discourse of children's rights may pose similar problems.

The revival of a conception of child as mini-adult gives rise to especial anxieties in the case of little girls. Here too a variety of models (in both senses of the word) is invoked to deal with the emulation of sexualized feminine fashion by little girls. In the first instance we have children's 'rights' to be fashionable underscored by children's 'needs' to be accepted by their peers. There is a dilemma here for the mother who wants her child to be happy and liked by others – not to mention consequences of the financial imperative to buy their child's social acceptability. In the following example, the mother of seven-year-old Kellie fulfilled her demand to buy her

> a mini-skirt and leggings. I bought them for her because it's how all the kids in the class dress. She would love a suspender belt. And she wants all those modern shoes with heels. I don't mind really, it's what's in fashion. ('Just like mummy wears?', *Guardian*, 19 January 1992)

Parents were reported to distinguish between the contexts in which girls dressed up in these ways (it was only OK at home), and to accept them wearing aspects of stereotyped adult femininity as long as they did not sport 'the whole package – pierced ears, scent, make-up, high heels' (*Guardian*, 19 January 1992), which was taken to make them vulnerable. The final word in this article comes from a parent who views preoccupation with fashion as indicating a healthy concern with taking care of herself necessary to her personal (but definitely feminine) development, which (*pace* Foucault), is seen as aiding the constitution of her self-concept:

> I think it's an encouraging sign that she takes care. She has to learn a sense of style and of herself, just like she has to learn simultaneous equations. (*Guardian*, 19 January 1992)

Dilemmas of agency

This increasing sexualization of young girls (which parallels the infantilization of women) highlights the dilemmas within a liberal discourse struggling to accord agency to children. Indeed Rex and Wendy Stainton Rogers (1992) note that the child has replaced the maiden in new mythologizations of the (sexual) corruption of innocence. An abused child may be a 'victim', but as such she or he has been rendered passive. By contrast, the current message for young children in the UK is that 'We can say no'. Does this mean that if they haven't said 'No', they are collaborators rather than victims? The opposition between 'innocent' and 'knowing' is still reproduced when the traditional notion of childhood as asexual is replaced by one of children's rights. Further, according agency to children may usher in a form of victim-blaming so that they are treated as responsible for their own abuse. Moreover, we should not forget how sexuality is central to the maintenance of the boundary between child and adult. Sexual activity in most cultures marks the transition to adult status.

Admitting infantile and child sexuality therefore challenges existing categorizations, and especially threatens the nostalgic sentimentalized notion of childhood (a challenge Freud both revealed and suppressed: Rush, 1977; Masson, 1984). The shift from one conception of childhood to another seems merely to confirm a double bind of being either a passive, asexual victim or an active collaborator (Kitzinger, 1990). What seems to be missing from this picture is an analysis of power.

Childhood as a social world focused on the domestic realm is, of course, central to the maintenance of asymmetrical gender relations, and the sanctity and the privacy of the home has masked the abuse of both women and children. A happy, cosy childhood is now synonymous with stability and tradition – significantly eliding personal and social history (as, for example, in Abbey National's slogan 'permanent values in a changing world' accompanying a selection of photos representing the development of a nuclear family over time, with financial investment conflated with stereotypes of personal security). Children represent that part of ourselves we want to protect and nurture. We relate to children through the lens of our own recollected childhood, and our efforts as adults to repress the frustration and powerlessness, and repair this (or, in some horror films, to avenge it). The mother quoted earlier denied the suggestion that she saw her child as an index of her own social status:

> No, I think it's more a reflection of my own childhood. We had to wear horrible jumpers that my mother knitted and I hated it. I think people can be lazy about how they dress their kids. Maybe they don't have the time or the imagination. (*Guardian*, 27 May 1991)

Significantly, she does not mention having the money.

Whose girl?

If the quintessential child is a little girl, then it should come as no surprise that her sexuality is presented ambivalently. The popular film *My Girl* (released in 1992, with the video version staying in the top ten rentals in the UK for over a month: *What's on TV*, November 1992) manages simultaneously both to sexualize her by tracing the development of her relationship with Thomas J, and to celebrate the essential innocence and purity of childhood (and thereby also the 'naturalness' of heterosexuality). While in the film (which in the UK is rated PG: suitable for children with parental guidance) eleven-year-old Anna Chlumsky kisses Macaulay Culkin, the feature on this in the magazine *Smash Hits* (a substantial proportion of whose readership is under ten) carries the title: 'What's it like kissing Mac?'

with the answer 'Yuck!' The subtitle reads 'Anna Chlumsky on snogging Hollywood's hottest property'. While she is sexualized in the description of 'snogging', then, the threat to Anna's essential childishness is warded off by her retort 'Yuck!' The text merits a closer look.

> This is Anna Chlumsky, Macaulay Culkin's co-star in *My Girl*. She's sitting in a posh hotel in Mayfair, West London with her mum, and she's giggling and telling *Smash Hits* all about *that* scene. You know the one? By the lake? Where she gets to kiss Macaulay? For their characters Vada and Thomas J it's a first kiss. And in real life, for both Anna and Mac, it was their first snog too! So what was it like? 'Yuck! I can't tell you if Mac's a good kisser, I've nothing to compare it to. We just wanted to get it over with, it took 15 takes in the end!'
>
> And do they really have the hots for each other?
>
> 'No, ahahahaha, we're good friends though. Whenever I go to New York I go and see him.' (*Smash Hits*, 5–18 February, 1992, emphasis in the original)

Note how the juxtaposition between telling *Smash Hits* 'all about *that* scene' and 'sitting . . . with her mum' succeeds in both indulging a gossipy voyeurism (of adult sexual confession) and securing her position as dependent child, albeit one who knows that 'snogging' is something to giggle about. She is accorded the desire to want to 'snog' or to 'have the hots', but her account safely refuses it.

According to *Smash Hits*, the film 'tells the story of how hard it can be growing up. Only this time, it's from a girl's point of view.' There are two points of interest here. Firstly, the film's claim to be 'from a girl's point of view' (with 'only this time' implying that most other accounts have been from that of the boys) is undermined by its title, *My Girl*, which is plainly from someone else's point of view (Thomas J/Macaulay Culkin, and the audience). However much the actual content of the film is represented as being 'from a girl's point of view', it is framed within a larger narrative which explicitly positions her as object rather than subject. Secondly, the storyline of 'how hard it can be growing up' suggests that what is difficult is the process of *transition from* childhood, thereby defining the arena of childhood itself as safe and trouble-free. The later description of her as 'a sweet, highly intelligent 11 year old' is next to a photo-shot with a text inset in the tradition of film gossip: 'Mac's co-star Anna Chlumsky: "Whenever I go to New York I go and see him."' This functions in similar ways to that of the text alongside nude pin-ups in British tabloids which reinforce by omission the sauciness and sexualization of the model by mentioning her intellectual rather than physical attributes.

While Anna is addressed as an active sexual agent, as when she 'gets to kiss', or asked 'does she have the hots', the text makes clear that the screen kiss was a 'first kiss' (for both of them). Hence the staging of a 'snog' (and it is made clear that it was no more than staged) works to highlight the children's *a*sexuality. Further, there is something peculiarly self-maintaining and contradictory going on. The act of performance (of the kiss) that both highlights, and merits the protestations of, this innocence violates precisely that which it sets out to secure (rather in the ways virginity tests do). It constructs what it seeks to deny, it produces awareness about sexuality while simultaneously trying to proscribe it. I focus on this presentation of *My Girl* because it reflects a set of social preoccupations which both challenge and remake concepts of childhood, such that the film succeeds both in acknowledging and in rejecting child sexuality. It both gives vent to the anxiety and contains it: it does this in the text by Anna's expressions of disinterest; and within the plot by making it impossible that the friendship could be maintained or develop (since the 'boyfriend' dies early on in the film).

Women and children

It seems there are striking resonances between cultural representations of childhood, and dominant traditional notions of femininity. The child, like the woman, requires care and protection. These so-called 'needs' are related to the legal position of women and children, with both groups historically treated effectively as possessions owned by men (Lowe, 1982; Smart and Sevenhuijsen, 1989). In his analysis of gender representations in advertising, Goffman 1979) noted how devices such as body posture portrayed women as passive, unaware, vulnerable and helpless – features he explicitly regarded as reflecting a cultural infantilization of women.

As separate?
However, the need to resist the elision between woman and child should be clear: girls are otherwise fated to occupy a position of uniform passivity and powerlessness. Despite the gendered assumptions that inform accounts of child development, childhood is a period of *relative* freedom from traditional gender prescriptions. Hudson (1984) notes that the young British women she interviewed preferred to identify themselves within a discourse of adolescence rather than one of femininity. She suggests that this is because the developmental 'stage' of adolescence, with its culturally masculine connotations, offers them access to a more active and varied range of subject positions. Childhood, or the discourse of development, may

then become a site of resistance for women. On a similar note, Diana Gittins' (1985) observation that age and gender are asymmetrical categories from the point of view of their meaning and function as power relations is relevant. While age is an 'eventually achievable' category, gender is treated as relatively immutable. Hence the denial of power on grounds of gender rather than age is final. The position of child may therefore have some advantages for girls and young women.

Woman as boy?

However, while women have come to play an ever-growing part in the public sphere of production, and feminism has, arguably, indelibly changed some aspects of women's consciousness, the cultural indices of this change seem mixed. Rosaline Coward (1984) and Judith Williamson (1987) have noted how the greater earning and buying power of women has been reflected in images of women who looked straight into the camera, but whose strength was mitigated by looking damaged or beaten up. Similarly, the arresting cover girls of the late 1980s who returned a level, piercing gaze resembled pretty boys, gamine tomboys. Why should the success and increasing status of women be associated with images that rob them of femininity? Is a powerful woman a boy? Does this add a new nuance to the saying that a woman in a man's world has to act like one? It seems that the variability, the relatedness of discourses of childhood and of femininity are in danger of folding into each other, of mutating one into the other. This has implications for both children and women, particularly in relation to definitions of sexuality.

Eternal truths?

Corresponding with the supposed media creation of the 'new man', we have seen a proliferation of images of men and babies in the UK. Most of these maintain some fairly traditional, stereotypical masculine attributes alongside the caring, nurturant associations of participative fatherhood. Recall here the theme of patriarchal lineage in the 1989 Kodak ad with its slogan 'only T grain has no grain as far as the eye can see', depicting a man holding a baby up high to survey the land he(?) will inherit, or that of a male intelligence outdoing female nurturance in the Norweb central heating advert ('When it's more than just a question of warmth'). A relatively new addition to the marketing scene is the production of male perfumes or fragrances (as opposed to 'aftershaves'). While women's perfumes continue to celebrate helplessness, compulsion and passivity (as in the early

1990s Opium advert's caption 'parfum de dépendence', with its explicit textual references to death), men's perfumes focus on passion and intimacy as healthy. A man's smell can (apparently) connote care, continuity and tradition. In 1989 Charles of the Ritz produced an image of man, woman and child to market its men's perfume. The text on the picture (presented in scrawly – do we read romantic? – writing and in poetry form) explicitly mobilizes 'signs of Man' (sic) that allude to big, meaningful concepts: of love, family, tradition, culture, with juxtapositions of body and stone emphasizing solidity, permanence, continuity. The image portrays woman and man above child, with the child's face buried in the man's shoulder, thus rendering only minimal gender cues, although the length of hair would perhaps connote a boy. No clothing is visible. The man's face is more clearly lit, and therefore defined, than the woman's. In fact the direction of the lighting is such that his head is positioned in between the light source and her face so that he puts her in shadow, and her lips touch his hand as he cradles the child's head, a nice touch of deference to his paternal authority.

At around the same time (1989–92), Calvin Klein introduced its marketing for a new 'eau de toilette', with its own paternal imagery. In 'Eternity' the mother figure is completely absent. Also in black and white, it portrays the man, this time prostrate, holding across his (bare) breast the head and torso of what looks like a child, *and* looks like a woman. The face is more visible now, the hair is short but in a style that a girl or woman might wear. The long-lashed eyes are closed and the angle of the small-featured face is such that it is hard to judge whether it is the face of a child, or the face of a woman in foreshortened perspective. The eyes are closed as if in rapture or blissful sleep, secure in his hands – one of which is on her/his forehead and the other around her/his shoulder. His hands, then, obscure other clues that might disambiguate the figure; the back is turned so breasts would not be visible, while his left hand sports a wedding ring. While a towel is discernible under his head, the scene is not unlike that of two people in bed together.

What does it mean if the figure held in the man's arms can be read as either representing a woman or a child? If this is so, then we are faced with two possible and invidious interpretations: woman as infantilized, or child as lover. Either way their positions have been collapsed together within the ambiguity of this visual representation. What is set in circulation is both the transgressive sexualization of children or/and the desexualization of women. We might speculate on the significations of the woman in the Ritz ad becoming replaced by the child in the Calvin Klein one. If the picture is read as of man and child, is it an image of protection or of abuse? The covert sexual connotations of men and baby ads have been noted by feminists (such as Smart, 1989), and the examples I have shown are typical in presenting images of physical power and intimacy between man and baby/child (and now woman?), in ways that emphasize the man's sexuality – most notably by having him bare-chested. Indeed, when in 1991 Norway announced the setting up of a new ministry for children, not only was this headed by a man (since this was said to demonstrate that it was being taken seriously), but publicity images depicted him within the now obligatory iconography of the new man, bare-chested – but with *two* babies (*Guardian*, 21 May 1991). It is surely no coincidence that concepts of virility and potency elide sexuality with power. The production of these ambiguous marketing images can be interpreted as reflecting a moment in contemporary culture when the category of the child is shifting to accord greater agency to children and, paradoxically, this threatens to confirm women's subordinate status. The texts marketing the 'new' involved father are explicitly linked to, present themselves as continuous with, the old patriarchal father, with the child/woman locked in an everlasting embrace of care and control.

If the period 1989–92 marked the sexual blending of gender and age categories, subsequent developments seem to pose some partial resolution to these ambiguities, but in less than helpful ways. While the general cultural sexualization of little girls continues apace, the sexual and gender anomalies of the male accessory market seem, like the pre-Oedipal themes they echo, to be resolved in favour of fixed gender identification, as in razor ads which depict the admiring little boy imitating his father, practising for the patriarchal position that will soon be his. Here themes of tradition and continuity are retained, but sexual nuances are safely secured within traditional gender roles (and displaced to the adult heterosexual couples of the Häagen-Dazs ice cream ads).

Outside the arena of arty black and white ads, the categories of gender and childhood have recently been re-wrought to create new identities forged across the twin Tory discursive practices of 'Back to Basics' and 'the market'. In a bizarre twist, the assertion of children's rights to equal participation in legal decisions and consumption of goods turns into a repudiation of childhood per se. The murder of two-year-old James Bulger by two ten-year-old working-class Liverpool boys in 1993 has severely strained the romantic concept of childhood, with natural innocence transmuting into original sin. Once it was determined that the children could be considered criminally responsible, their treatment in legal, press and political commentaries exhibited all the attributes of *in*humanity that characterize the portrayal of mass murderers and rapists (Cameron and

Frazer, 1987) with the judge ruling for 'detention without limit for "unparalleled evil"' (*Guardian*, 23 November 1993). It seems that if the actions were not those of children, we cannot accept them as adult either.

Where girls forgo child status if they are sexually active or even abused, violence and aggression are the cultural domains that mark the boundary for boys' exemption from childhood. In a climate of according greater agency to children, the costs of failing to act in ways conforming to our notions of childhood are vilification, abhorrence and excommunication from humanity. As the British press coverage of the Bulger case exemplifies, the enormity of the investment in particular cultural understandings of childhood is betrayed by the torrents of hate, fear and loathing, alongside pathologization of working-class families, that is unleashed at its violation. We have come full circle, then, from gender as central to membership of humanity even for children, to particular gendered positions elaborated for children that render them outside the socio-moral sphere. There are direct practical consequences too. Little boys who not long ago would have been sent to educational psychologists with 'behavioural difficulties' are now being referred for being 'evil' (Tom Billington, pers, comm., 1994). It seems it is preferable to maintain the horror of the domain of the natural (of violence or sexuality) rather than to admit the destructive impulses created by the too cultural and material deprivations that lie within our responsibilities. Such are the psychic and cultural resources that are simultaneously constituted and warded off by the patriarchally structured technologies of gender, age and development.

I want to finish by highlighting four arenas for feminist intervention in the cultural definition and regulation of gender and childhood. Firstly, we need to theorize the diversity of ways in which the woman–child relation is articulated, rather than colluding with the overdetermined ways in which women and children are collapsed together. But, secondly, we also need to ensure that analyses of the positions of women and of children are not treated as absolutely separate, because this fails to recognize the centrality of models of childhood to current forms of social organization, including, and perhaps especially, gender relations. Thirdly, we need to extend this analysis outside the privileged arena of glossy magazines, over-hyped films and local moral panics. The elision between woman and child, with corresponding attributions of both sexualization and desexualization is nowhere more evident than in representations of the 'Third World', especially as presented by aid and charity organizations (Burman, 1994b, 1994c, 1994d). We need to resist and challenge the genre of women and children peopling the appeal for money, where we, the readers, are positioned as the male providers and experts who will save them and watch over them. Fourthly and finally, it is therefore vital to draw attention to cultural–historical, as well as gender, specificities in order to resist the globalization and homogenization of development structured into patriarchal representations of children, men and women.

References

Barker, M. (1989) Investigation into the attitudes of children towards comics with regard to the particular comics read and sex of subject. Unpublished undergraduate project, Manchester Polytechnic.

Barker, M. (1990) *Comics: Power, Ideology and the Critics*. Manchester: Manchester University Press.

Bell, V. (1993) Governing childhood: neo-liberalism and the law. *Economy and Society* 22(3), 390–405.

Burman, E. (1992) Developmental psychology and the postmodern child. In J. Doherty, E. Graham and M. Malek (eds), *Postmodernism and the Social Sciences*. London: Macmillan.

Burman, E. (1994a) *Deconstructing Developmental Psychology*. London: Routledge.

Burman, E. (1994b) Poor children: ideologies of childhood in charity appeals. *Changes: An International Journal of Psychology and Psychotherapy* 12(1), 29–36.

Burman, E. (1994c) Innocents abroad: western fantasies of childhood and the iconography of emergencies. *Disasters: International Journal of Disasters Studies and Management* 18(3), 238–53.

Burman, E. (1994d) Appealing and appalling children. Paper for Manchester Hospitals Trust Psychotherapy Service, Gaskell House, June.

Cameron, D. and Frazer, L. (1984) The liberal organ: needs, rights and pornography in *The Guardian. Trouble and Strife* 4, 23–7.

Cameron, D. and Frazer, L. (1987) *Lust to Kill*. Cambridge: Polity.

Cavendish, K. (n.d.) *Psychology*. New York: NBC.

Chodorow, N. (1978) *The Reproduction of Mothering*. Berkeley, CA: University of California Press.

Coward, R. (1984) Pouts and smiles. In *Female Desire: Women's Sexuality Today*. London: Paladin.

Dingwall, R. and Ekelaar, J.M. (1986) Judgements of Solomon: psychology and family law. In M. Richards and P. Light (eds), *Children of Social Worlds*. Oxford: Polity.

Dingwall, R., Ekelaar, J.M. and Murray, T. (1984) Childhood as a social problem: a survey of the history of legal regulation. *Journal of Law and Society* 11(2), 207–32.

Dinnerstein, D. (1977) *The Rocking of the Cradle and the Ruling of the World*. London: Souvenir Press.

Fineman, M. (1989) The child advocacy movement in the United States. In C. Smart and S. Sevenhuijsen (eds), *Child Custody and the Politics of Gender*. London: Routledge.

Gesell, A. (1950) *The First Five Years of Life: A Guide to the Study of the Pre-school Child*. London: Methuen.

Gilligan, C. (1982) *In a Different Voice: Psychological Theory and Women's Development*. Cambridge, MA: Harvard University Press.

Gittins, D. (1985) *The Family in Question*. London: Macmillan.

Goffman, E. (1979) *Gender Advertisements*. London: Macmillan.

Hendrick, H. (1990) Constructions and reconstructions of British childhood: an interpretive survey, 1800 to the present day. In A. James and A. Prout (eds), *Constructing and Reconstructing Childhood: Contemporary Issues in the Sociological Study of Childhood*. Hampshire: Falmer Press.

Hennessy, E., Martin, S., Moss, P. and Melhuish, E. (1992) *Children and Daycare*. London: Paul Chapman.

Hudson, B. (1984) Femininity and adolescence. In A. McRobbie and M. Nava (eds), *Gender and Generation*. London: Macmillan.

Kitzinger, J. (1990) Who are you kidding? Children, power and the struggle against sexual abuse. In A. James and A. Prout (eds), *Constructing and Reconstructing Childhood: Contemporary Issues in the Sociological Study of Childhood*. Hampshire: Falmer Press.

Lowe, N. (1982) The legal status of fathers: past and present. In L. McKee and M. O'Brian (eds), *The Father Figure*. London: Tavistock.

Masson, J. (1984) *The Assault on Truth*. Harmondsworth: Penguin.

Messenger Davies, M. (1989) *Television is Good for Your Kids*. London: Hilary Shipman.

Moore, S. (1988) Getting a bit of the Other: the pimps of postmodernism. In R. Chapman and J. Rutherford (eds), *Male Order: Unwrapping Masculinity*. London: Verso.

Piaget, J. (1957) The child and modern physics. *Scientific American* 197, 46–51.

Riley, D. (1983) *War in the Nursery: Theories of Child and Mother*. London: Virago.

Rose, N. (1990) *Governing the Soul: The Shaping of the Private Self*. London: Routledge.

Rush, F. (1977) The Freudian coverup. *Chrysalis* 1, 31–45 [reprinted in *Feminism & Psychology*, (1996), forthcoming].

Smart, C. (1989) Introduction. In C. Smart and S. Sevenhuijsen (eds), *Child Custody and the Politics of Gender*. London: Routledge.

Smart, C. and Sevenhuijsen, S. (eds) (1989) *Child Custody and the Politics of Gender*. London: Routledge.

Solberg, A. (1990) Negotiating childhood: changing constructions of age for Norwegian children. In A. James and A. Prout (eds), *Constructing and Reconstructing Childhood: Contemporary Issues in the Sociological Study of Childhood*. Hampshire: Falmer Press.

Spender, D. (1980) *Man Made Language*. London: Routledge and Kegan Paul.

Stainton Rogers, R. and Stainton Rogers, W. (1992) *Stories of Childhood: Shifting Agendas of Child Concern*. Hemel Hempstead: Harvester Wheatsheaf.

Steedman, C. (1982) *The Tidy House: Little Girls' Writing*. London: Virago.

Steedman, C. (1991) A history of subjectivity. Paper for Feminist Research Seminar, Manchester Polytechnic.

Walkerdine, V. (1988) *The Mastery of Reason: Cognitive Development and the Production of Rationality*. London: Routledge.

Walkerdine, V. and the Girls and Mathematics Unit (1989) *Counting Girls Out*. London: Virago.

Williamson, J. (1987) Packaging the punch. *Womensreview* 1, 14–16.

4

Conflicting Opinions? 'Anorexia Nervosa', Medicine and Feminism

Julie Hepworth and Christine Griffin

In this chapter we use a poststructuralist form of discourse analysis informed by feminism to examine the legacy of the discovery by Gull (1874) and Laseque (1873) of 'anorexia nervosa' (hereafter AN) during the late nineteenth century. We consider various feminist approaches to AN, especially the work of Susie Orbach (1978, 1986), Kim Chernin (1985) and Sheila MacLeod (1981), examining the discursive continuities and disjunctures between the texts of Gull and Laseque and feminist analyses of AN over one hundred years later. We go on to consider the complex inter-relationship of such discourses in interviews with British health care workers who are involved in the diagnosis and treatment of AN. These semi-structured interviews were conducted by Julie Hepworth with twelve male and female psychiatrists, clinical psychologists, general practitioners, psychiatric nurses and feminist therapists who worked with clients/patients diagnosed as 'anorexic'. We end by examining the implications of our arguments for feminist theory and practice around AN, addressing questions of terminology, treatment, popular representations and recent developments in feminist psychology and cultural studies.

We argue that some of the elements contributing to the contemporary status of AN within the popular, medical and feminist domains are enmeshed within the language and the discursive forms through which AN was constructed during the late nineteenth century. This discursive structure is based on a traditional medical model: AN now has its own symptomatology within the official classification system of diagnostic criteria used by clinical psychologists and other mental health professionals (American Psychiatric Association, 1987, 1994). Such a model locates 'anorexics' in a relatively passive position (as 'ill'), and as 'manipulative' through their refusal of medical treatments (as well as food). The medical model appears antithetical to feminist approaches which emphasize the socio-cultural pressures on young women to be slim rather than individual (or family-based) pathology. Most feminist analyses continue to operate (albeit critically) with the concept of AN, and tend to represent women's eating disorders as involving external factors. However, they retain the category of AN, which positions women as passive sufferers of a particular condition.

It is significant that the focus of this interview study was those working with people diagnosed as 'anorexic' rather than on clients/ patients themselves. Both our feminist perspective and the use of a poststructuralist approach led us to adopt this strategy. We are not engaged in a search for the causes of AN. Rather, we are examining the construction of the category of AN and the discursive practices and subject positions which are made available through the complex process of that construction. This is not to imply that 'anorexics' are not also involved in the construction (and deconstruction) of AN, but we do wish to take a closer look at those who attempt to explain (and 'treat') AN from outside, as it were. Some feminists, of course, attempt to explain AN from inside, as former 'anorexics' (Chernin, 1985), but it is the *category* of AN which is our main concern, not those individuals who are seen to have this 'illness'.

The 'discovery' of anorexia nervosa

It is generally accepted that anorexia nervosa was 'discovered' by the British physician W.W. Gull (1874) and the French physician E.C. Laseque (1873) during the 1870s, as a disease with no identifiable organic cause which involved extreme dietary restriction. For Gull and Laseque, AN was not only more prevalent amongst young women, it was also a typically – even inherently – 'feminine' condition (Hepworth and Griffin, 1990). Similar practices of 'dietary restraint' or 'self-starvation' did not begin in the late nineteenth century, however, and nor have they been confined to young women of the Anglo-American middle classes (Tait, 1993). Prior to that period, 'fasting girls' had been dealt with under the aegis of religion rather than medicine, in the domain of clerics rather than physicians – or therapists (Hepworth, 1991).

The shift in the 'treatment' of dietary restraint (or what Tait calls 'dietary asceticism') coincided with more widespread political changes related to the rise of scientific medicine (Merchant, 1980). This move from the primacy of the religious sphere to that of the medical domain as the site of dominant discourses is also found in relation to the concept of adolescence, which was also 'discovered' during the late nineteenth century, this time by American psychologist G. Stanley Hall (Griffin, 1993).

A number of recent texts have examined the historical contexts in which fasting occurred amongst young women prior to the 'discovery' of AN (Brumberg, 1988; Tait, 1993). They have also traced the medicalization of such fasting practices which followed from the work of Gull and Laseque. We will turn now to the key discourses through which these two physicians (who operated in a state of traditional academic competition rather than mutual co-operation) constructed AN as a disease (see Hepworth and Griffin, 1990, for a fuller analysis).

AN was constructed as an inherently *female* condition partly through Gull and Laseque's focus on women patients. It was also defined as an inherently *feminine* condition which could develop from women's supposedly irrational nature. Laseque wrote about anorexia as an exclusively female condition, arguing that the cause of anorexia lay in women's emotional and unstable nature. He based his explanation of anorexia on supposed disturbances in women's marital, sexual and emotional lives. According to Laseque:

> A young girl, between fifteen and twenty years of age, suffers from some emotion which she avows or conceals. Generally it relates to some real or imaginary marriage project, to a violence done to some sympathy, or to some more or less conscient desire. At other times, only conjectures can be offered concerning the occasional cause, whether that the girl has an interest in adopting the mutism so common in the hysterical, or that the primary cause really escapes her. (Laseque, 1873: 265)

Anorexia was presented as a reflection of the failure of individual young upper- and middle-class women to move without fuss into their pre-ordained marital and domestic roles. Alternatively, women were discouraged from intellectual stimulation, and were commonly prescribed enforced passivity, limited reading and a quiet domestic life when conditions such as anorexia and hysteria had been diagnosed (Showalter, 1987). Drawing like Laseque on a dominant patriarchal discourse of femininity, Gull also constructed women as having an inherently 'feminine' irrational disposition which could develop into conditions such as AN.

The discourse of femininity associated specific qualities with the feminine, in direct opposition to those qualities and characteristics which were held to be synonymous with masculinity. This ideological representation of femininity constructed women as creative, emotional, deviant and mad, compared with the more rational, scientific and logical qualities associated with (white upper- and middle-class) masculinity (Merchant, 1980; Turner, 1987). As Joan Jacob Brumberg (1988: 142) puts it in her historical study of the rise of anorexia nervosa in Western societies: 'Victorian physicians . . .

attributed hyperactivity in anorexia nervosa to the basic perversity of the female adolescent'.

In their search for an acceptable cause for anorexia, both Gull and Laseque relied on the supposedly 'irrational' nature of women, and especially young women. AN was defined as a form of irrational behaviour which was inherently feminine and therefore only to be expected in young women, particularly those of the more affluent class. Such irrationality and 'mental perversity' was also held to be characteristic of the insane in general. According to Laseque (1873: 367): 'In comparing this satisfied assurance to the obstinacy of the insane, I do not think I am going too far'.

Gull and Laseque defined excessive restlessness as a 'symptom' of anorexia, and yet 'quietude' and 'contentment' were also seen as evidence of this pathological state. Gull referred to the mental state that could give rise to anorexia as 'mental perversion', whilst Laseque preferred to compare anorexics to 'the insane'. Thus we can see the emergence of the notion of an inherently female and feminine madness which could develop into specific nervous diseases. This argument had been similarly used in explanations of hysterias and neurasthenia (Showalter, 1987).

Gull's (1874) paper on AN represented his attempts to explain a condition through its categorization and integration into a medical paradigm. As self-styled 'experts', these male physicians contrasted their own supposedly rational attempts to explain the condition with the irrational nature of female anorexic symptomatology. The medical paradigm rested on a discourse of scientific discovery which searched for the organic causes of specific 'medical conditions' in order to arrive at a diagnosis (Gilbert and Mulkay, 1984). Gull attempted to find a specific organic cause for the condition he called 'anorexia nervosa' using the traditional medical model. When the search proved unsuccessful, Gull argued that AN resisted further definition.

At this point, Gull started to move away from his search for a physiological aetiology and began to look towards the psyche. It should not be assumed that Gull and Laseque's arguments followed a linear path, nor that each discourse was presented in sequential fashion within their texts. Their failure to identify a 'medical' cause of anorexia did produce a shift towards the psychological domain in search of an explanation, but these themes followed a cyclical rather than linear pattern. Gull continued to search for organic causes, even though he was beginning to suggest that anorexia originated from 'mental perversion'.

Although Gull's explanation for anorexia shifted from the organic and physiological to the psychological, it remained within the medical/scientific discourse. Laseque also made this move into the psychological realm, placing greater emphasis on the role played by the pressures of bourgeois family life in the emergence of AN (Tait, 1993). Whilst the diagnosis of AN was most often discussed in terms of the medical/scientific discourse, the various treatments for this 'new condition' were to be found within the clinical discourse around treatment regimes. Debates over which prescriptive treatments were suitable for AN took place in a context in which even Gull admitted that there was a marked absence of any relationship between the medicinal preparations prescribed and the patients' recovery: 'The medical treatment probably need not be considered as contributing much to the recovery. It consisted, as in the former case, of various so-called tonics, and a nourishing diet . . . The inclination of the patient must in no way be consulted' (Gull, 1874: 24).

As Gull moved away from attempts to determine an organic cause for anorexia, and redirected his attention towards the psyche, his methods of treating and controlling the condition changed. The controlling agent shifted from medical science to the rapidly developing discipline of psychiatry. The medical process of diagnosis, intervention and treatment was applied to the psyche with the overall aim of controlling the patient through the moral (or psychological) domain. According to Gull: 'The patients should be fed at regular intervals, and surrounded by persons who would have moral control over them; relations and friends being generally the worst attendants' (Gull, 1874: 26).

The introduction of 'moral control' and 'moral treatment' received much attention from the medical profession as instruments which could be employed by physicians in the emerging arena of 'mental illness' (Showalter, 1987). The situation had changed by the late nineteenth century, and the clinical discourse reflected this development. In practice, the therapeutic interventions of Gull, Laseque and their contemporaries showed considerable variation. By the end of the nineteenth century, the private home for hysterics was the preferred site of treatment, since incarceration in a public hospital or insane asylum had unpleasant associations with the workhouse for the predominantly bourgeois parents of young women who were diagnosed as anorexic (Brumberg, 1988).

AN is now incorporated into the APA's (1987, 1994) official diagnostic classification system using criteria that draw on some of those discourses identified in the texts of Gull and Laseque. The APA estimates that 95 per cent of those diagnosed as 'anorexic' are female, and AN is still seen as an inherently 'feminine' disorder which affects mostly young women. Amenorrhoea, or the cessation of menstrual periods, is one of the diagnostic criteria for AN, and the return of regular menstruation is one of the key indicators of 'recovery' (Dally, 1969). The gendered nature of AN was also reflected in the interviews with health care practitioners, even when questioned about their experiences of AN amongst young men (Hepworth, 1994).

> *Interviewer*: Have you seen any males who starve themselves?
>
> *Psychiatric Nurse Ms R*: I think it's a lot more severe [in males] in the fact that they can . . . take it on their, out on their bodies quite a lot more harshly so it's more a case of starvation. The case which I saw was a young lad who was very plump, always teased at school and all of a sudden it was just like a crash diet, and that was it, and you know, he then turned anorexic, which was a shame. I haven't really seen that many cases of lads, only a couple, but they've always been much more severe and they seem much younger lads. This lad was fourteen, quite young really.

The gendered nature of discourses around AN is apparent here in the representation of anorexia in males as more severe and involving 'much younger lads' compared to female 'anorexics'. It appears that females and males who are diagnosed as 'anorexics' are judged according to different sets of norms. A fourteen-year-old *female* with the type of eating disorder described by Nurse R would not be viewed as at all unusual, since the peak ages for the incidence of AN are fourteen and eighteen amongst young women (Halmi et al., 1979). Contemporary uses of the discourse of femininity construct male patients diagnosed as 'anorexic' as exceptional, and it was more common to refer to a system of differential diagnosis in the interviews we conducted:

> *Psychiatric Nurse Ms V*: . . . but anorexia in men seems to be diagnosed differently anyway. It's usually put down to depression or . . . endogenous depression. I know a couple of times I've seen men with eating disorders and they haven't been diagnosed as having eating disorders. They've been diagnosed as having something like endogenous depression . . . They usually follow the same pattern as females . . . people who have been diagnosed as anorexics. The outward symptoms seem to be basically the same, but for some reason the diagnoses are different.

It is significant that only psychiatric nurses used this argument about differential diagnoses. As the lowest-status and lowest-paid group of the health care practitioners interviewed, they have the most contact with 'patients', but the least input into the process of diagnosis. Clinical psychologists such as Dr K tended to discuss the possibility of

AN amongst males in terms of a problem of differential *disclosure*, thereby shifting the focus from clinician to patient:

> *Clinical Psychologist Dr K*: I haven't treated any men with it [AN], no. I've had my suspicions occasionally. I think it's quite difficult to get men to admit to an eating disorder. I can only think of one lad who I saw last year who had a number of again sort of social skills, self-esteem problems, who I feel his eating pattern was probably abnormal that he was very thin and so on, but not to the extent that I think he was anorexic, you would not necessarily label it as anorexia.

We are not making any statement here about the prevalence of differential diagnoses or differential disclosure, since this was not a study of the diagnostic process. However, the powerful connection between AN, femininity and female status which is brought about via the discourse of femininity shapes the way in which these health care workers responded to our questions and to their patients, both male and female. AN is a profoundly gendered category. We would not deny that there might be particular reasons why eating disorders are more prevalent amongst women, in terms of the inequality of social conditions that encourage women to monitor weight gain and strive to be thin (Wolf, 1990). However, eating disorders may in fact be more common in men than is realized because of the discursive structure through which AN is represented as a typically female condition. This process then contributes to the overwhelming prevalence of AN amongst women which is reflected in official statistics. Changing social perceptions might allow more males to report, or be diagnosed as having, specific eating disorders. However, one symptom of AN remains gender-specific: amenorrhoea completely excludes males from the process of diagnosis.

Recent medical, popular and feminist texts on AN have challenged the medical explanations found in Gull and Laseque, yet many have retained the concept of AN itself (for example, MacLeod, 1981; Chernin, 1985; Orbach, 1986). Feminist analyses have been successful in challenging the dominance of the 'anorexia as pathology' perspective, but the medical and clinical discourses have not disappeared altogether. Feminist texts have incorporated additional discursive dimensions concerned with socio-cultural pressures on young women to be slim and attractive to men. We will now provide a brief review of some key feminist texts on AN, examining various discursive continuities and disjunctures with the work of Gull and Laseque.

Feminist analyses of 'anorexia nervosa': Orbach, Chernin and MacLeod

There is no one unitary feminist theory of AN, but rather a series of analyses and speculations that acknowledge – in different ways – the roles of gender and the socio-cultural sphere in what is sometimes referred to as 'the slimmers' disease'. In this relatively brief section we can only illustrate some of the diversity of feminist approaches, concentrating on three texts that are generally taken as influential following the expansion of feminist work on AN after the publication of Susie Orbach's *Fat is a Feminist Issue* in 1978. We focus here on *Hunger Strike* (1986) by Susie Orbach, a book which dealt with AN rather than eating disorders in general; *The Hungry Self* (1985) by Kim Chernin; and *The Art of Starvation* (1981) by Sheila MacLeod.

We would not argue that these three texts constitute the full range of feminist approaches to AN during the early to mid-1980s, but they do give some indication of the breadth and diversity of feminist work. All three are British-based, so North American and other international work would not necessarily follow similar lines, although there are many overlaps (for example Brumberg, 1988; Bordo, 1988). The late 1980s to early 1990s also saw further texts on AN and eating disorders in general which incorporated the critiques of earlier feminist texts; offered more detailed historical analyses; drew on poststructuralism, feminist appropriations of psychoanalytic theories and feminist studies. We will mention some of these texts in our final section.

An enormous body of literature lies between and around the work of Gull and Laseque in the 1870s and that of Orbach, Chernin, MacLeod and other feminist writers over one hundred years later. This includes the work of Hilda Bruch (1974), and a considerable psychiatric and psychological literature, most of which manages (even after Orbach) to ignore or to minimize the impact of gender and/or the social domain on AN (see Malson, 1991 for critique). In the clinical and popular arenas, this work represents the dominant narrative surrounding AN. Whilst they have not been unaffected by feminist work, mainstream psychological texts have incorporated feminist arguments alongside their reliance on an individualizing discourse surrounding AN which pathologizes particular young women (or their families – especially mothers) as 'sick' and psychologically 'disturbed'.

Orbach, Chernin and MacLeod all retain the use of terms such as AN and/or 'anorexia'. Susie Orbach does discuss the historical origins of AN and she acknowledges feminist and other criticisms of the term (Orbach, 1986). She tries to avoid its pathological connotations in her emphasis on the socio-cultural context and pressures on women to be slim and attractive to men. Orbach states: 'I use anorexia in its broadest possible sense to describe those women who are invested in not eating and have become scared of food and what it can do to them' (Orbach, 1986: 13).

Kim Chernin's text is a discussion of women and eating disorders using a Kleinian psychoanalytic perspective based on object relations theory. She writes as a woman who has had a problematic relationship with food and eating (Chernin, 1985). Throughout the text, Chernin treats 'anorexia' as a disease entity – which is represented as being responsible for the death of many women, including for example the well-known US singer Karen Carpenter.

Sheila MacLeod also writes as a 'recovering anorexic' in a text which takes an existential approach to AN (MacLeod, 1981). Female identity is seen as central to the state of 'anorexia nervosa', which MacLeod views as a manifestation of an existential crisis resulting from women's confusion about their 'being-in-the-world'. Mac-Leod's text focuses on the meanings of AN for 'anorectic women', with AN serving as a symbol for both oppression *and* resistance, in which starvation has its own aesthetic. Ironically, although MacLeod writes as a 'recovering anorexic', and makes the voices of women diagnosed as anorexic visible in her text, she (like Chernin) still locates herself at something of a distance from other 'anorectic women'. In places she positions herself as both therapist/researcher *and* client/anorexic: 'My experience shows that getting the anorexic to eat is only half the battle' (MacLeod, 1981: 122).

All of these writers locate AN as a condition which is specifically female and closely related to femininity, especially as it is lived by young, white, middle-class women. As feminists, Orbach, Chernin and MacLeod do not follow Gull and Laseque in describing AN as inherent in feminine 'nature' (that is, feminine irrationality). Their texts operate through a different discourse of femininity. Orbach constructs AN as a product of patriarchal society and the pressures it imposes on women. Chernin represents AN and other 'eating disorders' as outcomes of the unconscious conflict within the mother–daughter relationship, and MacLeod views AN as a particular existential dilemma facing women and a specific aspect of female identity. These texts emerge from a very different historical and political context from that of Gull and Laseque. However, AN is still constructed (albeit critically) as a disease entity which is *gendered*. These feminist researchers are, like Gull and Laseque, engaged in a search for the causes of AN, although Orbach, Chernin and MacLeod would locate those causes in different arenas.

To some extent, Orbach, Chernin and MacLeod draw on the medical/scientific discourse in their discussions of AN, again within very different analytic contexts. Despite her forceful criticism of the medical aetiology of AN, Orbach can still state: 'Anorexia nervosa is perhaps the most dramatic outcome of the culture's obsession with regulating body size. In the last ten years this psychological syndrome has risen to epidemic proportions' (Orbach, 1986: 23). The medical/ scientific discourse is evident here in terms such as 'psychological syndrome' and 'epidemic proportions' alongside Orbach's stress on the role of socio-cultural forces, although even patriarchal society is psychologized as 'obsessed with body size'. MacLeod presents a rather different analysis, rejecting the view of AN as 'a matter of slimming that has somehow or other got out of hand' (MacLeod, 1981: 10), referring to 'anorexia nervosa' as a 'disease' throughout most of her 1981 text.

Despite the (different) feminist arguments presented in all three texts, some elements of the dominant discourses through which AN and other 'eating disorders' are constructed in the mainstream medical and clinical psychological literature remain. Feminist arguments have made an impression on the mainstream literature, but the two perspectives are not identical, because feminist literature starts from a position of marginality in relation to the medical and clinical–psychological mainstream. The central discursive conceptualization of AN as a pathological disease entity which is specific to women, and the main narrative form of a search for the causes of this 'disease', remain in place. Orbach, Chernin and MacLeod present different arguments about the 'female' nature of AN, and about the role of family relationships. They would all challenge the mainstream attempt to pathologize AN as a disease found in particular 'dysfunctional' individuals or families. However, the medical/scientific discourse of disease and feminist forms of the discourse of femininity do not sit easily alongside one another. Feminists face the difficult task of explaining why only *some* women 'become anorexic' if *all* Western women face similar (though not identical) socio-cultural pressures to be thin.

At this point the family discourse and the discourse of identity enter the picture as potential solutions to this dilemma. Kim Chernin draws on the family discourse most explicitly by concentrating on the mother–daughter relationship (Chernin, 1985). For Chernin, anorexia represents a retreat to the mother in an attempt by daughters to recapture the safety of the mother–daughter bond, reflecting the daughters' difficulties in separating from the mother (cf. Lawrence, 1984). Orbach and MacLeod also use the family discourse, but in different ways, when they examine the role of the mother–daughter relationship in the development of AN. These analyses criticize the practices of white middle-class nuclear families without a detailed examination of the system of compulsory hetero-sexuality or the nuclear family norm.

Janet Sayers has pointed to the strange absence of the father in many feminist analyses of AN (Sayers, 1988). This absence is notable in the context of debates over the possible relationship between child sexual abuse and women's subsequent eating practices (Berliner, 1993). The family discourse is extremely powerful, and the line between the patriarchal blaming of mothers and a feminist analysis of the mother–daughter relationship is not always an easy one to draw. For Chernin (1985: 43), 'this anguished concern about the mother is hidden just beneath the surface of the eating problem', whilst according to MacLeod (1981: 132), 'for the anorexic, the most important member of that family is her mother'. In these feminist texts, it is not only what is said about the relationships between mothers and daughters that is important, but also what is *not* said about father–daughter relationships.

The one discourse which is most obviously specific to twentieth-century texts on AN is that of identity. Again this appears in rather different guises in the Orbach, Chernin and MacLeod texts, and in each case it operates in conjunction with other discourses. The discourse of identity is generally used in the context of role theory to refer to the conflicts experienced by women (especially young white middle-class women) as a consequence of contradictory expectations about being a woman in contemporary patriarchal societies. Ex-amples include the demands of being a good mother, a successful career woman, a satisfactory (heterosexual) lover and so on. Orbach argues that AN represents one response to this role conflict as young women deny themselves food in an attempt to exert control by denying their need for nourishment: 'The anorexic's refusal to accept her culturally defined role is seen to be per se pathological, not an extremely complicated response to a confusing social identity' (Orbach, 1986: 25).

AN is constructed in the above quote from Orbach as both a refusal to accept the dominant roles associated with (white middle-class) femininity *and* as a response to the contradictions inherent in those roles. 'Anorexic' women are thereby located as both rebels *and* victims in terms of their attempts to 'find' a satisfactory female identity (Corr, 1994). For Kim Chernin, the discourse of identity concentrates on the mother–daughter relationship and the 'uncon-fessed confusions of identity' expressed in eating disorders are assumed to represent women's difficulties in separating from and surpassing their mothers (Chernin, 1985: 36). Sheila MacLeod (1981: 64) constructs AN as 'fundamentally about an identity crisis', in which women must fight to develop an authentic identity in the context of a society where only masculine identities have the right to exist.

Identity is constructed within this discourse along the lines of mainstream social psychology as a unitary aspect of the self upon which individuals strive to impose a degree of coherence. If different aspects of one's identity are in conflict or appear to contradict one another, this is assumed to result in decreased self-esteem and lowered levels of psychological well-being. The search for an 'authentic' identity is also a pervasive element in theories concerning socio-cultural pressures on young women which are assumed to prevent them from finding or expressing their 'true' selves (Mac-Leod, 1981). Identity is conceptualized here as a noun rather than a verb, as something you 'have' (or not) rather than in terms of a more dynamic process of identification (Griffin, 1989). The notion of multiple and contradictory identities is generally associated with psychopathology rather than everyday psychological functioning (see Condor, 1986 for critique).

The discourses found in feminist texts were also reflected in interviews with health care practitioners. Their use of the discourse of femininity has already been discussed in relation to emphases on differential diagnosis and differential disclosure rates between women and men regarding AN. All of these health care workers drew on the medical–scientific discourse in their speculations about the causes of AN, even when they expressed profound uncertainty in this area – as most did. For psychiatrists and GPs there was some reluctance to locate the causes of AN in the socio-psychological domain, which was also reflected in the perceived efficacy of different treatment regimes:

> *Dr J (a general practitioner)*: I'm sure some of it is genetic. I'm sure some
> of it is related to family dynamics . . . but to describe it as a
> psychiatric condition with the sort of notion that somehow if you
> could understand the psychodynamics that have led up to it then
> they'll get better I think is nonsense.

This approach was in stark contrast to that of the psychiatric nurses, clinical psychologists and the feminist therapist, who tended to use a multifactorial model of the causes of AN which stressed socio-cultural factors and family dynamics over (or in contrast to) genetic or organic causes. Unsurprisingly, the feminist therapist, Ms NJ, proved closest to the feminist perspectives of Orbach, Chernin and MacLeod. She described herself as following Orbach 'fairly closely' from a 'fairly classic feminist psychotherapy viewpoint' which focused on the mother–daughter relationship. For Ms NJ, AN reflected what can happen when women cut themselves off from society in an attempt to control their needs (especially involving sexuality), which are constructed as bad and illegitimate in patriarchal terms. Ms NJ described AN as 'literally a self-imposed starvation', and argued that her focus on the mother–daughter relationship did not involve blaming mothers for AN.

The discourse of identity was relatively common in the responses of psychiatric nurses, clinical psychologists and the feminist therapist:

> *Dr M (a clinical psychologist)*: I see the central issue as around control and self-identity.

Dr J (the GP), for example, who at one point drew heavily on dominant discourses of the bio-medical domain, also used discourses from feminist analyses, such as discourses of identity and femininity, but outside a feminist context:

> *Dr J*: I think the problem is to become an autonomous adult, who is essentially self-governing, making your *own* decisions about your *own* life on your *own* terms . . . It's an existential dilemma in fact . . . I don't think they start off that way but their problems about becoming an autonomous adult start to hinge around the dependency problems and the power struggles over their eating. And certainly one of the things that happens is they, a lot of them, then *use* those to becoming an autonomous adult and . . . this fits in with 'they won't eat because they don't want to grow breasts' type of argument.

One issue which was discussed by two women interviewed (the clinical psychologist, Dr M, and the feminist therapist, Ms NJ) was sexual abuse, although a causal link with AN was not represented as strong. As the responses of these health care workers indicate, the similarities and disjunctures between those trained under the medical model and peripheral or oppositional practitioners like the feminist therapist were no more clear cut than the discursive boundaries between the texts of Gull and Laseque and those of Orbach, Chernin and MacLeod. We would not deny, though, that feminist therapists and researchers *are* using different perspectives from mainstream psychiatrists and GPs. At the discursive level, however, these differences are not necessarily so obvious.

Asking different (and difficult) questions: implications for feminist understandings of 'anorexia nervosa'

In this final section we consider the implications of using a poststructuralist form of discourse analysis for feminist understandings of AN and 'eating disorders' in general. We do not wish to couch this discussion in terms of a traditional academic critique which labels earlier feminist work as somehow inadequate or misguided. Feminist theory and practice around 'eating disorders' has produced important shifts in the conceptualization and treatment of women's troubled relationship with food, eating and the body. The work of Orbach, Chernin and MacLeod must be seen in the particular political and conceptual context in which it was produced, when the deconstructive project of feminist poststructuralism was less pervasive.

The first series of moves by feminists working around AN was to locate such 'eating disorders' in a wider social, political and historical context. As such, feminists posited an alternative set of causes for such 'disorders' which emphasized the role of socio-cultural forces in Western patriarchal societies and challenged the pathologizing approach and practice of mainstream health care practitioners. Writers such as Orbach, Chernin and MacLeod were caught in a series of discursive dilemmas involving the representation of women diagnosed as anorexic as rebels and/or victims, questioning the construction of AN by a patriarchal medical profession and developing alternative terminologies to that of AN, with its associated metaphors of disease and individual pathology. There are no easy solutions to these dilemmas, especially for those who continue to experience problematic relationships to food, eating and the body, and for the relatives, friends and health care workers involved with them.

The use of discourse analysis within a feminist perspective enabled us to ask different (although no less difficult) questions about AN. Firstly, in examining the historical and political context in which AN emerged as a clinical/medical disease entity, we go further than Orbach, for example, in deconstructing the term. We do not dwell on the search for a different cause (or set of causes) for AN, but rather we examine the ideological baggage associated with this type of terminology. The solution is not necessarily to find an alternative name for AN, since the term is located so firmly within popular and medical discourses. It is possible, however, to talk of 'body distress' rather than 'eating disorders' in an attempt to avoid some of the pathological connotations of the latter term (Corr, 1994). Some women may find terms such as AN and 'eating disorders' useful in addressing issues concerning their relationship to food, especially if they are, or have been, in distress over this.

The deconstructivist project does not deny that some women do experience distress concerning their relationship to food, eating and their bodies. We would not set out to identify particular women as dysfunctional in terms of their 'distorted body image' or their relationship to food, unlike some clinicians (Dally, 1969). As feminists, we do not assume that some 'disordered' or 'distressed' women have got it wrong whilst others have 'adapted' more successfully to an oppressive patriarchal system. Western patriarchal capitalism creates the conditions in which women's relationship to the body, food and eating is rendered potentially problematic. Our varied class positions, ethnicities, sexualities, age, family histories, religious, educational and occupational backgrounds mean that for some women (and men) this relationship can be more distressing than for others. A deconstructivist feminist approach does not set out to deny that distress, nor to hand such women a pile of feminist theory texts in an attempt to 'raise their consciousness'. It does, however, blur the boundaries between 'disordered' and 'normal' practices surrounding food, without necessarily viewing AN as a form of 'slimming that has somehow or other got out of hand' (MacLeod, 1981: 10).

A discourse analytic approach enables us to examine the implications of language in detail, including the full consequences of using the terminology of disease *and* the ways in which we position ourselves in the narratives we produce. In other words, what subject positions do these discourses through which AN is constructed allow? We have already seen how Sheila MacLeod shifted between a traditionally feminist autobiographical mode in which she was able to draw on her own experience as a 'recovering anorectic', and the narrative form which dominates the mainstream clinical literature, in which she distanced herself from (other) anorexics, thereby constructing anorexics as Other, or not 'normal'. The concepts we use and the ways in which we use them are equally important, since they shape what we (can) say and do about women's relationship to food and eating.

A number of feminists in psychology and cultural studies have adopted poststructuralist forms of discourse analysis in their work on AN and 'eating disorders'. American feminist Susan Bordo locates AN in specific cultural, political and historical contexts, rather than searching for the causes of AN in individual women (Bordo, 1993). She is concerned with the complex and contradictory *meanings* associated with 'the slender [female] body' that emerged during the 1980s (Bordo, 1993: 207). Bordo is less concerned with the causes of AN, in the traditional sense, than with the complex possibilities of multiple cultural readings of the phenomenon. She argues that it is possible to read 'the characteristic anorexic revulsion towards hips, stomach and breasts . . . as expressing rebellion against maternal, domestic femininity', which is represented in the relative lack of the mother's power in patriarchal societies (Bordo, 1993: 207). Bordo goes on to suggest an alternative reading in which 'disidentification with the maternal body, far from symbolizing reduced power, may symbolize (as it did in the 1890s and 1920s) freedom from a reproductive destiny and a construction of femininity seen as constricting and suffocating' (Bordo, 1993: 209). Bordo is not implying that either reading is the 'correct' interpretation of women's experiences of AN. She is examining the role of AN as a cultural phenomenon at particular historical moments: 'when the regulation of desire becomes especially problematic (as it is in advanced consumer cultures), women and their bodies will pay the greatest symbolic and material toll' (Bordo, 1993: 212).

Working as a British feminist in social psychology, Helen Malson argues that the treatment of AN as 'pre-given medico-psychological entity' reinforces the individualization of the diverse problems experienced by women diagnosed as 'anorexic' and excludes gender and social issues (Malson, 1991: 31). She draws on the work of feminists who have used Lacanian theory to examine AN as an element in the construction of patriarchal femininity and sexuality. We would agree with Malson that it is important to 'question the status of "anorexia" as an individualised medico-psychological entity', and that the analysis of AN as gender- and culture-bound does not undermine its 'reality', nor 'question . . . the "reality" of its fatalities or its devastating consequences in many women's lives' (Malson, 1991: 38). We concur with her conclusion that

> the current strictures of prescribed 'femininity' which focus so heavily on the appearance of the female body, and rely for their power on the extruded and fundamentally conflictual position of Woman as Other, must surely take a central place in our understanding of anorexia as a socially specific expression of the impossibility of women's subjected position in contemporary patriarchal society. (Malson, 1991: 38)

Note

This research was carried out as part of Julie Hepworth's PhD (Hepworth, 1991) conducted in the School of Psychology, University of Birmingham, supervised by Christine Griffin, and partially supported by a one-year research studentship from the Economic and Social Research Council.

References

American Psychiatric Association (1987) *Diagnostic and Statistical Manual of Mental Disorders* (3rd edn revised). Washington, DC: APA.

American Psychiatric Association (1994) *Diagnostic and Statistical Manual of Mental Disorders* (4th edn). Washington, DC: APA.

Berliner, L. (1993) Sexual abuse effects or not? *Journal of Interpersonal Violence* 8(3), 428–31.

Bordo, S. (1988) Anorexia nervosa and the crystallization of culture. In I. Diamond and L. Quinby (eds), *Feminism and Foucault: Reflections on Resistance*. Boston, MA: Northeastern University Press.

Bordo, S. (1993) *Unbearable Weight: Feminism, Western Culture and the Body*. Berkeley, CA: University of California Press.

Bruch, H. (1974) *Eating Disorders: Obesity, Anorexia Nervosa and the Person Within*. London: Routledge and Kegan Paul.

Brumberg, J.J. (1988) *Fasting Girls: The Emergence of 'Anorexia Nervosa' as a Modern Disease*. London: Harvard University Press.

Chernin, K. (1985) *The Hungry Self: Daughters and Mothers, Eating and Identity*. New York: Times Books.

Condor, S. (1986) Sex role beliefs and 'traditional' women: feminist and intergroup perspectives. In S. Wilkinson (ed.), *Feminist Social Psychology: Developing Theory and Practice*. Milton Keynes: Open University Press.

Corr, K. (1994) Feminist research on 'eating disorders'. Unpublished draft chapter for PhD, University of Birmingham.

Dally, P. (1969) *Anorexia Nervosa*. London: Heinemann.

Gilbert, G.N. and Mulkay, M. (1984) *Opening Pandora's Box: A Sociological Analysis of Scientists' Discourse*. Cambridge: Cambridge University Press.

Griffin, C. (1989) 'I'm not a women's libber, but . . .' Feminism, consciousness and identity. In S. Skevington and D. Baker (eds), *The Social Identity of Women*. London: Sage.

Griffin, C. (1993) *Representations of Youth: The Study of Youth and Adolescence in Britain and America*. Cambridge: Polity Press.

Gull, W.W. (1874) Anorexia Nervosa (apepsia hysterica, anorexia hysterica). *Transactions of the Clinical Society* 7, 22.

Halmi, K.A., Capser, R.C., Eckert, E.D., Goldberg, S.C. and Davis, J.M. (1979) Unique features associated with the age of onset of anorexia nervosa. *Psychiatry Research* 1, 209–15.

Hepworth, J. (1991) A post-structuralist analysis of the late 19th century medical discovery of anorexia nervosa and contemporary discourses on anorexia nervosa used by health care workers. Unpublished PhD thesis, University of Birmingham.

Hepworth, J. (1994) Qualitative analysis and eating disorders: discourse analytic research on anorexia nervosa. *International Journal of Eating Disorders* 15(2), 179–85.

Hepworth, J. and Griffin, C. (1990) The 'discovery' of anorexia nervosa: discourses of the late 19th century. *Text* 10(4), 321–38.

Laseque, E.C. (1873) On hysterical anorexia. *Medical Times and Gazette* 2, 265–6.

Lawrence, M. (1984) *The Anorexic Experience*. London: Women's Press.

MacLeod, S. (1981) *The Art of Starvation*. London: Virago.

Malson, H. (1991) Hidden a-genders: the place of multiplicity and gender in theorizations of anorexia nervosa. *BPS Psychology of Women Section Newsletter* Winter, 31–42.

Merchant, C. (1980) *The Death of Nature: Women, Ecology and the Scientific Revolution*. San Francisco: Harper and Row.

Orbach, S. (1978) *Fat is a Feminist Issue*. London: Hamlyn.

Orbach, S. (1986) *Hunger Strike: The Anorectic's Struggle as a Metaphor for our Age*. London: Faber and Faber.

Robertson, M. (1992) *Starving in the Silences: An Exploration of Anorexia Nervosa*. Sydney: Allen and Unwin.

Sayers, J. (1988) Anorexia, psychoanalysis and feminism: fantasy and reality. *Association for the Psychiatric Study of Adolescents*, 361–71.

Showalter, E. (1987) *The Female Malady: Women, Madness and English Culture 1830–1980*. London: Virago.

Tait, G. (1993) 'Anorexia nervosa': asceticism, differentiation, government. *Australia and New Zealand Journal of Sociology* 29(2), 194–208.

Turner, B. (1987) *Medical Power and Social Knowledge*. London: Sage.

Wolf, N. (1990) *The Beauty Myth*. London: Chatto and Windus.

Part 2

THEORETICAL ADVANCES

5

Feminist Discourses and Women's Heterosexual Desire

Wendy Hollway

Would you like to express
your sex without stress?
Would you like to discover
Physical conversations
of a different kind?
(Au Pairs, *Sense and Sensibility*)

There is no emancipatory discourse concerning women's hetero-sexual desire; that is, there is no currently available way of conceptualizing women's pleasure and sexual desire (active sexual wants) in heterosexual sex which is regarded as consistent with principles of women's liberation. For radical feminism, heterosexual sex is the eroticization of power difference. For psychoanalytic feminism, particularly Lacanian, desire is engendered by difference, and that difference is inaugurated by the phallus, that is, it is patriarchal.

To agree with the introductory statement does not mean, however, that there is no currently available practice of egalitarian and pleasurable heterosex: I do it, for one. What then is the relationship between sexual practice and this discursive state of affairs? Either I am wrong (lying or conning myself); or so-called rare experience need not affect feminist discourses (Thompson, 1994); or these discourses need some development. In both the second and third cases, it is necessary to conceptualize practices which transcend the determination of discourse. I shall argue the third case.

Discourses of unpleasurable heterosex are supported by recent British empirical work which provides a picture of women who are far from satisfied with their heterosexual relationships, both young women (Holland et al., 1994) and older women in long-term relationships (Duncombe and Marsden, 1993). However, to explore further the limitations of this picture, theoretical work is needed, because what people can report, and how that is made sense of by researchers, is affected by the availability of relevant discourses.[1] Looked at from the perspective that experience is mediated by discourse, the lack of an emancipatory discourse of women's heterosex means that it is very difficult to communicate the experience of pleasurable, egalitarian heterosex, both at the level of simply talking about it, and also at a theoretical level of conceptualizing women's heterosexual desire as consistent with a feminist politics. I shall argue that a feminist discourse on heterosexuality is needed within which the full range of women's experiences can be located; from the experience of disempowerment to the sense of oneself as autonomous sexual agent; from the eroticizing of power difference to the experience of equality and sexual pleasure at the same time.

In summary, the lack of an emancipatory discourse concerning women's heterosexual desire means that there is a serious gap in feminist political discourse: a gap where there could be articulated a possibility of women creating the conditions of sexual pleasure, satisfaction and fulfilment of desire in relationships with other loving and loved adults.

Let me make it clear from the start that the purpose of such a discourse is not to pretend that heterosexual couples can live (and fuck) happily ever after; nor to create an idealized norm against which individual women may fail. It is to de-privatize the actual in some women's lives (how many we cannot know); to articulate the possible, so that women can make better informed choices; and to distinguish the healthy and happy from the oppressive.

There is no emancipatory discourse of women's heterosexual desire

> No questions are being asked in political discourse on sex about hope and sorrow, intimacy and anguish, communion and loss. (Dworkin, 1987: 56)

Since the great feminist debate about women's orgasms in the early seventies (Koedt, 1973), there has been a notable absence of feminist enquiry about 'normal' heterosexual sex, during a time when American and British feminism has concentrated massively on the oppressiveness of male sexuality as manifest in rape, pornography, prostitution and sexual harassment. Male power is understandably the central conceptual tool of these radical feminist critiques of male heterosexuality which have dominated feminism for the past decade, but there is remarkably little attempt to understand how this is negotiated between men and women in real relations. Now there is a sudden resurgence of feminist discussion about women's heterosexuality.[2] This literature is either based on the argument that there can be no emancipatory heterosexuality for women under the conditions of patriarchy (for example Kitzinger, 1994; Schacht and Achison, 1993), or based on the absence of an emancipatory discourse concerning heterosexuality as a problem for feminism (Hollway, 1993; Jackson, 1995; Smart, 1994; Segal, 1994).

The most obvious recent British example of the resurgent interest is the Special Issue of *Feminism & Psychology* 2(3) (Kitzinger et al., 1992) and subsequent *Reader* (Wilkinson and Kitzinger, 1993) on heterosexuality, whose editorial summarized the contributions as 'one long grey stream of heterosexual misery' (Kitzinger and Wilkinson, 1993: 12). In a response to the Special Issue I hazarded the opinion that the way that the terms of contribution were set up for heterosexual feminists' personal accounts made it likely, within the recent context of feminist debate on sexuality, that contributors would be hampered by a sense of guilt as well as an absence of discourses which make sense of 'the pleasures, desires and satisfactions in their sexual relationships' as opposed to the 'painful contradictions' (Hollway, 1993: 412). Several of the heterosexual feminist contributors did testify to the difficulty of responding to 'a public challenge to us to account for the ambiguities of our position' (Thomas, 1994: 317), or felt 'rounded up for confessions in a public forum' (Gergen, 1992: 62). One reviewer of the Special Issue simply said: 'No woman, certainly no feminist, would be likely to want to see herself summed up by a term which defines her primarily in relation to men' (Swindells, 1993: 44). Smart (1994) argues that when the earlier second-wave celebration of women's heterosexual practices was rejected within feminism, guilt was put back in a dominant place, especially because accusations of sleeping with the enemy came on top of white, middle-class women's longer-standing sexual guilt, characteristic of the Christian tradition.

The idea that there is something fundamentally inconsistent about the very terms 'feminist' and 'heterosexual' derives from the developments in radical feminist theory in the 1980s which can be encapsulated in the slogan 'sleeping with the enemy'. The fact that the majority of women continued to do just that was accounted for variously in terms of being a powerless victim of heteropatriarchal power (how can women leave if they've got no independent resources?), or, for those of us with independent resources, it involved false consciousness. The slogan 'any woman can' (be a lesbian) laid down the lesbian feminist gauntlet. However, as Stevi Jackson has recently commented: 'If "any woman can" I, as a financially independent woman surrounded by lesbian friends, ought to have been able to. I could have opted for political correctness via celibacy, but I chose not to' (Jackson, 1994: 14).

Choice is a rare – and brave – term in relation to feminist heterosexuality, particularly in a theoretical climate dominated by social constructionism, in which choice is often regarded as an illusory discursive product of liberal individualism. So Jackson's theoretical position is in this light problematic, but also a fluent expression of the dominant position:

> What is specific to heterosexual desire . . . is that it is premised on gender *difference*, on the sexual 'otherness' of the desired object . . . Since it is gender hierarchy which renders these anatomical differences socially and erotically significant, it is hardly surprising heterosexual sex has been culturally constructed around an eroticization of power. (Jackson, 1994: 3)

While the dominant position derives primarily from radical feminism, Jackson is also echoing the orthodox feminist psychoanalytic account of the construction of desire in gender difference (see Chodorow, 1994 for a clarifying, full account). Adams presents it with a Lacanian accent:

> Both the boy and the girl have to submit to castration to allow the emergence of desire, that investment of the object with erotic value which makes the object relation possible . . . The whole economy of desire is rooted in the phallus *and* this phallus is attributed to the father . . . So if desire is the investing of the object with erotic value, this investment is not made in relation to difference as such, but in relation to a gendered difference . . . Desire is *engendered* by difference. (Adams, 1989: 248)

Lacan took the proposition directly into the realm of heterosexuality, when he made his 'great, scandalous claim that there is no sexual relation', which Gallop interprets as his 'announcement of the impossibility of heterosexuality' (1982: 129). According to Gallop, the arena of gender difference is crucial to feminist transformation: 'any feminist upheaval . . . must undo the vicious circle by which the desire for the father's desire . . . causes her to submit to the father's law' (1982: 71).

The conjunction of radical feminist and psychoanalytic feminist thought in conflating power, difference and desire (albeit from such different epistemological starting points) has made it very difficult to get a theoretical glimpse of any desire, let alone a heterosexual desire, based on equality.[3]

The structural reality of men's privileged access to power and the effects of the dominance of heterosexuality in reproducing women's inequality are amplified in contemporary feminist discourses in which 'compulsory heterosexuality' (Rich, 1980), 'heteropatriarchy' (Jeffreys, 1990) or 'the heterosexual matrix' (Butler, 1990)[4] have become shorthand for the description of a system in which women are represented as having no choice and no meaningful access to power. The implications for a theory of change, and hence a meaningful feminist politics, are profound. It is this problem which has led to the accusations of 'victim' feminism which have so divided feminists of late, particularly in the USA, with other feminists, who want to stress women's agency and (some) power, being labelled 'power' feminists (for example, Roiphe, 1993 and Paglia, 1992).

In the most dogmatic versions of radical feminist discourse, women are represented as inevitably victims in and of heterosexuality. A paradigmatic example, in my view, is Schacht and Achison's article on heterosexual instrumentalism, in which heterosexuality is defined as 'an eroticized hegemonic ideology of male dominance' (1993: 37). (Schacht and Achison are careful to say that 'some sexual acts between women and men are egalitarian' (1993: 39), but since the claim is inconsistent with every feature of their analysis, the qualification is theoretically meaningless and politically redundant.)

This radical feminist emphasis on male power leads to the position that women who have sexual relations with men are necessarily engaged in relations of dominance and subordination: referred to by Dworkin (1981) as the 'eroticization of inequality' and now labelled as 'the eroticization of power difference' (Jeffreys, 1990; Kitzinger, 1994). For Jeffreys, the possibility that women could have orgasms in heterosexual sex under the conditions of patriarchy is seen as a serious problem (Jeffreys, 1990; see also Kitzinger, 1994). Kitzinger asks (problematizing lesbian sado-masochism as well as heterosexuality): 'how then can we have sex without reenacting power differences?' and answers 'I suspect that we can reshape sexual desire only by reconstructing the social and political conditions within which sexuality is defined' (Kitzinger, 1994: 207). This position seems to me to express the core dilemma of contemporary western feminist theory and politics of sexuality.

The same dilemma poses some questions for discourse theory. Is women's sexuality, and particularly heterosexuality, caught in a matrix of discourses? To what extent have feminist approaches been limited by the historical construction of women's sexuality? Is feminism neglecting an extra-discursive terrain? To what extent do our practices and/or our desires transcend discourses?

Power, discourse and subjectivity

By taking the stance that an emancipatory discourse concerning heterosexuality is politically desirable for contemporary feminism, I am making the assumption that the production of discourses can have political effects. The relation between 'word' and 'world' has, however, proven extremely difficult to theorize. The dominance of discursive approaches in social science has led to a remarkable avoidance of the extra-discursive. A recognition of the fact that all understanding of the world is mediated through language has been falsely reduced to a premise that the world can be understood as discursive. This has left out crucial questions about the relation of discourses to practice and to subjectivity, and therefore to agency and choice.

Foucault (1978) famously argued that, far from sex being repressed in modern cultures, as Freud would have it, sex was being actively produced in discourses ranging from that of the confessional to those of public hygiene. He implicated psychoanalysis in positioning a wide range of people through four key discourses: the masturbating child, the homosexual, the hysterical woman and the reproductive heterosexual couple. Foucault's work contributed to an understanding of how deviancies have been produced in relation to the sexual norm of the reproductive couple, and that regulative discourses and practices concerning sexuality have not focused therefore on adult heterosexuality, which remained a hallowed space, protected from public intervention, in the name of the man's right to rule in his own domain.

The implication in Foucault is that a person's sexuality is forged within these discourses. I believe that is too deterministic. To be sure, the nineteenth century witnessed enormous activity in this area, with significant effects, but Foucault's historical analysis relies on the premise that there were sexual practices going on which had been largely outside the sphere of discourse. This extra-discursive sphere could be seen as doubly private, not just located in the 'private' realm of the family, but not talked about there either.[5] However, when sex is not talked about, this absence is not equivalent to an absence of meaning in sex.

Whilst I have been indebted to discourse analytic approaches in my work on sexuality and heterosexuality (Hollway, 1983, 1984a, 1984b, 1989), my central concern has been to theorize the relation between subjectivity, discourse and gendered power relations in a way which does not reduce subjectivity to the sum of positions in discourses, nor women to an object position in power relations with men (and thus to victim status):

In displacing the individual as a simple agent the post-structuralists achieved a massive and important step. However . . . in this view the subject is composed of, or exists as, a set of multiple and contradictory positionings of subjectivities. But how are such fragments held together? Are we to assume, as some applications of post-structuralism have implied, that the individual subject is simply the sum total of all positions in discourses since birth? If this is the case, what accounts for the continuity of the subject, and the subjective experience of identity? What accounts for the predictability of people's actions, as they repeatedly position themselves within particular discourses? Can people's wishes and desires be encompassed in an account of discursive relations? (Henriques et al., 1984: 204)

My earlier work left me convinced of the importance of theorizing sex as signification, but dissatisfied with available accounts of desire. Putting these two together in my response to the heterosexuality Special Issue, I tried to give a theoretical explanation of some fragments of an account of my own heterosexual desire (Hollway, 1993). Amongst many responses (see *Feminism & Psychology* 4(2), 1994 and 5(1), 1995), I was criticized for analysing these desires as if they were outside an 'ideological location' (Brown, 1994: 322), for my recourse to a notion of individual history (Thompson, 1994: 327) and (by implication) for excluding 'structural features of male dominance' from my account (Ramazanoglu, 1994: 321). In each case, the premise seems to have been that when an account is based on women's desires which do not simply reflect the well-known contours of male dominance through heterosexuality, it contradicts an analysis which recognizes those wider inequalities. This was despite the fact that my analysis was based on problematizing pleasure and desire as signification. Yet paradoxically, there is a tendency to dismiss such desires because they are 'ideologically' constructed in discourse; a tendency demonstrated in Thompson's dismissal of my exploration of the signifier 'strong arms' (Hollway, 1993) as tantamount to a Mills and Boon narrative (Thompson, 1994: 326), in Jackson's dismissal as 'a traditionally feminine emphasis' (Jackson, 1994: 5) and also in Brown's charge that I come 'perilously close' to the pseudo-reciprocal gift discourse, when I talk about the significations of openness and giving in heterosexual penetration (Brown, 1994: 324; see Hollway, 1995 for the reply). The whole point of analysing sex as signification is to locate desire and pleasure within social forces, understood through a non-reductive analysis of language, power relations and individual history. I think the misreadings are triggered by my insistence on the importance of the psyche as something which is not a simple reflection of the social, because the dualism which is still so influential in social science has meant that there is no available account of the social and the psyche as mutual productions (see Henriques et al., 1984; Hollway, 1989).

In summary, the problem seemed to be that sex is readily seen as social when it signifies dominance and submission, because this is consistent with available theoretical discourse, but when significations reflect successful resistance to patriarchal relations, for example openness, reciprocity and mutual giving, they are dismissed. Dismissals of individual history and the psyche result in a simplification of the question of how determinative are the wider patriarchal inequalities within which my heterosexual practice, like everyone else's, is located. Because this is unfamiliar theoretical terrain, I shall try to summarize my main arguments.

I have used case examples in order to understand the operations of power and desire in heterosexual couple relations. In the kind of discourse analysis which I used to interrogate the transcripts, I found I needed four strands to the analysis: a simple discourse analysis; a psychodynamic account of the reasons for reproducing or modifying the take-up of positions in discourses; an analysis of the part played by individual history, both conscious and unconscious, in adult social relations; and an emphasis in each of the above analyses on intersubjectivity as formative in the ongoing reconstruction of self, in the past and in the present. Without these components, the account of power relations was unsatisfactory.

For the initial discourse analysis, I identified several discourses concerning sexuality ('male sexual drive', 'have/hold' and 'permissive') and distinguished between the different positions available to men and women. For example, I gave a reading of Jim's account of his early attraction to girlfriends in terms of movement in the account among subject and object positions in three discourses, the power these conferred and the contradictions produced (Hollway, 1989: 61–3). I then reanalysed the same account adding a psychodynamic explanation (1989: 63–6), demonstrating that it was necessary to look for a motive to account for someone's emotional investment in specific positions in discourse, in order to understand the reproduction of gender-differentiated discourses. I concluded that 'over and again in my material, I found that the positions that people took up in gender-differentiated discourses made sense in terms of their interest in gaining them enough power in relation to the other to protect their vulnerable selves' (1989: 60). In this way a connection was made between the power asymmetry of gender-differentiated discourses at the social level and the way this power inequality gets reproduced through individuals; individuals who are agents when they engage in social relations, however constrained their possibilities. Clearly structuralist notions of power are inadequate for the above kind of discourse analysis.

The last two factors, individual history and intersubjectivity, further complicate this picture of the mutual productions of the social (discourse) and the psyche in gendered power relations. I argue that the uniqueness of meaning for each individual is achieved along an axis which registers past events, not cognitively, but in terms of the unconscious. This unconscious registration pervades the meanings involved in the experiencing of later events. I give examples of two women, for both of whom making love without contraception signifies on this axis as securing commitment, because of the implications of having a baby for men addressed by the have/hold discourse. I then situate them differently in relation to individual histories (within discourses) and power relations (Hollway, 1989: Chapter 4). This analysis develops the use of the unconscious in the idea of positions in gender-differentiated discourses being taken up because the power they confer acts as a defence against anxiety. It gives the concept of the unconscious a social basis through theorizing its historical development in relation to meaning and discourse.

Throughout an individual's history, meaning has been achieved, consciously and unconsciously in relation to others. Since infancy, we have used significant others as vehicles for containing some of the ambivalent feelings which it is difficult to acknowledge in ourselves. Defence mechanisms such as projection and introjection operate intersubjectively and continue, more or less unassuaged, throughout life. Much of my discourse analytic work has demonstrated the workings of these unconscious dynamics between women and men where splitting occurs according to normative femininity and masculinity, through gender-differentiated discourses.

So, to take an example from my case material, Will could consciously believe that he did not mind whether Beverley decided for or against an abortion, until, contrary to both their expectations, she decided for an abortion. At that point, Will experienced his own strong wish for Beverley to have their baby, a wish that had been projected by him, because to contain it made him feel vulnerable and out of control, and introjected by Beverley, where it corresponded to standard feminine positioning in discourse (for a detailed analysis see Hollway, 1989: Chapter 5).

Erotic domination

Who can love someone who is less than human unless love itself is domination per se? (Dworkin, 1987: 168)

There is no currently available substitute for psychoanalysis, or, more broadly, psychodynamic accounts of child and adult identity, once it is acknowledged that individual history plays an important part in the reproduction of, or change in, sexual relations (see Hollway, 1996). One of the transformative strengths of recent psychoanalytic feminism is its emphasis on intersubjectivity and the earliest relations with others in the formation of the gendered self (Chodorow, 1978, 1994; Dinnerstein, 1978; Eichenbaum and Orbach, 1982; Benjamin, 1984, 1990, 1995; Ernst and Maguire, 1987). This counteracts the determinist tendencies of a Lacanian analysis noted above. Surprisingly, the contributions of feminist psychoanalysts have not been incorporated into dominant feminist discourses concerning sexuality, even in those areas where transgressive sexual desires appear to be central, for example in sadomasochism, where there is overwhelming evidence of the importance of individual history (see Kaplan, 1993; Welldon, 1988). Many feminists dismiss psychoanalysis wholesale because its practice has been oppressive to women and in particular to lesbians (for example Kitzinger, 1987; Jeffreys, 1990; Kitzinger and Perkins, 1993).

In my view, a feminist theory of sexuality which does not engage with the unconscious effects on adult sexual practices of the formative relations of childhood is going to provide an inadequate base for a feminist politics which, by any definition of politics, needs to understand how people can change:

> No political movement can give expression to our real hopes and longing if it condemns without understanding the alienated forms in which these longings have appeared. (Benjamin, 1984: 308)

In her work, Jessica Benjamin has explored directly the question of erotic domination, both in its gendered aspects and in its relation to 'the earliest issues of intimacy and separation in infancy' (1984: 292). She asserts the importance to all human infants of the 'vital connection to another being' (1984: 293) and the process of acquiring a self through differentiation from others, in particular the other who is the primary carer, usually the mother. A common consequence is a 'conflict of differentiation':

> that between the need to establish autonomous identity and the need to be recognized by the other. The child's independent acts require a recognizing audience and so reaffirm its dependency on others. (Benjamin, 1984: 293)

While adults may have achieved some stability in relation to these issues of dependency and separation, it is in the sexual relationship that they resurface because of its exclusive status in the contemporary West as the location of intimacy.

The denial of dependency, which is characteristic of the way boys are required to give up the mother in order to establish masculinity, produces the problem of domination. However, the conflict of differentiation is not peculiar to boys and neither are we talking about dynamics that are determinative for all boys or all girls. For both sexes, the need for recognition is in conflict with the struggle for autonomy and can produce an artificial resolution by imagining that one can be independent without recognizing the other person as an equally autonomous agent. The current structuring of motherhood exacerbates this tendency in children, and boys already have an extra investment in differentiation because of their exceptionally testing Oedipal drama, which is therefore more likely to culminate in false differentiation. The artificiality of this solution resides in the fact that if we deny the other's agency, 'if we overpower her, there is no one to recognize us' (Benjamin, 1984: 295). Benjamin illustrates the dialectic of control thus:

> If I completely control the other, then the other ceases to exist, and if the other completely controls me, then I cease to exist. True differentiation means maintaining the essential tension of the contradictory impulses to assert the self and respect the other. (Benjamin, 1984: 295)[6]

Erotic domination is a way of 'repudiating dependency while attempting to avoid the consequent feeling of aloneness' (Benjamin, 1984: 296). In voluntary sado-masochism, partners rely on each other, with one maintaining boundaries while the other allows the boundary to be broken. Each relies on the other for the repudiated part. Autonomy and the need for recognition are split, in contrast to true differentiation. The desire for erotic domination

> is an attempt to relive an original effort at differentiation that failed . . . Behind this failure is a replay of the original thwarted impulse to discover the other person as an intact being who could respond and set limits at the same time. (Benjamin, 1984: 303–4)

Contained in this account is the suggestion of 'true differentiation' as the basis for a sexuality which differs from the scenario of erotic domination. The capacity for true differentiation starts when the relations between infant and mother (or other primary carer) contain 'the germ of mutual recognition' (Benjamin, 1984: 305). Whereas Lacanian theory claims that any such possibility does not survive the Oedipal phase (see Adams, 1989), object relations approaches are based on the premise that human beings are basically object- (or person-) seeking. Depending on the quality of early object relations, people can achieve relations in adulthood in which the need for recognition and the wish for autonomy can coexist, albeit in tension (see also Klein, 1963; Person, 1988; Gaylin and Person, 1988). Supposing this capacity can exist in relations between women (which few would want to challenge), the question becomes whether it can be accomplished across gender difference as currently structured, given that the capacity for real recognition and differentiation is undermined by gender difference.[7]

In summary, I am arguing that the meanings of sex, notwithstanding their location within patriarchy, can reflect the themes which result from two adults who have achieved a reasonably successful differentiation, which minimizes the psychic investment in establishing control – engaging in domination – and whose desire can therefore be structured around the pleasures of being recognized and loved as an autonomous being. To maintain that this is possible within the wider institutionalization of compulsory heterosexuality is not to place such people outside social forces, nor is it to deny the empowerment necessary to achieve such a position (Ramazanoglu, 1994: 321). In my view, this possibility is the absence at the heart of feminist discourses of sexual desire and the reason why the 'eroticization of power difference' has come to define the practice of heterosexual sex within feminist discourse.

Heterosexual love

. . . the secret of love is to be known as oneself. (Benjamin, 1984: 301)

Empirical work on women in heterosexual relations continually stresses the connections for women between sex and love, intimacy or emotions. Two examples: 'many wives reported that to enjoy sex they needed to be talked to in a loving and gentle way' (Duncombe and Marsden, 1993: 224); and Stevi Jackson's conclusion from reading the empirical literature on young girls is that their 'capacity for sexual arousal may be bound up with understanding this sensation as love' (Stevi Jackson, 1993: 209). (See also Duncombe and Marsden, 1993; Holland et al., 1994; Lees, 1986; Thomson and Scott, 1991; Hite, 1974.) While feminists and others routinely emphasize the social construction of emotions and of pleasure (Jackson, 1994, 1995; Brown, 1994), I would argue that in the theorization of this area, just as of desire, the relation between the historical construction of subjectivity and the contemporary world in which these women are attempting to negotiate satisfying relationships and enjoyable sex needs to be kept in view. To theorize the desire for intimacy in terms of the need for recognition is clearly relevant here.

Generally, in feminist discourse, love is seen as captured by the discourse of romance. The propensity to be sceptical of claims to successful love (including, I suspect, of my own account of heterosex) is reinforced by the daily experience of women who claim love when all one can see from the outside is domination and objectification, as in 'women who love too much' (Norwood, 1985).

The distinction between 'love', as people aspire to it, and this debased version could perhaps be clarified by introducing a parallel distinction to Benjamin's between true and false differentiation. The parallel is between true and false recognition. I would suggest that women (and occasionally men) striving for recognition can feel recognized by finding themselves viewed as sexually desirable (in men's case maybe as financially desirable, though the parallel is not close). This is evidenced in the widespread phenomenon of women who are trapped in their desire to be the objects of men's sexual desire. For an understanding of this phenomenon, the Lacanian account does appear useful. However, the distinction between true and false recognition could rescue it from universalism.

The artificiality of the solution of false recognition lies, I would suggest, in the fact that vulnerable aspects of the self, aspects that contradict the idealized image of sexual perfection, have to remain hidden, thus contradicting the reasons for the search for recognition. Like false differentiation, this is an intersubjective affair, since the capacity of the other to accept what is hidden requires that the woman can acknowledge it and accept it herself and vice versa. This depends not only on her present partner, but on the history of true or false recognition that she has experienced. I echo this idea in my commentary on sexual pleasure: 'It is surprisingly hard to accept someone's love, no holds barred . . .' (Hollway, 1993: 414).

When the interconnection between power and desire is over-emphasized, we are left with a psychic determinism which is no more useful for theorizing change than the social determinism inherent in radical feminism.[8] For such reasons, I have preferred to look at the connections between power and anxiety. The resultant insights, like those of Benjamin above, derive from object relations or Kleinian psychoanalysis, which is based on an understanding of pre-Oedipal relations. It points to a time before power relations are gendered, when power is articulated in adult–child relations, giving rise to anxiety and defences against it, so that the basis for future power dynamics in intimate relations are laid here, before Oedipal dynamics come into operation.

The connections between power and anxiety make sense of the uses of control to protect one's vulnerability in love relationships. So, for example, Martin, one of my research participants, says

. . . in a love relationship you make the most fundamental admission about yourself – that you want somebody else. It seems to me that that is the greatest need, and the need which, in relationship to its power, is most strongly hidden and repressed. Once you've shown the other person that you need them, then you've made yourself incredibly vulnerable.

In consequence, his partner, Martha, cannot find true recognition:

I want to be treated as a complete person, someone who has feelings and ideas and intuitions that are actually worth taking notice of. No room is allowed for me to be myself, fully, because it might be too powerful an intrusion on his actions. (Hollway, 1984a: 246–7)

True recognition is the other face of true differentiation because recognition of the other does not then have to compromise one's autonomy, which is what Martin feared. The power to deny someone's needs, a power which, when put into practice, Martha experienced as so undermining, can be transformed into the power to meet someone's needs for recognition and autonomy and their power to meet yours. This for Benjamin is 'the secret of love' (1984: 301). The tension which Benjamin believes is a part of the resolution persists precisely because one is always dependent upon the other not to betray that trust; that is their power. In terms of sex, each has the power to satisfy or to frustrate the other's pleasure, a giving or withholding which signifies something more fundamental, namely recognition.

This version of power is gendered and asymmetrical just as long as differentiation and recognition are split between heterosexual partners (typically between men and women, but not always). If both have developed a capacity to hold both within themselves – that is a capacity for true recognition and true differentiation – then this power is symmetrical; there is equality in this arena, which, though limited, is primary when it comes to egalitarian significations of sex. Equality here does not mean no power and no difference. It means no power difference resulting from the needs for recognition and differentiation.

The tension of autonomy and dependency, Benjamin's 'conflict of differentiation', means that issues of power and trust are still played out in sex, but not necessarily in erotic domination. Being the active or passive one can mean giving rather than receiving sexual pleasure, looking after rather than being looked after. Controlling someone else's experience of pleasure is a far cry from controlling their pain. Issues of trust and power are rehearsed, but with a benign outcome. Giving up control when you trust someone to look after you as well as you could yourself feels better than looking after your needs yourself, or catering for your own pleasure.

It is significant for a discussion of egalitarian sex whether these alternative positions can be swapped over. When you know how both emotional positions feel, then you can experience each in the act of doing either: activity/passivity, control/abandon, pleasuring/being pleasured, cradling/being cradled, fucking/being fucked. This analysis assumes the permeability of individual boundaries, at least at the unconscious level, and the possibility of identification across difference: being the instrument of your pleasure turns me on; your abandon makes me come. In these circumstances, who is fucking whom is an irrelevance, one exchangeable signifier among many.

This kind of heterosex resists fixed gender difference, and I suggest that this resistance is achieved through identification of similarities, as opposed to being caught in the discourses and fantasies of gender difference.[9] All characteristics are potentially gendered, but they are not always forever gendered, since gender difference is never a total success; it is beset by contradictions, particularly in the contemporary world where women's positions have changed so dramatically. Material conditions, institutions, discourses and the human capacities of relating provide spaces for similarities to transcend differences. These can be expressed in heterosexual sex and contribute to true recognition.

Discourse and the extra-discursive

Social constructionism has emphasized, often using discourse theory, how people's social positions construct who they are, and has been criticized for being too deterministic and having no theory of agency or change (Giddens, 1991). This debate is crucial for my theoretical position here, namely that emancipatory heterosexual practice is possible, even though an emancipatory discourse of heterosexual sex does not exist. How is the practice conceivable, if not through discourse? I have discussed three ways of conceptualizing this question, in each being careful to locate the analysis within the social. First, and most simply, there is practice as a product of the possibilities provided because of the contradictions produced between discourses. Second, we can see practice as informed by individual histories, which are themselves located within discourse and power relations, but with meanings achieving unique significance through the workings of the unconscious. Third, I have raised the possibility of an 'extra-discursive' space concerning heterosexual sex, provided by the doubly private realm within which so-called normal sex has been practised. This space is social in that it is constituted through practice (and through fantasy as well as fact), rather than through discourse as talk. It therefore creates spaces for variety which is reproduced through what sex signifies in families, passed on between generations more through what is not said than what is said; through the reading of parental sexual practice within the wider context of the parental relationship. These three approaches are not mutually exclusive and together they provide ways of understanding the complexity, variability, contradiction and uniqueness through which practices of heterosex can escape the oppressiveness of dominant forms of heterosexual relating.

And in future?

In this chapter, I have suggested some ways of theorizing the possibility of egalitarian heterosex. In the absence of any such public accounts, I have started from my own experience. For discourse analysis, *any* individual's experience is valid and requires understanding theoretically. This contrasts with typical radical feminist formulations, such as Thompson's: discussing my own case, she asserts 'the fact that there are exceptions to the general rule of female subordination within heterosexual relations does not negate the general rule' (Thompson, 1994: 326–7). What theoretical and political status should experiences like mine have, when oppressive heterosexuality is so widespread? Thompson claims that it is an exception and that until exceptions constitute a majority, radical feminism should ignore them (Thompson, 1994: 328). But a theoretical recourse to 'exceptions' leaves any theory dogmatic and resistant to change.

My contention is that a position such as Thompson's discounts the necessity for heterosexual relations to be a site of political changes, along with many other sites, and therefore undermines the possibility of change in this arena. The effects that we may already be seeing include the distancing of many heterosexual women from feminism, and the colonization of issues concerning heterosexuality by the right wing without much of a struggle, because the feminist agenda has recently been unable to incorporate any positive emancipatory discourses about heterosexual relating.

The production of a discourse which resonates with more women's experiences nonetheless requires more empirical work, informed, I hope, by some of these ideas, preliminary though they are. I would like to suggest that heterosexual feminists interested in this research area, and who themselves relate to what I'm talking about (plenty have told me so informally), generate some empirical material in this area. I am not calling for work which suppresses aspects of heterosex which contradict equality; rather for discourse analytic work which has access to theoretical tools which can do justice to the full range of experience.

Notes

1 For example, on the basis of interviews with heterosexual couples, Gilfoyle et al. (1992) identified a 'reciprocal gift discourse', but modified it, prior to publication, to 'pseudo-reciprocal gift discourse', following criticism that the label 'connoted too much equality and mutuality' (happily, they document this in a footnote: 217). In the absence of a feminist discourse which recognizes the possibility of equality and mutuality, the interviewees' accounts were basically marked up as ideological, informed by a discourse unable to theorize the possibility of equality or mutuality.

2 Kitzinger et al., 1992; Wilkinson and Kitzinger, 1993; Smart, 1994; Margaret Jackson, 1993; Hollway, 1993, 1995; Segal, 1994; Holland et al., 1994; Duncombe and Marsden, 1993; Stevi Jackson, 1994, 1995. The fact that the British Sociological Association annual conference 1994 took the theme 'Sexualities in social context' accounted for some of this recent production. A further factor is recent funding for research related to HIV transmission.

3 But see Ethel Person and other psychoanalysts such as Kernberg, summarized in Chodorow, 1994.

4 However, in a recent interview, Butler explains that she ceased to use the concept of 'the heterosexual matrix' because it 'became a kind of totalizing symbolic, and that's why I changed the term in *Bodies that Matter* to heterosexual hegemony' (Butler, 1994).

5 Lesley Hall's (1991) analysis of early twentieth-century male sexuality suggests that not only were many men unable to position themselves successfully as men in heterosexual practices, but that some men and women just did not know what to do, because nobody had ever talked about sex.

6 For me this casts light on the dilemma of the so-called 'willing wimp', which seems to be a product of the limitations of current feminist discourse on heterosexuality (see, for example, Ramazanoglu, 1994; Jackson, 1994, 1995). The 'willing wimp' conjures up for me the idea of a man acquiescing in being controlled by his female partner, possibly in the name of feminism. This could not be based on true differentiation, and it does not surprise me that most women do not desire such partners, be they men or women. Men who are not trapped in erotic domination cannot find fulfilment in such partnerships either.

7 'To Freud the difference between the sexes precedes the appearance of the sexes and . . . the integrity of such separated sexes depends upon the power of just this original difference to connect them, with its distance, to each other' (Fineman, 1979: 118).

8 Lacan has been criticized for the determinism of his version of the Oedipal entry into culture and gender (Henriques et al., 1984: 216). Orthodox psychoanalytic theory has been criticized for assuming an inevitable link between the achievement of gendered identity on the one hand and sexual object choice on the other. In their critique of the relation of psychoanalysis to lesbian sexuality, O'Connor and Ryan (1994) have undertaken a detailed deconstruction of this assumption, demonstrating it to be an important task for feminist theory to uncouple the relationship between identity and object choice. Certainly, the case within psychoanalytic feminism for the eroticization of power difference would be undermined by such work.

9 Elsewhere I argue that similarities between women and men have been left under-theorized; that identification is a useful theoretical tool in this regard, and that 'it will be necessary to understand the ways in which identification works across the major social divisions of difference' (Hollway, 1994: 544; see also Hollway, 1996).

References

Adams, Parveen (1989) Of female bondage. In T. Brennan (ed.), *Between Feminism and Psychoanalysis*. London: Routledge.

Benjamin, Jessica (1984) Master and slave: the fantasy of erotic domination. In Ann Snitow, Christine Standell and Sharon Thompson (eds), *Desire: The Politics of Sexuality*. London: Virago.

Benjamin, Jessica (1990) *The Bonds of Love*. London: Virago.

Benjamin, Jessica (1995) Sameness and difference: toward an 'over-inclusive' theory of gender development. In A. Elliott and S. Frosh (eds), *Psychoanalysis in Contexts: Paths between Theory and Modern Culture*. London: Routledge.

Brown (1994) Pleasures untold: heterosexuality, power and radicalism. *Feminism & Psychology* 4(2), 322–5.

Butler, Judith (1990) *Gender Trouble: Feminism and the Subversion of Identity*. London: Routledge.

Butler, Judith (1994) Gender as performance: an interview with Judith Butler. Interviewed by Peter Osborne and Lynne Segal. *Radical Philosophy* 67 (Summer), 32–9.

Chodorow, Nancy (1978) *The Reproduction of Mothering: Psychoanalysis and the Sociology of Gender*. Berkeley: University of California Press.

Chodorow, Nancy (1989) *Feminism and Psychoanalytic Theory*. London: Yale University Press.

Chodorow, Nancy (1994) *Femininities, Masculinities, Sexualities: Freud and Beyond*. London: Free Association Books.

Dinnerstein, Dorothy (1978) *The Rocking of the Cradle and the Ruling of the World*. London: Souvenir Press.

Duncombe, Jean and Marsden, Dennis (1993) Love and intimacy: the gender division of emotion and 'emotion work'. *Sociology* 27(2), 221–41.

Dworkin, Andrea (1981) *Pornography*. London: Women's Press.

Dworkin, Andrea (1987) *Intercourse*. London: Arrow Books.

Eichenbaum, Luise and Orbach, Susie (1982) *Outside In . . . Inside Out*. Harmondsworth: Penguin.

Ernst, Sheila and Maguire, Marie (eds) (1987) *Living with the Sphinx: Papers from the Women's Therapy Centre*. London: Women's Press.

Fineman, Joel (1979) Psychoanalysis, bisexuality and the difference before the sexes. In M. Nelson and J. Ikenberry (eds), *Psychosexual Imperatives: Their Role in Identity Formation*. New York: Human Sciences Press.

Foucault, Michel (1978) *History of Sexuality: An Introduction*. Harmondsworth: Penguin.

Gallop, Jane (1982) *Feminism and Psychoanalysis: The Daughter's Seduction*. London: Macmillan.

Gaylin, William and Person, Ethel S. (eds) (1988) *Passionate Attachments: Thinking about Love*. New York: Free Press.

Gergen, Mary (1992) Unbundling our binaries: genders, sexualities and desires. *Feminism & Psychology* 2(3), 447–9.

Giddens, Anthony (1991) *Modernity and Self-Identity*. Cambridge: Polity.

Gilfoyle, Jackie, Wilson, Jonathan and Brown (1992) Sex, organs and audiotape. *Feminism & Psychology* 2(2), 209–30.

Hall, Lesley (1991) *Hidden Anxieties: Male Sexuality 1900–1950*. Cambridge: Polity.

Henriques, Julian, Hollway, Wendy, Urwin, Cathy, Venn, Couze and Walkerdine, Valerie (1984) *Changing the Subject: Psychology, Social Regulation and Subjectivity*. London: Methuen.

Hite, Shere (1974) *The Hite Report*. London: Wildwood House.

Holland, Janet, Ramazanoglu, Caroline, Sharpe, Sue and Thomson, Rachel (1994) Power and desire: the embodiment of female sexuality. *Feminist Review* 46, 21–38.

Hollway, Wendy (1983) Heterosexual sex, power and desire for the other. In S. Cartledge and J. Ryan (eds), *Sex and Love: New Thoughts on Old Contradictions*. London: Women's Press.

Hollway, Wendy (1984a) Gender difference and the production of subjectivity. In Henriques et al. (1984).

Hollway, Wendy (1984b) Women's power in heterosexual sex. *Women's Studies International Forum* 7(1), 63–8.

Hollway, Wendy (1989) *Subjectivity and Method in Psychology: Gender, Meaning and Science*. London: Sage.

Hollway, Wendy (1993) Theorizing heterosexuality: a response. *Feminism & Psychology* 3(3), 412–17.

Hollway, Wendy (1994) Beyond sex differences: a project for feminist psychology. *Feminism & Psychology* 4(4), 538–46.

Hollway, Wendy (1995) A second bite at the heterosexual cherry. *Feminism & Psychology* 5(1), 126–30.

Hollway, W. (1996) In D. Richardson (ed.), *Theorizing Heterosexuality: Telling It Straight*. Milton Keynes: Open University Press.

Jackson, Margaret (1993) *The Real Facts of Life: Feminism and the Politics of Sexuality c. 1850–1940*. London: Taylor and Francis.

Jackson, Stevi (1993) Even sociologists fall in love: an exploration in the sociology of emotions. *Sociology* 27(2), 201–20.

Jackson, Stevi (1994) Heterosexuality as a problem for feminist theory. Unpublished paper presented at the British Sociological Association Conference.

Jackson, Stevi (1995) Heterosexuality, power and pleasure. *Feminism & Psychology* 5(1), 131–5.

Jeffreys, Sheila (1990) *Anticlimax: A Feminist Perspective on the Sexual Revolution*. London: Women's Press.

Kaplan, Louise (1993) *Female Perversions*. Harmondsworth: Penguin.

Kitzinger, Celia (1987) *The Social Construction of Lesbianism*. London: Sage.

Kitzinger, Celia (1994) Problematizing pleasure. In L. Radtke and H. Stam (eds) *Power/Gender: Social Relations in Theory and Practice*. London: Sage. pp. 194–209.

Kitzinger, Celia and Perkins, Rachel (1993) *Changing Our Minds: Lesbian Feminism and Psychology*. London: Onlywomen Press/New York: New York University Press.

Kitzinger, Celia and Wilkinson, Sue (1993) Theorizing heterosexuality. In S. Wilkinson and C. Kitzinger (eds), *Heterosexuality: A 'Feminism & Psychology' Reader*. London: Sage.

Kitzinger, Celia, Wilkinson, Sue and Perkins, Rachel (eds) (1992) *Heterosexuality*. Special Issue of *Feminism & Psychology*, 2(3).

Klein, Melanie (1963) *Our Adult World and its Roots in Infancy*. London: Heinemann.

Koedt, Anne (1973) The myth of the vaginal orgasm. In *Radical Feminism*. New York: New York Times Books.

Lees, Sue (1986) *Losing Out*. London: Hutchinson.

Norwood, R. (1985) *Women Who Love Too Much*. London: Arrow Books.

O'Connor, Maureen and Ryan, Jo (1994) *Wild Desires and Mistaken Identities: Lesbianism and Psychoanalysis*. London: Virago.

Paglia, Camille (1992) *Sex, Art and American Culture*. New York: Vintage.

Person, Ethel S. (1988) *Dreams of Love and Fateful Encounters: The Power of Romantic Passion*. New York: Norton.

Ramazanoglu, Caroline (1994) Theorizing heterosexuality: a response to Wendy Hollway. *Feminism & Psychology* 4(2), 320–1.

Rich, Adrienne (1980) Compulsory heterosexuality and lesbian existence. *Signs* 5(4), 631–57.

Roiphe, Katie (1993) *The Morning After: Sex, Fear and Feminism on Campus*. New York: Little, Brown.

Schacht, S.P. and Achison, Patricia (1993) Heterosexual instrumentalism: past and future directions. *Feminism & Psychology* 3(1), 37–54.

Segal, Lynne (1994) *Straight Sex: Rethinking Heterosexuality and the Politics of Pleasure*. London: Virago.

Smart, Carol (1994) Desperately seeking the post-heterosexual woman. Unpublished paper presented at the British Sociological Association Conference, University of Central Lancashire, April.

Swindells, Julia (1993) A straight outing. *Trouble and Strife* 26 (Summer), 40–4.

Thomas, Alison (1994) Heterosexual feminist identities: some reflections. *Feminism & Psychology* 4(2), 317–19.

Thompson, Denise (1994) Retaining the radical challenge: a reply to Wendy Hollway. *Feminism & Psychology* 4(2), 326–9.

Thomson, Rachel and Scott, Sue (1991) *Learning about Sex: Young Women and the Social Construction of Sexual Identity*.London: Tufnell Press.

Welldon, E. (1988) *Mother, Madonna, Whore*. London: Free Association Books.

Wilkinson, Sue and Kitzinger, Celia (eds) (1993) *Heterosexuality: A 'Feminism & Psychology' Reader*. London: Sage.

6

Identity, Politics and Talk: A Case for the Mundane and the Everyday

Sue Widdicombe

In this chapter, I shall be concerned with the ways that issues of identity and politics are addressed in two broad strands of discourse analytic work, namely that which is informed by poststructuralist ideas (Althusser, 1971; Foucault, 1972, 1981) and that which is informed by ethnomethodology (Garfinkel, 1967) and the philosophy of language (Wittgenstein, 1953; Austin, 1962). Although they share a common framework in terms of the assumption that identities and subjectivity are constituted in language which is thus the appropriate site of study, I am concerned here with the significant differences between these analytic approaches.

In particular, I focus on the way that, under the influence of poststructuralism, identity has come to be regarded as a moral and political issue, not just an intellectual concern (for example, Bhavnani and Phoenix, 1994; Wilkinson, 1991). Consequently, interpreting identities solely in terms of their political significance has become an integral feature of discourse analyses associated with poststructuralist ideas. This kind of discourse analysis is gaining increasing popularity amongst feminist and critical social psychologists; its primary appeal lies in the way that it seems to enable researchers to use discourse analysis as a tool in making sweeping political claims. Moreover, as poststructuralist discourse analysis becomes more trendy, the ethnomethodological variety, which focuses not on political features of identity but on the details of talk in interaction, has come to be regarded as unfashionable and naive. There is a corresponding neglect of the mundane and everyday; for example the ways in which identities are constructed, negotiated and made relevant in talk, and the ways in which people construct their meaning and significance. The postmodern trend thus represents a move away from earlier feminist concerns to focus on women's accounts of identities and experiences in their own terms (for example, Wilkinson, 1986).

In the first part of this chapter, I shall argue that pressure to produce political conclusions has had a number of unfortunate conceptual, methodological and practical consequences. In the second part, I shall present an analysis of two extracts from my interviews with members of youth subcultures in which they negotiate the relationship between political activities and subcultural identity. The analytic approach that I adopt is the less fashionable variety. Instead of adopting an explicitly feminist or any other political perspective in the interpretation of these accounts, I focus on the ways that members negotiate the political significance and basis of their activities in the details of their talk.

Conceptual issues

The political dimension of discourse, and therefore of identity and subjectivity, is built into the definition of discourse. Discourses are regarded as products and reflections of social, economic and political factors, and power relations (Gavey, 1989; Parker, 1992). They are thoroughly implicated in and maintained through the part they play in institutional and material practices. It is through discourse that material power is exercised and power relations are established and perpetuated (Gavey, 1989). Since identity and subjectivity are said to be constituted through a person's positions in different discourses they are, by implication, thoroughly political. In addition, different positions in discourses are said to vary in terms of the power they offer individuals.

The concept of discourse is then used to establish at the outset the kinds of questions that it is legitimate (or useful) for discourse analysts to ask. For example, it is argued that in order to understand identity and subjectivity, we need first to identify the relevant discourses and the positions they make available, and then examine the power relations that are facilitated, the historical and structural conditions giving rise to particular discourses and their ideological effects (Wilkinson, 1991; Parker, 1992). The political formulation of discourses thus informs an explicit political frame for doing discourse analysis.

Alongside these analytic guidelines, a set of reasons is given for why analysts should examine them. Specifically, it is argued that analysts should be motivated to make political interventions or to expose the ideological operations of particular discourses. In this way, discourse analysis is set up merely as a political exercise. Any work that does not conform to these criteria, such as discourse analyses which are purely descriptive and therefore not 'progressive', are described as 'traditional positivist methods *masquerading as* discourse analysis' (Burman and Parker, 1993: 11; emphasis added).

Therefore political interpretations are regarded as an intrinsic feature of doing discourse analysis, or at least *worthy* discourse analysis (but see Parker and Burman, 1993: 166). It is tempting to draw parallels with the ways that mainstream psychology has operated according to the principle of exclusion, by claiming that research which does not conform to scientific criteria cannot be considered worthwhile; but this problem is neatly circumnavigated by claiming that political criteria are employed to avoid assimilation into mainstream empiricist psychology (Parker and Burman, 1993: 170). The research agenda is thus set up to exclude detailed analysis of the ways people themselves give meaning to their identities and actions; unless, that is, this kind of analysis can be made to yield political conclusions.

Methodological issues

The analytic rush to identify discourses in order to get on with the more serious business of accounting for their political significance may be partly responsible for the tendency towards ascriptivism. That is, the tendency to impute the presence of a discourse to a piece of text without explaining the basis for specific claims. To illustrate this point, consider the following extract taken from Gavey's (1989) analysis of sexual coercion in heterosexual relationships. The speaker, Sue Davis, was earlier asked to describe a sexual experience that 'looking back on, you now feel uncomfortable about or regret in some way?' (Gavey, 1989: 468)

36   I: What, if any, were some of the initial consequences of this event? (gap of half a line)

37   Sue: Um (pause) Well, he must have gone away with a fairly disillusioned attitude towards sex as far

38   as his first encounter had gone. I um felt just depressed about the whole incident. I didn't like it. I hadn't

39   wanted it, and I'd simply done it because I didn't want (pause) I seemed to have sex a lot at the time

40   because I didn't want to hurt someone's feelings. As though I was strong and they were not. Um, and I

41   know my feeling in those days was that sexual activity by itself isn't important, it was how I felt about

42   someone that made it important or not important. I still feel that way a bit. You know, it's (pause)

43   although I've been stuck with one person for many years it's (pause) sex without the love is just (pause) it's

44   no different from wiping your bottom after you've gone to the toilet,
     or brushing your hair. It's a physical
45   activity. It's an enjoyable one, um, well it can be an enjoyable one.
     (taken from Gavey, 1989: 469)

The reader is informed that the discourse of permissive sexuality can be found on lines 39, 41, and 43 to 45, and that within this discourse Sue is positioned as a liberated woman. Lines 37 and 39 to 40 illustrate the male sexual needs discourse, through which is constituted her identity as a person who is responsive to male needs. But what exactly is it about the words or phrases found on these lines that substantiates the claim that they are informed by or illustrate particular discourses? Without some indication of the empirical grounding of these discourses, there is little to inspire confidence that Sue's experiences are permeated with these discourses. Indeed, the primary warrant for the identification of these discourses lies not in the analysis of this account, but through Gavey's reference to Hollway's (1984, 1989) prior identification of their existence. But Hollway (1984: 231) simply tells us that she delineated three discourses through a combination of her own knowledge and what was suggested by the data; we are not given access to how exactly the data suggested these discourses. The reader is left all the more in the dark since 'I didn't want to hurt someone's feelings' (line 40) does not seem to be entirely synonymous with satisfying men's need to have sex; yet this statement is the most obvious candidate for the male sexual needs discourse which we are assured is located on line 40.

Nonetheless, as mentioned above, it seems that the ways that discourses are manifested in talk are less important than the political claims which can be made having ascribed discourses to a piece of text. Again by way of illustration, this is what Gavey has to say about this account:

> Given the subject positions adopted by Sue Davis [sexually liberated woman who is also responsive to male needs], nonconsent in the situation she encountered would have been almost inconceivable. Thus the whole notion of consent and the meaning of choice in such contexts are rendered problematic. What is important here is that these subject positions reproduce a form of heterosexual gender relations in which women lack power.
> One value of a poststructuralist approach is its assertion that subjectivity is produced through discourses that are multiple, possibly contradictory, and unstable. Sue Davis, for example, does not escape from any ill effects of this unwanted sexual experience. It left her feeling 'flat' (line 32) and 'depressed' (line 38) (see also lines 7–8 and 49). This suggests that her experience was not constituted solely by her positionings in the permissive

sexuality discourse and the male sexual needs discourse. (Gavey, 1989: 470)

This interpretation, like the guidelines for doing poststructuralist discourse analysis, treats accounts as though they are produced in a social interactional vacuum. Yet accounts generated through interviews, whatever else they may be doing, are primarily produced to address the interactional business deemed relevant to the particular circumstances. Moreover, consideration of the interactional circumstances within which Sue Davis' account is produced gives rise to very different analytic conclusions. In particular, a closer analysis of this account highlights important features of people's talk which are missed when analysts ignore the social functions of language use.

Remember that Sue has been asked to produce an account of a sexual encounter which now gives her cause for embarrassment or regret. She then provides an account of an occasion when she had sex without wanting to. In the initial part of this extract, she describes feelings that make this incident appropriate to the interviewer's request ('I um felt just depressed about the whole incident'), and she also gives a reason for those feelings ('I didn't like it. I hadn't wanted it'). Having sex (or indeed doing anything) when you don't want to is an accountable matter and Sue's subsequent provision of an explanatory account shows that she does take it to be incumbent upon her to warrant her actions. Notice how she begins to portray her motives for having sex on *this* occasion: 'I'd simply done it because I didn't want (pause)'. She then corrects this statement by producing another through which she indicates that this incident was one of a series of such encounters: 'I seemed to have sex a lot at the time because I didn't want to hurt someone's feelings.' The implication is that in general the motivation for unwanted sex was dependent upon the perceived personal consequences to the other person of not having sex; hurting their feelings presumably because they would then feel rejected. She also states that it was 'As though I was strong and they were not.' The implication is that it was by virtue of the belief in her own strength at the time that she felt in a position to protect their feelings.

At the same time, she indicates that such protection was of minimal personal cost. She does this by trivializing the kind of sex of which this particular incident was an example in several ways. First, I noted above that she switches from an account of having had sex on this occasion to portraying the frequency of this kind of sexual encounter. She thereby makes clear that this was not an isolated incident, and hence indicates its character as 'nothing special'. Second, she draws an explicit distinction between sex with love and sex without love, and she characterizes the latter as not important sex (lines 41–2). Third, she reinforces this assessment by drawing analogies with mundane activities which are part of anybody's daily routine: 'it's no different from wiping your bottom after you've gone to the toilet, or brushing your hair' (line 44). Therefore, the statements that Gavey points to as illustrative of the 'permissive sexuality' discourse on closer inspection function to trivialize certain kinds of sexual encounters; they are not primarily designed to characterize herself as a 'sexually liberated woman'.

So, Sue accounts for having unwanted sex by characterizing herself as someone who can protect another person's feelings because she is strong and because at the time she regarded this kind of sex as generally trivial and insignificant and hence of little cost to herself. A case could be made for the way that these descriptive strategies function to avoid implying that she was the helpless victim of sexual coercion with no choice in the matter. Yet Sue's status as helpless victim is exactly the conclusion that Gavey draws from her analysis. Politically, some conclusions may be more appealing than others, but to gloss over inconvenient aspects of talk does a disservice to those on whose behalf researchers claim to speak. Moreover, it seems that political interventions are more usefully made from an understanding of the more mundane ways that people characterize their selves and the meanings they impute to their actions.

The point is that by elevating their own political agendas as the pre-established analytic frame, researchers may actually undermine the practical and political utility of the analyses they undertake. A further, but related, methodological issue concerns the belief that only by analysing discourse at a broad level can political concerns be realized. There is thus an implicit assumption of incompatibility, or tension, between a focus on the mundane and on the political. In particular, it is assumed that producing detailed descriptions of the ways in which social life is conducted and sustained within the mundane contexts of social interaction does not allow the researcher to make political claims. Consequently, discourse analysis can only be a political analysis in so far as it goes beyond the discourse that is the object of analysis.[1]

Nevertheless, the pursuit of political agendas through broad analysis misses an important point. For it seems that it is precisely in the mundane contexts of interaction that institutional power is exercised, social inequalities are experienced, and resistance accomplished. I am not suggesting that these are necessary features of all accounts, simply that in this sense, detailed analysis may be more politically acute than the kind which elevates the researcher's politics and uses this to guide interpretation of what people have to say.

Practical issues

The practical implications of poststructuralist discourse analysis appear to be twofold. First is the empowerment of people by giving them a voice (or letting them remain silent; Bhavnani, 1990). It is, then, curious that this aim is related to the kind of analysis which fails to attend to the details of what people are saying and doing with their talk. Second, it has been suggested that by constructing more politically sound discourses, researchers can provide people with 'better' ways of understanding themselves or constructing their own subjectivities.

There is, however, an important sense in which researchers' albeit laudable intentions in this respect may be thwarted by the analytic procedures they adopt. I want to develop this argument, based on my own work, and from my observation of a certain parallel between the current trend in discourse analytic work and the work of sociologists of youth subcultures. Specifically, New Subcultural Theory (for example, Hall and Jefferson, 1976; Hebdige, 1979; Brake, 1985) adopted an explicit political, neo-Marxist framework for interpreting the emergence and meaning of these phenomena. In this way, members' lives were interpreted solely in political terms, as symbolic resistance to oppression which was said to be represented in style (for critiques, see Cohen, 1980; Davis, 1990). The claims that style signified resistance were derived from conceptual tools such as semiology (see, for instance, Barthes, 1971); working-class youth were not considered articulate enough to express what their lives 'really' meant. Subsequently, these ideas have filtered into common usage and, in particular, the media so that in simplified form, the 'resistance through rituals' thesis is available as a resource for outsiders to make sense of the meanings of members' lives, selves and identities. However, our analysis of members' accounts in a variety of interactional contexts shows that they are permeated with resistance to precisely these kinds of cultural resources and assumptions (Widdicombe and Wooffitt, 1995).

In so far as analytic interpretations become available as cultural resources, they become resources to be resisted. However benevolently constructed, category ascriptions, together with knowledge about the meaning of identities thereby made relevant, function as powerful mechanisms of social control through the way they infuse individual's lives at the level of social interaction. They provide the means through which other people assume they already know something about members' selves and lives without speaking to them. And this is why resistance is a likely response. I will now illustrate this argument, using my interview data.

In the analysis that follows, I have not tried to impute a political meaning to subcultures. Instead, I analyse the ways that respondents fashion their talk to address the political significance of subcultural identities; in particular the ways that they undermine subcultural identity as the basis of their political activities.[2]

The first extract comes from an interview with two male punks ('Sue' is the interviewer, and author of this chapter; see Appendix for an explanation of the transcription symbols and why they were employed).

Extract 1

```
 1   Sue:   d'you think it's making a p'litical statement anymore?
 2          (0.2)
 3   Ben:   ⌈well people do:
 4   Joe:   ⌊.hh
 5          (.)
 6   Joe:   ⌈I– I
 7   Ben:   ⌊there are plenty a people who who still like the overtly
 8          political in– er– in the scene you know there's things like
 9          Class War (.) which is like which is like real sort of mickey
10          mouse politics (bu– ⌈th's)
11   Joe:                       ⌊if– if you got like there's um: (.) like–
12          like I said mm the thing– the thing that– tha– tha we started
13          off w–was the Cronsack Club thing .hhh I mean that was like
14          basically like a political (vision) in– inta putting on bands
15          which er which were. basically bands which couldn't get gigs
16          anyway .hhh an like hm– that was li– all the money went t–
17          sort of right back into supporting an getting decent venues an
18          that sort of stuff an that y'know .hh (an) a– ts it's like th– the
19          One in Twelve Club up in u:m: Bradford there's also one in
20          Leeds an that you know .hh an like ⌈they'll be
21   Sue:                                      ⌊ahha
22   Joe:   (y'know) so it's like it's all s– so people don't get ripped off an
23          that y'know .hh an it's all– it's not sort of like. it's not sort of
24          y'know it's not. I don't know a– ° what's the word for it° >but
25          I mean< it's all– it's all still sort of like really y'know
26          like s–s– strai ⌈ght cut
27   Ben:                  ⌊right on
28   Joe:   an that and right on. I mean there's it's not really (.)
29   Ben:   I mean yeah the whole sort of (.) whole sort of er punk rock
30          or (scene) it's still you know right on er–
31   Joe:   it's still totally like I mean all the people who're into it're still
32          totally sort of like politically aware if you want to use that
33          word an that
34   Ben:   it seems like er like large amounts are being into sort anti
```

35		poll tax (.) things you know ⌈an like
36	*Sue*:	⌊mmhm
37	*Ben*:	they will be th– that's that's the most sort of important
38		thing ⌈at the moment
39	*Joe*:	⌊it's like if you think if you've got any sort of
40		march be it like a CND one or: or a vivisection or a: poll tax
41		one or a::. whatever there ar– there'll always be like a. like a
42		majority of s–sort of like– punky type people there an that
43		y'know
44		(.)
45	*Sue*:	mmhm
46	*Ben*:	there're still lots of people in–involved in like y'know like
47		an–. like animal stuff y'know like er: go on hunt sabs and
48		(.) anti vivisection things y'know ⌈like
49	*Sue*:	⌊mhmm
50	*Ben*:	mm anti fur shop stuff
51		(0.2)
52	*Ben*:	like the vegan police as they're known ngh
53	*Joe*:	hah hah HUH HUH
54	*Ben*:	things th– ⌈were quite QUITE
55	*Joe*:	⌊( )
56	*Ben*:	quite prevalent a:h a few years ago that aren't so sort of now
57		(.)
58	*Joe*:	well there's still MAssive amounts of people into that sort of
59		thing you know like an mm you know
60	*Sue*:	mm ⌈hm
61	*Joe*:	⌊an jus like y'know like lots of em political stuff an like
62		getting involved in that way an, fanzines (.) .hhh

Consider Ben's initial response to the question. He does not produce a direct affirmative or negative response to it; instead, and after a noticeable silence, he says 'well people do:'. The implication is that *some* people do, but that this does not include himself. Subsequently, in lines 7 to 10, Ben formulates, and derogates, the political dimension of punk to which he says 'plenty a people' subscribe. Specifically, he describes the nature of the political dimension through the provision of an example, 'there's things like Class War'. Class War is a radical anarchist organization, which was said at the time to be popular amongst punks.[3] He then produces a negative assessment of this feature of the subculture; he describes it as 'real sort of mickey mouse politics'. So he derogates the political dimension of punk which he made relevant by implying that it is not serious politics. But notice how he describes this as 'the *overtly* political in the scene' thereby implying that there may be other, more covert political dimensions of the subculture. And in the subsequent turns, both participants produce descriptions of activities which, it may be inferred by contrast, are truly political.

But why should he *initially* produce and then dismiss a political aspect of the subculture? To address this question, we need to consider what respondents may take to be the assumptions built into the question to which this is a response: is it making a political statement *any more*? In particular, it can be suggested that it is informed by what is generally known about punk; that in the past it was making a political statement through its connection with anarchy. Thus, his response acknowledges and makes explicit the kinds of assumptions that inform the question. By making them explicit, he is able to dismiss them as the true political dimension of the subculture.

I will return to analysis of Extract 1 later in this chapter, but I want now to present a second extract from a conversation with ex-gothic alternative types.[4] The first speaker, Tom, directly addresses the stereotyped assumptions on which the question (whether members are rejecting the system) is based. He describes it as 'the old question' and says that he has 'bin asked this one so many times'. By pointing to the frequency and status of the question, he also indicates its basis in what is generally assumed about category members. In addition, he makes explicit the stereotyped feature of the subculture assumed by the question: 'you mean a form of anarchy really' (line 9).

Extract 2

```
 1  Sue:   d'you think that sort've looking different is– in some way
 2         at least um (.) rejecting the sort of system?
 3         (0.4)
 4  Tom:   ⌈ah hhh it's the old question really
 5  ?:     ⌊hhh
 6  Tom:   heh heh heh ⌈bin asked this one so many times
 7  ?:                ⌊I get
 8         (.)
 9  Tom:   (mm– a ff–) you mean a form of anarchy really (.)
10  Sue:   ahha
11  Tom:   e:rm, I suppose in some ways it is ⌈because
12  ?:                                       ⌊(      )
13  Tom:   we don't– we DON'T want to be like everybody else and
14         we don't w– t– we don't want people telling us what to do
15  Sara:  you don't want to conform to the norm do you Tom
```

Unlike the speaker in Extract 1, he does not dismiss this characterization of the subculture but he nonetheless modifies it: 'I suppose in some ways it is'. In this way, he is able to display agreement that their lifestyle constitutes a form of anarchy while producing his own version of what this actually means: 'because we DON'T want to be like everybody else . . . we don't want people telling us what to do'; and the second respondent says 'you don't want to conform to the norm'. There is, furthermore, a crucial difference between what is implied in the question and the subsequent modification. In particular, the question suggests that anarchy, or rejecting the system, is accomplished through appearance; whereas the modified version makes relevant a more personal basis in terms of what category members don't want to do.

In both Extracts 1 and 2, participants go on to describe their own activities. For example, in lines 11 to 23 of Extract 1, Joe describes their involvement in an organization aimed at 'putting on bands', and he describes similar clubs elsewhere in England. He ascribes a political dimension to these activities in three ways. First, he makes explicit the inherently political character of the club; he says that it is 'basically like a political (vision)' (line 14).[5] Second, he describes the aims of the club, 'so people don't get ripped off an that'; thus he portrays the club as a means of resisting commercial exploitation. Third, after some difficulty in finding an appropriate descriptive term, Ben and Joe jointly produce a description of the club as 'straight cut an that and right on'. They thus reinforce the earlier claim that their activities are politically informed. So, they draw an implicit contrast between the overtly political but trivial interests of some punks which are based in anarchist organizations, and the intrinsically political and genuine nature of their own activities.

The political dimension of the subculture is reinforced in subsequent parts of Extract 1 by portraying a range and diversity of activities concerned with specific socio-political issues in which members are involved: anti-poll tax, CND, 'animal stuff y'know like er: go on hunt sabs and (.) anti-vivisection things . . .' (lines 47 to 48), as well as fanzines (line 62). Thus, the range and diversity of activities, or 'lots of em political stuff' (line 61) is used to warrant the claim that punks are making a political statement.

Similarly, in Extract 2, Lucy affirms that members are rejecting the system and she describes their behaviour and attitudes as the vehicles through which this is accomplished (lines 17 to 22).

Extract 2 continued

```
15   Sara:   you don't want to conform to the norm do you Tom
16   Lucy:   it's like (.) u:m (.) er we we reject the system the way it is
17           at the mo:ment not, e:r (.) in the way we behave .hh our
18           attitudes an that
19   Sue:    ⌈mmhm⌉
20   Lucy:   ⌊li:ke⌋ we won't buy certain things from certain shops
```

21		.hh like you know anybody er connected with <u>apart</u>– er
22		apartheid and er things we won't buy .hh you'll find that the
23		majority .hh of the: <u>al</u>ternative subcultures come from
24		vegetarian or <u>vegan</u>, or: .hh ⌈you know
25	*Sue:*	⌊mmhm
26	*Lucy:*	some sort of <u>o</u>ther form of rejecting <u>some</u> sort of stuff like
27		.hh it's it's all tied .hh personally people won't tch won't
28		consciously think about that type but. over<u>all</u> we <u>are</u> in the
29		<u>way</u>. the way we are and the way we behave .hh the things
30		we <u>go</u> to the .hh some bands stand for this and some bands
31		stand for that .hh the way we do <u>that</u> yes we are re<u>j</u>ecting the
32		system .hh ah although we <u>cannot</u> <u>openly</u>. .hh pro<u>c</u>laim this
33		saying oh <u>every</u>body with red hair everybody with <u>dy</u>ed hair
34		is rejecting the system
35	*Sue:*	⌈yeah⌉
36	*Lucy:*	⌊but ⌋ in our <u>own</u> little ways, our <u>own</u> little <u>a</u>ctions we <u>are</u>
37	*Sue:*	⌈mmhm⌉
38	*Lucy:*	⌊hhh ⌋ it's because unless you. everybody that wants to
39		be <u>different</u>. does. does that out of <u>some</u> sort of moti<u>v</u>ation
40		be it either political social or: (.) tch or personal
41	*Sue:*	mmhm
42	*Lucy:*	they're doing this in order to. please themselves .hh
43		<u>s</u>econdly comes the overa:ll opinion of, wanting to <u>c</u>hange
44		the system (really)
45	*Sue:*	mmhm
46	*Lucy:*	originally <u>black</u>– where did black come ↑from a<u>n</u>archists
47		.hh you fe– find that most– well a fair per<u>c</u>entage of us
48		belie:ve in this y'know don't believe in the <u>means</u> of
49		a<u>chieving</u> ⌈it
50	*Sue:*	⌊ahha
51	*Lucy:*	but believe in the overall <u>theory</u> of it
52		(0.4)
53	*Lucy:*	y'know bu–
54		(0.2)
55	*Lucy:*	( ) many people like the younger ones don't think about it
56		f– to <u>them</u> it's just .hh oh I do it because my <u>big</u> <u>brother</u> does
57		it y'know wha I mean but <u>old</u>er ones like us um we do think
58		about things an an awful <u>lot</u> that's why so many of us go to
59		<u>marches</u>.
60	*Sue:*	mmhm
61	*Lucy:*	<u>do</u>. <u>organised</u>. things you know like CND or: whatever er
62		.hhh campaigning for vege<u>tar</u>ianism you know shouting
63		outside McDonald's <u>burger</u> <u>bars</u> <u>don't</u> buy the y'know
64		you're <u>k</u>illing the rain forest you're <u>k</u>illing us all y'know uh
65		heh heh s– suppose yes we are in a way

We can observe two further features of Lucy's initial response. Notice that her affirmation is built around repeating certain aspects of the interviewer's question, 'd'you think that sort've looking different is– in some way at least um (.) rejecting the sort of system?' She repeats the phrase 'reject[ing] the system' (line 34), but she does not repeat the part of the question which implicates appearance as the means of rejecting the system. Moreover, by specifying behaviour and attitudes as the means by which the system is rejected, she dismisses the common assumption that appearance is the primary vehicle through which this is realized.

The second feature of Lucy's response concerns the way that she modifies the interviewer's reference to 'the system' by specifying 'the system the way it is at the mo:ment'. Compare the different inferences made available through these two formulations. The first could be taken to imply that rejecting the system is an overarching feature of members' lives; consequently, and given common assumptions about young people's behaviour, it could be taken to imply that rejection is merely a result of adolescent perversity or blind rebellion. By specifying the target of rejection as the contemporary system, it is implied that rejection is contingent upon negative aspects of the current system and that if the system changed in desirable ways, members would cease to reject it. It is thus implied that their behaviour constitutes an informed rather than a blind response and she thereby avoids the negative inferences made available in the question.

There are further features of these extracts that I want to examine.[6] In both, respondents produce interesting depictions of the people involved in political activities. Consider, for example, the sequence of turns in Extract 1 on lines 29 to 38. On lines 29 to 30, Ben produces a summary assessment of the political dimension of the contemporary subculture. He says, 'I mean yeah the whole sort of (.) whole sort of er punk rock or (scene) it's still you know right on er–'. It is noticeable that the ascription to punk of being 'right on' is marked by a variety of vagaries such as 'sort of' and an alternative characterization which is unfortunately not clearly discernible. A preliminary observation is, then, that there may be a problem entailed by imputing politically correct views to the subculture.

This observation is further warranted by the way that Joe reformulates Ben's assessment in the next turn: 'it's still totally like I mean all the people who're into it're still totally sort of like politically aware . . .'. Like Ben, he uses the phrase 'it's still' indicating a continuation of a political dimension; he also formulates the maximum case of political concern, '*all* the people are *totally* politically aware' (cf. 'the *whole* scene is *right on*'). The significant feature of his reformulation, then, is the way that Ben's reference to 'punk rock or (scene)' is changed to 'all *the people* who're into it'. He thereby shifts the focus from the subcultural category to its membership; that is, he attributes political awareness to the members and not to the category itself.

However, in his subsequent turn, Ben modifies the reference to 'all the people who are into it' (implying punk), to 'large amounts'. Thus, he modifies Joe's formulation of the maximum state of affairs, *all* the people, and he deletes the implicated reference to their membership of the subculture. Furthermore, whereas the previous formulations portray an overarching political awareness, Ben describes their support of a specific issue, the anti-poll tax campaign. For Ben, his interest is warranted not by any qualities of the punks themselves, such as their political awareness, but is contingent on the contemporary relevance of the specific issue. That is, he says 'they will be th– that's that's the most sort of important thing at the moment'.

How, then, can we make sense of the actions accomplished through these reformulations? Observe how Ben's description of 'punk rock' as 'right on' could be taken to imply that the latter is a criterial or consensual dimension of the subculture. Joe's subsequent attribution of such views to the people or members avoids some problematic inferences of the attribution of views to the subculture – in particular, that they are merely part of the subcultural image. Nonetheless, portraying *all* members as politically aware invokes the possibility that political awareness may be regarded as a consensual feature of membership and thus that their views are merely a result of conforming to an image or prescribed behaviour. Consequently, punks' political concerns could be regarded as non-genuine or shallow. The final component of this sequence avoids these problematic inferences. First, Ben's reference to 'large amounts' indicates that not all punks share political concerns; so that this cannot be regarded as constituting a criterial attribute of membership. Second, being right on or politically aware makes relevant a certain kind of overarching image (which, it may be implied, members adopt because of its positive connotations). By contrast, specifying a particular issue, the poll tax, focuses attention on socio-political issues as the significant determinant of their views.

The point is that in this interactive sequence respondents display a sensitivity to and then avoid the idea that their political concerns are informed by membership of the subculture. Moreover, in subsequent parts of Extract 1, their portrayal of an association between membership of the subculture and political activities rests on the description of the numbers involved, and not the category-bound nature of the activities. For example, 'there're still lots of people in–involved in like y'know an–. like animal stuff' (lines 46 to 47); and 'there's still MAssive amounts of people into that sort of thing' (lines 58 to 59). It is also noticeable that Joe does not refer explicitly to these people as punks, although we may infer their affiliation with the subculture. The exception to this descriptive strategy occurs on line 42 where he characterizes the people who go on marches as 'punky type people'. But even here, punk is employed to qualify the category 'people' and not to indicate the primary significance of their identity as punks.

These descriptive strategies allow respondents to negotiate a problem; portraying the political dimension of the subculture without making membership the basis for their activities. A similar problem is addressed in Extract 2. For example, on lines 22 to 27, Lucy says that 'you'll find that the majority .hh of the: alternative subcultures come from vegetarian or vegan, or: .hh you know some sort of other form of rejecting some sort of stuff like .hh it's it's all tied'. So she characterizes the type of people who join alternative subcultures as the kind of people who are *already* rejecting other things and she says that 'it's all tied'. She thereby reinforces the claim that members are rejecting the system (in its broadest sense) without making the activities that constitute rejection contingent upon membership. Her claim is further warranted by making explicit alternative reasons for rejection. On the one hand she mentions a desire to affiliate with a particular category or be a particular kind of person and she rejects this: 'personally people won't tch won't consciously think about that type'. Instead, she makes rejection an overarching and intrinsic feature of their lifestyle: 'overall we are in the way . . . we are and the way we behave the things we go to . . .' (lines 28 to 30).

There are three further ways in which Lucy rejects the idea that rejecting the system is a consequence of category membership. First, she states explicitly that not everybody who could be categorized as a member, on the basis of their appearance, is rejecting the system: 'we cannot openly. .hh proclaim this saying oh everybody with red hair everybody with dyed hair is rejecting the system' (lines 32 to 34). It is therefore implied that such behaviour cannot be a criterial feature of membership and therefore of alternative subcultures. Second, she emphasizes the personal and mundane nature of activities that constitute rejection: that is, she emphasizes that rejecting the system is done 'in our own little ways, our own little actions' (line 36). Third, she makes relevant the motivations for their actions.

She points to the *variety* of motivations: 'everybody that wants to be different. does. does that out of some sort of motivation be it either political social or: (.) tch or personal'. This formulation achieves two effects: it indicates that action *is* motivated (rather than, say, driven by conformity), while simultaneously implying that the specific motivation depends on the individual – in other words, it is personal. Moreover, in line 42 she says that 'they're doing this in order to. please themselves'. In this way, she reinforces her claim that activity is informed primarily by personal inclinations or desires. But if this were presented as the sole motivation, she might be open to the charge of pure self-interest. This potential problem is avoided through the production of a secondary motivating factor, 'the overa:ll opinion of, wanting to change the system (really)' (lines 43 to 44).

In the final part of her account, Lucy draws a distinction between younger and older members. This distinction enables her to contrast different motivations for involvement in political activities. Thus, she says that the 'younger ones don't think about it'. Instead their involvement is a result of conforming rather than a genuine concern with socio-political issues: 'I do it because my big brother does it' (lines 56 to 57). By contrast, 'older ones like us um we do think about things an awful lot' (lines 57 to 58). She thus makes relevant a real concern with such issues, and she claims that this constitutes the basis of their activities: 'that's why so many of us go to marches', 'do. organised. things' like CND, 'campaigning for vegetarianism' and so on (see lines 61 to 62). This descriptive sequence is followed by a summary assessment or upshot: 'suppose yes we are in a way [rejecting the system]'. The implication is again that their participation in these activities, while not primarily motivated by a desire to reject the system, may be interpreted in these terms.

A final feature of these accounts that I want to consider concerns the ways that speakers formulate the basis of their claims about the political dimension of the respective subcultures.

from Extract 1

39	*Joe*:	it's like if you think if you've got any sort of
40		march be it like a CND one or: or a vivisection or a: poll tax
41		one or a::. whatever there ar– there'll always be like a. like a
42		majority of s–sort of like– punky type people there an that
43		y'know

The respondents in Extract 2 employ a similar formulation in this further extract in response to the question of whether the subculture is making a political statement:

Extract 3

1	*Sue*:	and is it making some sort of political statement
2		(.)

3 *Sue*:   er political in a: wider sort of sense=
4 *Sara*:   =it must be cos like when you go on the marches i– (.) it's
5   always people that look like us that go: .hh hh heh
6   ⌈ huh heh
7 *Lucy*:   ⊦ huh huh
8 *Tom*:   ⌊ heh heh
9 *Sara*:   ah hah hah
10 *Lucy*: I think you'll find (s   ) well I've actually known s– straight
11   people that go as well I mean you'd be surprised . . .

These observations are presented as evidence of the political awareness of punks (Extract 1) and the political statement made by alternative subcultures (Extract 3). Given this, one might reasonably expect the evidence to be formulated in terms of what members do; that is, we might expect a statement such as 'punks go on marches'. But they do not produce this kind of formulation. Instead, they focus on the marches. So, in Extract 1, the speaker says: 'it's like if you think if you've got any sort of march . . . there'll always be like a. like a majority of s– sort of like– punky type people there', and in Extract 3 the speaker begins her response with the statement, 'it must be cos like when you go on the marches i– (.) it's always people that look like us that go'. This makes the basis of their claims an observable or empirical phenomenon derived from direct experience; it also implies that anyone who goes on or witnesses demonstrations will come to the same conclusion. Basing their claims on empirical observation warrants the factual status of their claims and thus clearly avoids making them contingent upon what is generally known about the subcultural category.

To summarize, there are three points that I want to draw out from the analytic observations. The first concerns the implications of the ways that respondents affirm the political dimension of the subculture, by first acknowledging and then dismissing stereotyped assumptions concerning the basis and nature of the political dimension: for example, that punk is about anarchy and that this is manifested through their attachment to organizations like Class War. Similarly, in Extract 2, respondents reject the cultural assumption that appearance is the vehicle through which they reject the system. I argued earlier that academic and popular discourse on youth subcultures provided outsiders' resources through which to impute meaning to members' lives. I also said that because these resources are constructed in the absence of members' accounts, they are assumptions to be resisted.

Clearly, these analytic conclusions are very different from the rather more grandiose claims about power and oppression that are derived through analysis which adopts an explicit political agenda.

Nonetheless, we can begin to see how, in the details of their talk, members display and achieve resistance not to their subordination but to what is generally known or assumed about their lives, their lifestyles and identities. In more general terms, far from being an obstacle to understanding the political significance of identities, a detailed analysis of talk shows the site where power and resistance are played out, in this case through the way that social category ascription can function as a means of social control.

The second point is that respondents make their claims about the political dimension of the subculture contingent on specific activities in relation to specific socio-political issues. However, in affirming the political dimension of the subculture, respondents must also address certain problematic inferences thereby made available: for example, that political activities are a criterial feature of the subculture or the subculture image, or that their activities are motivated merely through their membership of the subculture. Such inferences could, in turn, implicate the shallow or non-genuine nature of their political concerns. In addition, members' behaviour could be interpreted merely as a result of blind conformity to the political features of the subculture, or adolescent perversity. Such inferences are potentially relevant because of cultural knowledge about the subculture and young people's behaviour.

In these extracts, respondents display a clear sensitivity to these kinds of problematic inferences; in particular they employ a variety of descriptive strategies through which they avoid the potential inference that political activity is merely informed by their membership of the subculture. This is accomplished, for example, in the details of their description of the people involved; by making relevant primarily personal motivations; and through an explicit denial that activities are informed by the desire to be a particular kind of person. Furthermore, they indicate that the majority, but not all, members are involved; and in Extract 2 Lucy distinguishes between different types of members. In these ways, they make clear that political activism cannot be regarded as a consensual or normative feature of the subculture.

My analysis of the subtle ways that speakers negotiate the relationship between subcultural identity and political activity may have wider implications. In particular, it is often assumed that collective identification and affiliation (perhaps through conscious-ness-raising) is a precursor to collective political action outside the discipline of psychology. This concern is shared by feminist psychologists (such as Burman, 1994) and social identity theorists (such as Tajfel and Turner, 1979; Tajfel, 1981). But this analysis suggests that if the basis of political action is seen to lie in collective identification, then this may constitute a threat to individual integrity and the authenticity of this action. There is some resonance here with research which shows that when women portray their own activities or beliefs which could be classified as feminist, they make clear that these activities are not contingent upon being a feminist (Griffin, 1989). Indeed, the phrase, 'I'm not a feminist but (I do or believe things that could be seen as feminist)' seems to have become a common rhetorical strategy through which people may point to personal choice and motivation as the basis of their behaviour. Given that people do have a strong sense of themselves as individuals (Kitzinger, 1992), the most effective way of marketing particular political aims is likely to be through appealing to personal choices and decisions rather than by appealing to collective identities or shared oppression.

The third and most important point is to reiterate the value of attending to what people say, and to the tacit reasoning and communicative competencies through which identities and other discursive actions are produced, made relevant and negotiated to address real interactional and inferential issues. It is in the context of interaction that issues of identity are live, practical concerns. Discourse analysis which overlooks this in the search for abstract discourses about which political statements can be made misses significant features of social life at its most basic level of interaction. Moreover, by not attending to the ways that people portray the significance of their own identities, researchers do a social injustice to those people who they claim are the objects of their concern.

Notes

1 Wetherell and Potter's (1992) *Mapping the Language of Racism* represents an attempt to bridge the two analytic approaches. On the one hand, they are critical of the abstract, reified and disembodied poststructuralist notion of discourses. This suggests that discourses are potent causal agents in their own right, as though they automatically work to produce subjects and objects. Wetherell and Potter emphasize, by explicit contrast, their conceptualization of language as essentially a social practice, meaning that it is *used* in particular contexts. Moreover, they state that 'a focus on discourse as social practice has led us to analyse discourse in terms of its entry into the world of practical affairs: everyday conversation and texts. This means that . . . the focus is very much on the implementation of those discourses in actual settings' (Wetherell and Potter, 1992: 90). To mark clearly this difference, they use the notion of interpretative repertoires rather than discourses. On the other hand, they say that their aim, 'to capture the ideological operation of a wide range of different interpretative repertoires operating in a culture' could only be accomplished through an analysis which went beyond the discourse collected ('we commonly did not have complete examples of such things available in our materials'; Wetherell and Potter, 1992: 103).

2   For the purposes of this chapter, I have selected two accounts in which respondents clearly make relevant a political dimension to their lives. But I could equally have selected accounts in which respondents explicitly denied the assumption that their affiliation with a subculture was political.

3   At the time these interviews were conducted (1989) it was the subject of media attention, partly because disturbances at anti-poll tax and other demonstrations were attributed to a minority of extremists from organizations like Class War.

4   The label 'alternative types' was used by respondents who could not clearly be categorized as either gothic or punk, but whose style fused elements from both. The description was sometimes used by ex-gothics who wished to dissociate themselves from this subculture while maintaining identification with a broad style and lifestyle which is seen as alternative to being straight or following High Street fashions.

5   Although the word following 'political' on line 14 is not clear, its formulation as 'basically like a political' something is clear.

6   Unfortunately, space does not permit a thorough analysis of the full extract. Consequently, I have restricted my observations to just certain parts.

Appendix: Transcription notation

The transcription notation I have used in this chapter is a selection from Jefferson's system (presented in Atkinson and Heritage, 1984). I find it useful in the presentation of the accounts since it provides some indication of how something was said. Not only can this clarify the meaning of certain phrases, it also brings the words alive in a way that 'tidied up' transcription does not.

[	overlapping utterances
=	continuous utterances (i.e. where there is no interval between adjacent utterances)
(0.2)	indicates a timed interval or pause within a stream of talk, timed to approximately the nearest tenth of a second.
(.)	indicates a pause shorter than this
so:	a colon indicates an extension of the sound of syllable it follows (more colons extend the stretch)
.	a stopping fall in tone (sounds like the end of a sentence)
,	a continuing intonation (sounds like the kind of pause you get between clauses within a sentence)
↑	a marked rise in intonation
own	indicates emphasis
DON'T	indicates that the word, or part word, is spoken much louder than the surrounding talk
° °	the speech between the degree signs is quieter than the surrounding talk
> <	the utterances enclosed between these signs is spoken faster than the surrounding talk
( )	single parentheses indicate transcription doubt, empty parentheses indicate that I couldn't work out what was said at all
.hh	an audible aspiration and (hh) inhalation
if–	a dash indicates the sharp cut-off of the prior word or sound.

References

Althusser, L. (1971) *Lenin and Philosophy and Other Essays*. London: New Left Books.

Atkinson, J.M. and Heritage, J. (eds) (1984) *Structures of Social Action: Studies in Conversation Analysis*. Cambridge: Cambridge University Press.

Austin, J.L. (1962) *How to do Things with Words*. Oxford: Oxford University Press.

Barthes, R. (1971) Rhetoric of the image. Working Papers in Cultural Studies 1, Centre for Contemporary Cultural Studies, University of Birmingham.

Bhavnani, K.-K. (1990) What's power got to do with it? Empowerment and social research. In I. Parker and J. Shotter (eds), *Deconstructing Social Psychology*. London: Routledge.

Bhavnani, K.-K. and Phoenix, A. (1994) Shifting identities shifting racisms: an introduction. In K.-K. Bhavnani and A. Phoenix (eds), *Shifting Identities Shifting Racisms: A 'Feminism & Psychology' Reader*. London: Sage.

Brake, M. (1985) *Comparative Youth Culture: The Sociology of Youth Culture and Youth Subcultures in America, Britain and Canada*. London: Routledge and Kegan Paul.

Burman, E. (1994) Experience, identities and alliances: Jewish feminism and feminist psychology. In K.-K. Bhavnani and A. Phoenix (eds), *Shifting Identities Shifting Racisms: A 'Feminism & Psychology' Reader*. London: Sage.

Burman, E. and Parker, I. (1993) Introduction – discourse analysis: the turn to the text. In E. Burman and I. Parker (eds), *Discourse Analytic Research: Repertoires and Readings of Texts in Action*. London: Routledge.

Cohen, S. (1980) Symbols of trouble: introduction to the new edition. In *Folk Devils and Moral Panics: The creation of the Mods and Rockers*. London: Martin Robertson [first edn 1972].

Davis, J. (1990) *Youth and the Condition of Britain: Images of Adolescent Conflict*. London: Athlone Press.

Foucault, M. (1972) *The Archaeology of Knowledge* (trans. A.M. Sheridan Smith). London: Tavistock Publications.

Foucault, M. (1981) *The History of Sexuality*. Vol. 1: *An Introduction* (trans. Robert Hurley). New York, Vintage/Random House.

Garfinkel, H. (1967) *Studies in Ethnomethodology*. Englewood Cliffs, NJ: Prentice-Hall.

Gavey, N. (1989) Feminist poststructuralism and discourse analysis: contributions to feminist psychology. *Psychology of Women Quarterly* 13, 459–75.

Griffin, C. (1989) 'I'm not a women's libber but . . .': feminism, consciousness and identity. In S. Skevington and D. Baker (eds), *The Social Identity of Women*. London: Sage.

Hall, S. and Jefferson, T. (eds) (1976) *Resistance through Rituals: Youth Subcultures in Post-war Britain*. London: Hutchinson.

Hebdige, D. (1979) *Subculture: The Meaning of Style*, London: Methuen.

Hollway, W. (1984) Gender difference and the production of subjectivity. In J. Henriques, W. Hollway, C. Urwin, C. Venn and V. Walkerdine (1984) *Changing the Subject: Psychology, Social Relations and Subjectivity*. London: Methuen.

Hollway, W. (1989) *Subjectivity and Method in Psychology: Gender, Meaning and Science*. London: Sage.

Kitzinger, C. (1992) The individuated self. In G. Breakwell (ed.), *The Social Psychology of Identity and the Self Concept*. London: Academic Press/Surrey University Press.

Parker, I. (1992) *Discourse Dynamics: Critical Analysis for Social and Individual Psychology*. London: Routledge.

Parker, I. and Burman, E. (1993) Against discursive imperialism, empiricism and constructionism: thirty-two problems with discourse analysis. In E. Burman and I. Parker (eds), *Discourse Analytic Research: Repertoires and Readings of Texts in Action*. London: Routledge.

Tajfel, H. (1981) *Human Groups and Social Categories: Studies in Social Psychology*, Cambridge: Cambridge University Press.

Tajfel, H. and Turner, J.C. (1979) An integrative theory of intergroup conflict. In W.C. Austin and S. Worchel (eds), *The Social Psychology of Intergroup Relations*. Monterey, CA: Brooks/Cole.

Wetherell, M. and Potter, J. (1992) *Mapping the Language of Racism: Discourse and the Legitimation of Exploitation*. Hemel Hempstead: Harvester Wheatsheaf.

Widdicombe, S. and Wooffitt, R. (1995) *The Language of Youth Subcultures: Social Identity in Action*. Hemel Hempstead: Harvester Wheatsheaf.

Wilkinson, S. (1986) Sighting possibilities: diversity and commonality in feminist research. In S. Wilkinson (ed.), *Feminist Social Psychology: Developing Theory and Practice*, Milton Keynes: Open University Press.

Wilkinson, S. (1991) Feminism and psychology: from critique to reconstruction. *Feminism & Psychology* 1, 5–18.

Wittgenstein, L. (1953) *Philosophical Investigations*. (ed. G.E.M. Anscombe). Oxford: Basil Blackwell.

7

Romantic Discourse and Feminist Analysis: Interrogating Investment, Power and Desire

Margaret Wetherell

The object of romantic desire is, by definition, he (or she) who dominates and disappoints. (Lynne Segal, 1990: 274)

This chapter uses romance and romantic discourse as a device for interrogating discourse analysis and its significance for feminism. I want to review some of the distinctive features of discourse theory as it 'takes on' romantic talk and writing, and also highlight some of the dilemmas confronting this approach to cultural representations which have certainly troubled feminist discourse analysts. My aim is not to argue a case about romance, or even to make a serious contribution to feminist scholarship on romantic texts (such as Modleski, 1984; Radway, 1984; Snitow, 1984; Treacher, 1988; Miles, 1991). More speculatively, I want to give my view of some of the crossroads and decision points I think we have reached, or are reaching, in the study of discourse and gender.

I write as a social psychologist and my reference point is thus discourse analysis as it has been developing within that discipline (Potter and Wetherell, 1987; Parker, 1992). In more general terms, my topic is my reading of some of the relatively global premises characteristic of discourse work, found also in studies of rhetoric and in the social constructionist movement within social psychology as a whole (for example, Harré, 1979, 1986a; Gergen, 1985, 1991; Billig, 1987, 1991; Shotter, 1993). These premises concern the constitution of identity and subjectivity, the nature of experience and communication, ideology and the role of representation in social life. These basic assumptions will take centre stage in this chapter as opposed to the empirical claims and methods discourse researchers also advance as they develop their analyses of texts and talk (Edwards and Potter, 1992; Wetherell and Potter, 1992).

Three pieces of romantic discourse from three very different genres are presented in Boxes 7.1, 7.2 and 7.3 as a stimulus. I have

Box 7.1   Wings of Desire

Marion to Damiel

This, finally, must be serious.
I've often been alone but I've never lived alone.
When I was with someone I was often happy
but it seemed like a coincidence.
Those people were my parents
but it could have been others.
Why was this brown-eyed boy my brother
and not the boy with the green eyes on the opposite platform?
The taxi-driver's daughter was my friend
but I might as well have put my arm around a horse's neck.
I was with a man, I was in love
and I might as well have left him
and walked off with the stranger I met in the street.
Look at me, or don't.
Give me your hand, or don't.
No, don't give me your hand and look away.
. . .
I've never toyed with anyone
yet I've never opened my eyes
and thought, 'Now, this is serious.'
At last it is becoming serious.
I've grown older.
Am I the only one who wasn't serious?
Is it the times that lack seriousness?
I was never alone, neither on my own, nor with others.
But I would have liked to be alone.
After all, being alone means to be whole.
Now I can say it, as from tonight I'm alone at last.
I must put an end to coincidence.
The new moon of decision.
I don't know if there is destiny
but there is a decision.
So decide!
. . .
We two are now more than us two.
We incarnate something.
We are sitting in the place of the people
and the whole place is full of people
who are dreaming the same dream.
We decide everyone's game.

continues

Box 7.1   *continued*

I am ready.
Now it's your turn.
Now you've got to decide.
Now or never!
You need me.
You will need me.
There's no greater story than ours!
a man and a woman.
It will be a story of giants
invisible but transferable,
a story of new ancestors.
Look, my eyes.
They are the picture of necessity,
of everyone's future.
Last night I dreamed of a stranger.
It was my man.
Only with him could I be alone.
Open up to him,
wholly, wholly, open for him.
Welcome him wholly into me.
Surround him with the labyrinth of shared happiness.
I know
it's you.

Extract transcribed from the film *Wings of Desire* directed by Wim
Wenders. Screenplay in collaboration with Peter Handke.

---

transcribed one of the final speeches from Wim Wenders' film *Wings
of Desire* (written in collaboration with Peter Handke), borrowed a
bit from Ann Oakley's autobiography *Taking it Like a Woman*
(1984), and, finally, reproduced a sequence from a Barbara Cartland
novel – *Moments of Love* (1982). These extracts are there to act as
illustrative moments in my tour of broad premises, although they also
deserve, of course, much more detailed analysis.

Transcendence, redemption and closure

David Harvey (1989) in his discussion of *Wings of Desire* argues that
Wenders' film vividly encapsulates the postmodern dilemma. The
first half of the story quite brilliantly plays with and illustrates images
of fragmentation, contingency, the loss of the centre, and the failure
of overarching systems of meaning to make sense of life. While, in

---

Box 7.2   South of the Baltic Sea

The morning spent waiting for him was perhaps the best time. (She would not like him to misunderstand this.) . . .

The minute he arrives she realises that their time together is again beginning to be over. He stands there and seems both a stranger and her intimate lover. . . .

The hours are crowded with experiences, not just of the two of them together (though that would, of course suffice) but of this place, its ambience, its difference from the cultures they know best. They get lost together in the rain, they stand together in a church and kiss. They sit, listening to mournful music in the minor key, in warm restaurants where everything is submerged in vodka. . . .

She can't remember what she said. . . . Why doesn't he say that she is beautiful? Why doesn't he say he loves her incredibly, more than he has ever loved anyone, and for ever; that he wants to spend his life with her; that she is everything to him? Why doesn't he buy her red roses and swim the sea with chocolates? She wouldn't believe it if he did. . . . She distrusts romantic chivalrous gestures in men. It means they are treating women as sex objects. So why does she want it? Why is she hurt by his pragmatism? The last thing she needs is to live with him, with his self-interest, his self-centred depressions, his magisterial exercise of male power. The last thing she wants is to be like his wife. She knows what she wants: she wants him to love her now wholeheartedly, to think of no one and nothing else when he makes love to her. . . . She wants him to feel about her as he does about no one else, to be so conscious of her individuality that whether or not he loves another woman does not matter. She definitely does not want him to claim more than his fair share of her.

Extract from Oakley, 1984: Scenes 3, 4, and 5, pp. 50–3.

---

radical contrast, the last part of the film, in the scene I have transcribed, seems to suggest some sort of solution: the coming together and mutual affirmation of the main characters, the trapeze artist, Marion, and the angel Damiel. Their love, their romance, is presented as an escape from coincidence and fragmentation, a movement away from the postmodern condition towards unity, wholeness, togetherness, community and humanism.

The second extract, taken from Ann Oakley's autobiography, is a more reflexive account, with feminist inflections, as Oakley ponders the contradictions of romance. It is the beginning of a story about a passionate and adulterous affair. But, like the film transcript, it also describes a desire for a specific Other, linked to the search for a

---

Box 7.3   Simonetta and Pierre

'I am . . . happy,' Simonetta managed to stammer. 'I am . . . happy, Pierre . . . but I thought it would be . . . impossible for me to . . . m.marry you.'

'You will be my wife,' he said, 'and I will never allow you to cry like this again.'

He turned her face up to his. Then he was kissing away the tears from her eyes, her cheeks and lastly her mouth.

At the touch of his lips Simonetta felt thrill after thrill flash through her and it was like coming back to life from the dead.

Once again he was carrying her up into the sky and there was the rapture and wonder of being close to him, of belonging to him.

'I . . . love . . . you . . . I love you . . . I love . . . you,' her heart was saying.

Extract from Cartland, 1982: 298.

---

moment of transcendence. Although it is presented as autobiography, as part of Oakley's own experience, Oakley carefully says elsewhere in her book that the 'she' in her story, the narrator, is a literary device and fictional. 'She' is presented as the paradigm of all the contradictions to which Oakley sees modern women as exposed.

So, by romance, then, what I mean, at least for the purposes of this chapter, is a text which presents an image of redemption, of salvation and rescue. Usually, but not necessarily, this is presented as a heterosexual passion. Perhaps, characteristically, Barbara Cartland's metaphors, in the third extract, present this transcendence of 'earthly' ties most unambiguously and most unashamedly.

Romantic texts seem to be distinguished by forms of closure on many levels. These texts represent, first, the closing off of emotional ambivalence. The desire is for a movement away from contingency towards unity and towards an emotional paradise of reciprocity and certainty. Romance is also, literally, the story which very frequently ends all stories. The story behind the story, the revealed meaning. So, after all, the couple loved each other; that, particularly in the Mills and Boon genre, is what it all seems to be about. In fiction, and in films, romantic discourse often appears as a form of relief from the search for meaning; we move from the image of the couple (usually, newly met) locked in a maelstrom of ambiguities, partial disclosures, interpretations and formulations of their relationship to the predictable ending of romance which stifles other interpretations and imposes its authority over other accounts. In the end he loved her. That is the final story, and that is all we seem to need to say.

Because of this closure, romantic discourse sometimes presents a very static image. The couple are left forever locked in their embrace. They daren't move because movement would in some way spoil the effect. I can't help wondering, as other feminists have wondered, what happens when daily life has to be resumed and Marion and the angel Damiel or Simonetta and her man have to do a bit of shopping, negotiate cleaning the toilet, and so on. But that, of course, is not the point, and not the frame.

Romance, of course, is also usually gendered. It is a story that, typically, women are supposed to want and men to reject. Women are supposed to do the romance in relationships and men are supposed to do the sex. In popular culture, women and girls are assigned romantic fiction and men and boys pornography (Snitow, 1984; Walkerdine, 1984). Particularly within the genre of romantic fiction, the Harlequin and the Mills and Boon, women and men are also empowered differentially by romance and given contrasting positions and identities.

Romantic discourse is frequently contradictory on this issue of power, and perhaps this is part of its ambiguous appeal. On the one hand, romance seems to erase power in its image of mutuality. But, on the other hand, men are often represented as the initiators of romance and women as the receivers. Men are heroic in the throes of love, women are simply in the throes. Indeed, in many genres, for a relationship to count as romance, what is important is that the man, rather than the woman, recognizes it as such. I will come back to that contradictory message about power later, for as Tania Modleski (1984) has argued, it is all more complex than it might appear.

What, then, does discourse analysis, social constructionism and feminism have to say about all this? When we look at romance through the lens of discourse analysis, two distinctive features of this approach are clarified as well as three particular challenges or problematic issues. The two distinctive features concern the perspective on experience and the approach to subjectivity or identity. The three dilemmas concern: first, the explanation of what Wendy Hollway (1984) has called 'investment'; second, the relationship between discourse and the 'social'; and, third, the implications for feminist politics.

Discourse, experience and the formulation of identity

One emphasis of discourse analysis and social constructionism becomes clear if we develop a contrast with traditional, humanist, psychological interpretations of romantic love (Johnson, 1984). These look at romance as primarily an emotional *experience*: an experience outside time, history and culture which has an authority in itself, an authority which originates in being. From this perspective, the question asked about representations such as those in the three extracts might be these: Are the descriptions authentic? Are some of these accounts more 'true to life' than others? Do these words accurately describe the emotion? The premise would be that the words, the discourse, and the experience can always be separated. The emotion exists outside the words and thus we can inquire into how well the words fit the experience.

For me, the most interesting thing about discourse analysis, and the aspect which gives it a radical potential for feminist psychology, is that it rejects this model of the process of representation and this model of language and emotion. Discourse analysis emphatically privileges the linguistic or the social/linguistic over what has conventionally been understood as the psychological; it argues that experience, and thus subjective psychological reality, is constituted through language and the process of representation. It is not the case that representation reflects, and is secondary to, the experience (Harré, 1986b; Potter and Wetherell, 1987; Gergen, 1990; Shotter, 1993).

Discourse analysis proposes that, even in the case of the apparently 'overwhelming' emotions found in the three extracts, the experience, the psychology, the feeling, is always inevitably identified, labelled and constructed through narrative, language, and stories. It is the narrative which packages and thus, in some sense, creates and produces the identity and the desire, and, indeed, it is the narrative we adopt which defines the experience as one of those sorts of experiences and not some other kind of experience.

To put it another way, the discourse analyst says that it is not the case that every woman and man in love magically find themselves uttering, creating and discovering afresh, for the first time, these words as the mirror or reflection of their experience, although they may well feel they are doing just that. The words instead are second-hand, already in circulation, already familiar, already there, waiting for the moment of appropriation. The woman and the man, the heterosexual couple, recognize their experience and determine its quality through the words which are available.

The point I'm making is, as Roland Barthes says (1979), that to fall out of love, or more particularly, to fall out of romance, is not just to lose a relationship but, primarily, involves the loss of a language: a discursive method of figuring oneself and the other person and putting the two together. Discourse analysis focuses on that method of figuring while feminism questions the politics, the consequences and the alternatives. Together discourse analysis and feminism produce a radical and liberating scepticism.

James Averill (1985), in his social constructionist analysis of romantic love, points out that romantic love provides a 'paradigm' of emotion, a model and a rationale for feeling and action. In taking on the paradigm the individual confirms the broader cultural networks of which the paradigm is an aspect. Romance is, supposedly, highly individual, yet it is also another of those moments through which the individual affirms their sociality and instantiates their culture.

The second strength of discourse analysis for me, or the second interesting argument from a feminist perspective, is the view of identity or subjectivity which emerges as a result of this model of representation. If we say that experience is constituted through narrative then we are also saying that our self-knowledge, our self-accounts, our self-descriptions are discursively organized (see Edwards and Potter, 1992). We are saying that a sense of identity is always an invention, a construction, a melding and meeting point of discourses.

I'd like to paraphrase some comments of Stuart Hall's to draw this point out. Hall argues that the 'who am I?', the 'real me' is always formed in relation to cultural narratives. Identity, he says, 'is formed at the unstable point where the "unspeakable" stories of subjectivity meet the narratives of history, of a culture' (Hall, 1988a: 44).

There are a number of implications here. First, if we accept this position then, ultimately, we have to learn to live with ambivalence, with contradictions, with fragmentation because the discourses from which we construct a sense of self are inconsistent, contradictory, varying and embody the relics of many different social and ideological struggles (see Connell, 1987: 219–28). If there is no real me then there are multiple accounts of what I am like and if, like me, you have an authoritarian predilection for definite answers, for wanting to find out what is 'really' felt, the core meaning, then this is very frustrating. Because, although there are always attempts at unification and definition, 'real feelings' will be always contingent, always escaping, always changing, as the person comes to be positioned and re-positioned within different narratives and versions.

But, secondly, it means, as Hall also argues, that because we eventually do stop talking, or stop positioning ourselves, because we do, from moment to moment, settle, in conversation and in our accounts, on one version of ourselves, and often maintain this version for a considerable length of time (or, indeed, find that others have settled for us), identity is also about closure and difference. It is about refusing all the possible versions of 'me', and going at a particular moment for one; it is about closing off some narratives and marking a point of difference.

Hall suggests this moment of closure should be seen as a kind of stake or a kind of wager. He points out (1988a: 45) that it is a moment which says – I need to say something, something . . . just now. Right now, this is what I mean, this is what I am. The self, subjectivity, identity are these points of unfinished closure where we place a full stop. As the feminist psychoanalyst Jane Gallop (1982) similarly argues, identity, as part of feminist strategy, must be continually assumed and immediately called into question. I will return to this point later.

That argument, I think, is fascinating and in relation to romance and the projects of feminism it is, again, potentially liberating. If we see romantic discourse as both enchanting and usually, also, deeply problematic for women, perhaps deeply oppressive, then it may be possible to close off identity and subjectivity in relationships differently. Or, at least, if romance proves impossible to shake off, there is the comforting knowledge of the constructed nature of this feeling. That move, I think, can be more reassuring and more empowering than grounding romance in the authority and authenticity of unquestionable experience.

These, then, are some ways in which discourse analysis clarifies romance, and makes a new contribution. But romance also raises some special challenges for discourse analysis. These points of debate, as I noted, are of three kinds. Crudely speaking, there is the psychologist's problem; the dilemma discourse analysis presents for the social theorist; and the political challenge of how to move forward from this base as a feminist. I'll take each of these in turn.

Questions about investment

The psychologist's issue is this (it is Wendy Hollway's (1984) point of interrogation in her analyses of heterosexual relationships). Why do we position ourselves within romantic discourse? What's in it for us, what explains the irrational charge of desire? And why are some people immune? Why do women do it, if they do, more than men? Why select one man or woman as the object of romantic desire and not another? Explain that if you will.

This question of investment or attachment is important and complex, and one solution is to place discourse analysis in some relation with psychoanalysis – most commonly in studies of romance, in relation to some version of object relations theory and/or Lacanian psychoanalysis. Analyses of romantic discourse and its gendered nature from a broad object relations perspective (see Edley and Wetherell, 1995: 38–65; Miles, 1991; Treacher, 1988) refer us back to the subjectivity of the child in the pre-Oedipal stage, to the patterning of early relationships (most usually with the mother). These accounts see the child's trajectory as moving from a state of connection with the mother to one of disconnection, separation and autonomy as the mind is built up from the residues of significant relations with the 'objects' (people) in the environment.

Psychoanalysts who observe the interaction between mothers and babies in the first few months of life argue that this relationship tends to be quite unlike any other human relationship in its emphasis on 'merger' and 'symbiosis'. It is distinguished by the extreme dependency of the child upon mother, by the degree of sensitivity most mothers show to the child's needs, by the blurring of identity between mother and child, and by the potential for absorption of each in the other.

The British object relations theorist Donald Winnicott (cf. Greenberg and Mitchell, 1983: Chapter 7; Frosh, 1987: Chapter 4) argues that at birth the baby's sense of self is best described as 'undifferentiated'. The baby, whether male or female, experiences true symbiosis with the mother. She or he has, initially, no sense of where the mother ends and self begins, no sense of what is 'me' and what is 'not me', and only a limited or non-existent grasp of the properties of objects and its own powers in relation to these.

A sense of self emerges, however, through early interactions with the mother. Children learn through frustrations and delays in the gratification of needs, and as the mother begins to turn her attention to other matters, that there are boundaries to their experience which define where self ends and the world begins. Babies learn that they are not omnipotent but dependent. Indeed, at around six months, anxiety at separation when the mother is absent becomes possible, although it was not evident before, because children can now perceive their mothers and themselves as distinct individuals.

This process of separation and gradual individuation is one which all humans are thought to experience. It is a process which object relations theorists see as pivotal in the development of self-esteem, a self-concept, a sense of physical security, and a self-confident and optimistic attitude to life. But for boys it is suggested that individuation has a further dimension of a much stronger dis-identification from the mother, as a core gender identity begins to form. The boy, unlike the girl, is forced into a much stronger repudiation of the mother. Masculinity, in these terms, can be seen as a piece of additional 'neurosis' men acquire as they learn to dis-identify from the feminine and from their mothers. Robert Stoller (1985), for example, describes masculinity as a state of constant vigilance, the formation of a barrier against symbiosis since it is only through a carefully maintained difference from the feminine that a man can be confident of being 'man enough'.

Romance, in this scenario, represents a form of nostalgia, the hankering for a return to some early sense of wholeness, subjective unity and self/other diffusion. Romance represents a desire for perfect mothering. Hollway argues that men, because of the precarious and particular character of their sexual/gender identity, resist diffusion and their desire for the Other, or for the scrutinizing Mother, because of the intense vulnerability summoned up by this degree of connection and intimacy. Men typically make romance, love and intimacy safe, Hollway argues, through the projection of the desire for mutual self-affirmation on to women.

Angela Miles (1991) and Amal Treacher (1988) argue from slightly different standpoints that the perfect male hero in romantic fiction is someone who is totally caring and absorbing. The woman reader's desire, in fact, is for a male mother – someone who offers symbiosis but safely contained within phallic difference. Treacher and Miles ruefully note the impossibility of the fantasy – where is the man who can be relied upon to 'mother' another? Ann Oakley in Box 7.2 similarly wonders whether such 'perfect encompassing love', ideal in fantasy, might prove stifling in reality.

Lacanian psychoanalysts also remark on the fantastic nature of the desires expressed in romance and their doomed nature. Lacan argues that the basic point about desire for an object (*objet petit à*), a desire for another, is that it is interminable, forever restless, and unsatisfied. There can be no permanent closure of the kind premised in romance. As Toril Moi puts it, 'there can be no final satisfaction of our desire since there is no final signifier or object that can be that which has been lost forever (the imaginary harmony with the mother and the world)' (Moi, 1985: 101). Lacan argues that before acquiring language and becoming a subject within the symbolic order, the child passes through an imaginary stage. In this stage the child's sense of self as unitary and bounded depends on the mother who supplies the child with this illusion of completeness. Hence is initiated the search to be again seen as whole and total in the eyes of others and, therefore, the eternal captivation of the imaginary.

The desire for the romantic object is, in part, a fantasy concerning the benevolent gaze of the original Mother/Other who can see the subject whole, unified, and 'self-identified'. Romance, remember, is the discourse distinguished by the image of unity and redemption/ rescue, and characterized by the absence of contingency. It also contains highly narcissistic strivings for recognition. The desire is for the idealized other to confer perfection on self and recognize the special, endearing and unique nature of that self through their loving gaze.

However the psychoanalytic argument is developed, the appeal is the location of narratives of romance and other 'voices of the mind' in family histories, giving 'depth', explaining repetition and the 'driven' character of narrative construction. But there are important differences between the object relations account and those found in Lacanian psychoanalysis, and these differences are vital for the dialogue between discourse analysis and psychoanalysis. With object relations accounts there is a danger that romance is once more grounded in experience (this time, the mother of all experiences, so to speak). The constructive effects of discourses in immediate, moment to moment and longer-term formulations of self and Other, just celebrated in the previous section of this chapter, become overwhelmed by an experiential and relational process placed in the distance of the past and subsequently frozen.

From a Lacanian perspective, however, the relations of signification in which the child and mother move are central from the start. The subsequent search for an object of romance, for closure, recognition, the polish and completion of the image, along with the dialectics of desire, are understood as taking part within a symbolic order which is gendered (patriarchal) and which presents a cultural context of meaning. It becomes possible, in other words, to examine the intertwining of personal imaginaries with social imaginaries and to consider the nature of the symbolic resources articulating the images which become the objects of desire.

Discourse and the social

As Toril Moi (1985), Lynne Segal (1990) and many other feminists have pointed out, the greatest danger with an appeal to the psychoanalytic and the psychodrama of the family is the disappearance of the particularities of the material and social context in which family relations and child development are played out. And this signals the challenge to discourse analysis raised by the sociologist and the social theorist. Is there another kind of bedrock here, after all, beyond the words, a social bedrock which grounds romantic narratives? Do the determinants of romance lie in what is often called the extra-discursive – in material and social reality, in social institutions, social practices and in social processes such as the sexual division of labour?

With regard to romantic discourse, what might be these other determining 'conditions of existence'? First, perhaps the cultural institutions which produce romantic discourse, the formats and profit margins under which they operate and the general technology of representations. Second, there are the social practices governing sexual relations and self-presentation. It is important to remember that love and romance have become the principle through which people have come to organize their economic and domestic relationships with each other. There is also the social history of romance – and the view, for example, that the emergence of romantic love depends on the appearance in the late Middle Ages of a strong concept of the individual which, in turn, is tied to the social and economic changes characterizing that period. We need to ask, too, about the take-up of romantic discourse, in terms of class, gender, ethnicity, age, and so on. Who becomes positioned romantically and just who finds this form of articulation a felicitous one? What is the status, for instance, of the older woman in the market-place of romance?

Talk of 'conditions of existence' suggests that here, at last, we might have causes beyond the words, or at least a mode of study which is more pressing and urgent than discourse analysis. My view is that a strong ontological distinction between the discursive and the extra-discursive is a mistake, both methodologically and epistemologically (see Wetherell and Potter, 1992: Chapter 3). To ignore the constitutive role of discourse is to ignore a central social force. How social objects (relationships, marriages, individuals, practices) are constituted in talk is pivotal to the nature of those objects. Talk about these things does not play a reflective or after-the-event role; it is the medium of the formation of social objects and social practices. However, clearly also, it is sterile to study discourse as though it were a mere literary matter. Talk and texts need to be continually placed in their inter-textual social context.

As we move to this positioning of the texts of romance in the texts of the social, then it becomes more and more appropriate to talk of discourse as ideology, and investigate how it might operate as ideological practice sustaining and justifying relations of power. This is a move I would want to endorse for feminist discourse analyses. The enormous advantage of the concept of ideology is that it raises the question – just in whose interests is the romantic nexus of power/knowledge and subject positioning? Who benefits here?

The literary critic Terry Eagleton (1983) argues, and this is a classic point about ideology, that its presence can be most positively felt in the significant silences, in the gaps and absences in discourses. For me, the gap, the significant silence in romantic discourse is, as I said earlier, life after the moment of redemption/rescue, once the mutual eye gaze drops away. In other words, the silence concerns mundane life, the kitchen sink part of the kitchen sink drama and just who is left standing at that sink gazing out the window, maybe listening to Simon Bates on the radio (Gill, 1993).

Feminist politics

It has been frequently suggested that discourse analysis is antithetical to and even explodes the possibility of political action (for example, Soper, 1990, and see the discussion of postmodernism and feminism initiated by Linda Nicholson, 1990, and Judith Butler, 1990). How can feminism, for example, be based on a deconstruction of the category 'female'? Doesn't politics depend on organizing around common experience and taking a stand? And what relevance can struggles over representation have for these political efforts? That is the third dilemma – does discourse analysis inevitably lead to an ambivalent and inadequate feminist politics? Isn't it bound to be irrelevant, reactionary and elitist?

Of course that can be true, it depends on the discourse analysis. But a politics based on the notion of the common experience of women can also get it wrong and indeed may sometimes feel even more marginalizing to black and working-class women (bell hooks, 1989). For me, the political impact of discourse analysis lies in the point just made, that things which are discursive are no less real in their effects, and changes in the social and economic are always intertwined with changes at the level of discourse and subjectivity.

It is fashionable at the moment to argue for what Hall (1988a, 1988b) calls, building on the work of poststructuralist theorists, a politics of articulation. That is, a politics which tries to combine two contradictory movements – opening and closing. Closing in the sense that effective political action involves putting, at some point, a stop to talking: in feminist terms it involves defining a community of women, and an identity from which to act. But also opening – in that this community of women must not be taken for granted; the way it is constructed and imagined must be continually open to question (see also Gallop, 1982).

For me, feminist psychology is and could be a model of this new method of politics. What might a feminist politics of articulation look like in practice? It is, I think, about tracing out the power dynamics of different discourses of femininity, about investigating the ways the imagined community of women has been constructed in different contexts, openly questioning the formulation of dominant discourses about women, and pushing forward subordinated and barely formulated alternatives. In this guise it is vital to work with ambiguity, ambivalence and openness with the recognition that femininity is a negotiable category which takes its shape as a particular type of identity within contrasting discourses. Accepting that there is not one thing there to be discovered, femininity should be seen as a method of description, not a psychological attribute.

It involves also living with the uncomfortable knowledge that discourses have multiple uses and multiple meanings (Wetherell and Potter, 1992). Romance, for example, can be read as disabling women, fixing us into potentially oppressive sexual relations. But romantic fiction may be also a source of resistance to men's power, and pleasurable precisely because it reveals the man squirming uncomfortably on the hook of his love for the heroine. His feet cut from under him, he grovels on bended knee. Romance, according to Tania Modleski (1982), can be read as a fantastical way of getting back at men, at rewriting their power plays, which become like the feeble efforts of the rabbit on the highway ducking and diving but still magnetized by the headlights of the approaching car. Unfortunately this feels like a solipsistic pleasure but the point is that discourse doesn't have just one political meaning.

We have to live with the fact, then, that nothing is simple, there is no inherent meaning, everything is ambiguous. But, of course, feminist psychology must also be about taking stands and fighting, probably and usually other psychologists and their control of women's lives. And for this we have to mobilize around some identities and some, rather than other, senses of community. Arbitrary closure is satisfying – this is the reality and it needs changing: we have to act on that basis, but perhaps keeping our fingers crossed behind our backs, the way that children do when telling a half-truth – not because we are insincere or uncommitted but because we are aware that sincerity, the feeling of rightness, and the aura of truth-telling is often the best, but sometimes also the most oppressive and dangerous, discursive effect.

Note

I would like to thank Ros Gill, Anna Dempsey, Derek Edwards, Jonathan Potter, and Jamie MacIntosh for their helpful thoughts and comments on this paper.

References

Averill, J. (1985) The social construction of emotion: with special reference to love. In K. Gergen and K. Davis (eds), *The Social Construction of the Person*. New York: Springer-Verlag.

Barthes, R. (1977) *Roland Barthes by Roland Barthes*. New York: Hill and Wang.

Barthes, R. (1979) *A Lover's Discourse: Fragments*. London: Cape.

Billig, M. (1987) *Arguing and Thinking: A Rhetorical Approach to Social Psychology*. Cambridge: Cambridge University Press.

Billig, M. (1991) *Ideology and Opinions*. London: Sage.

Butler, J. (1990) *Gender Trouble: Feminism and the Subversion of Identity*. New York: Routledge.

Cartland, B. (1982) *Moments of Love*. London: Pan.

Connell, R. (1987) *Gender and Power*. Cambridge: Polity.

Eagleton, T. (1983) *Literary Theory*. Oxford: Blackwell.

Edley, N. and Wetherell, M. (1995) *Men in Perspective*. Hemel Hempstead: Harvester Wheatsheaf.

Edwards, D. and Potter, J. (1992) *Discursive Psychology*. London: Sage.

Frosh, S. (1987) *The Politics of Psychoanalysis: An Introduction to Freudian and Post-Freudian Theory*. London: Macmillan.

Gallop, J. (1982) *Feminism and Psychoanalysis: The Daughter's Seduction*. London: Macmillan.

Gergen, K. (1985) The social constructionist movement in modern psychology. *American Psychologist* 40, 266–75.

Gergen, K. (1990) If persons are texts. In S.B. Messer, L.A. Sass and R.L. Woolfolk (eds), *Hermeneutics and Psychological Theory*. New Brunswick: Rutgers University Press.

Gergen, K. (1991) *The Saturated Self*. New York: Basic Books.

Gill, R. (1993) Justifying injustice: broadcasters' accounts of inequality in radio. In E. Burman and I. Parker (eds), *Discourse Analytic Research*. London: Routledge.

Greenberg, J. and Mitchell, S. (1983) *Object Relations in Psychoanalytic Theory*. Cambridge, MA: Harvard University Press.

Hall, S. (1988a) Minimal selves. In *Identity: The Real Me* (ICA Document No. 6). London: Institute of the Contemporary Arts.

Hall, S. (1988b) The toad in the garden: Thatcherism among the theorists. In C. Nelson and L. Grossberg (eds), *Marxism and the Interpretation of Culture*. Urbana: University of Illinois Press.

Harré, R. (1979) *Social Being*. Oxford: Blackwell.

Harré, R. (1986a) The step to social constructionism. In M. Richards and P. Light (eds), *Children of Social Worlds*. Oxford: Polity.

Harré, R. (1986b) Social sources of mental content and order. In J. Margolis, P.T. Manicas, R. Harré and P.F. Secord (eds), *Psychology: Designing the Discipline*. Oxford: Blackwell.

Harvey, D. (1989) *The Condition of Postmodernity*. Oxford: Blackwell.

Hollway, W. (1984) Gender difference and the production of subjectivity. In J. Henriques, W. Hollway, C. Urwin, C. Venn and V. Walkerdine, *Changing the Subject*. London: Methuen.

hooks, b. (1989) *Talking Back: Thinking Feminist, Thinking Black*. London: Sheba.

Johnson, R.A. (1984) *The Psychology of Romantic Love*. London: Routledge.

Miles, A. (1991) Confessions of a Harlequin reader: the myth of male mothers. In A. Kroker and M. Kroker (eds), *The Hysterical Male: New Feminist Theory*. London: Macmillan.

Modleski, T. (1984) *Loving with a Vengeance*. London: Methuen.

Moi, T. (1985) *Sexual/Textual Politics*. London: Methuen.

Nicholson, L. (ed.) (1990) *Feminism/Postmodernism*. New York: Routledge.

Oakley, A. (1984) *Taking it Like a Woman*. London: Jonathan Cape.

Parker, I. (1992) Discourse Dynamics. London: Routledge.

Potter, J. and Wetherell, M. (1987) *Discourse and Social Psychology*. London: Sage.

Radway, J. (1984) *Reading the Romance: Women, Patriarchy and Popular Literature*. Chapel Hill: University of North Carolina Press.

Segal, L. (1990) *Slow Motion: Changing Masculinities, Changing Men*. London: Virago.

Shotter, J. (1993) *Cultural Politics of Everyday Life*. Milton Keynes: Open University Press.

Snitow, A. (1984) Mass market romance: pornography for women is different. In A. Snitow, C. Stansell and S. Thompson (eds), *Desire: The Politics of Sexuality*. London: Virago.

Soper, K. (1990) Feminism, humanism and postmodernism. *Radical Philosophy* 55, 11–17.

Stoller, R. (1985) *Presentations of Gender*. New Haven, CT: Yale University Press.

Treacher, A. (1988) What is life without my love? Desire and romantic fiction. In S. Radstone (ed.), *Sweet Dreams: Sexuality, Gender and the Popular Imagination*. London: Lawrence and Wishart.

Walkerdine, V. (1984) Some day my prince will come. In A. McRobbie and M. Nava (eds), *Gender and Generation*. London: Methuen.

Wetherell, M. and Potter, J. (1992) *Mapping the Language of Racism: Discourse and the Legitimation of Exploitation*. Hemel Hempstead: Harvester Wheatsheaf/New York: Columbia University Press.

8

Pragmatism, Extravagance and Feminist Discourse Analysis

Corinne Squire

Discourse analysis is a much talked-about field in psychology, and it is increasingly something that feminist psychologists want to do. Many point to the convergences between feminist and discourse analytic concerns; a short list might include qualitative methods, experience, everyday language, reflexivity, and undecideability (Wetherell, 1986; Gavey, 1989; Hollway, 1989; Burman, 1991). There is, though, no necessary coincidence between feminist and discourse analytic interests in psychology, and a number of writers have emphasized the uncertain, even anti-feminist implications of discourse analysis (Gavey, 1989; Burman, 1991).

These divergences in view are complicated by doubts about how to define the two fields. Feminist psychology is a diverse category, encompassing a full range of psychological methods and theories (Squire, 1989; Morawski, 1992). It is described variously as a psychology by, about or for women, devoted to understanding gender relations or to improving women's condition. I shall characterize it broadly as the sector of psychology that analyses the effects of gender inequities on women's and men's subjectivities and tries to comprehend how these subjectivities might be changed; such a definition sacrifices precision for inclusiveness. Discourse analysis is similarly blurry. If a method, is it a form of conversation analysis or a Foucauldian archeology? If theory defines it, is its orientation towards a sophisticated, language-sensitive cognitivism, or towards linguisticism, or towards overarching accounts of power relations of for instance class, gender and race (Potter and Wetherell, 1987; Potter et al., 1990; Billig, 1991; Edwards and Potter, 1992; Parker, 1992; Burman and Parker, 1993)? Again, I am going to operate with a general definition of discourse analytic psychology, as an examination of the relationships between units of talk, writing, or other representational forms, and of the significance of these relationships for our subjective experience.

Given the intensity and variety of opinions on the question 'Can there be a feminist discourse analysis?', it is important to sort out the possibilities and problems that discourse analysis presents to feminist psychology. This chapter argues that the possibilities appear most often in two stories: narratives of pragmatism (West, 1989) and of extravagance (Wollen, 1987). These stories have had widespread and powerful presences in Western twentieth-century explanations of the world, and occur in both feminist and discourse analytic psychology. This chapter suggests that a feminist discourse analysis should deploy these narratives consistently, and in conjunction.

The instrumentalist case

Existing arguments for feminist discourse analysis are either instrumentalist, or they focus on feminists' and discourse analysts' theoretical convergence in a turn to language. The instrumentalist justification, based on the relative status of the two fields, suggests that while discourse analysis may share some of feminist psychology's concerns, its particular merit is that it provides a respectable institutional front. What feminist psychologists say is listened to, understood and valued more if they talk discourse analytic talk (Gavey, 1989). Discourse analysis is, indeed, an increasingly popular research framework. It supports a journal, *Discourse & Society*, and a clutch of discourse research units in universities and colleges. Mainstream psychological publications covering more general fields, like *Philosophical Psychology*, the *British Journal of Social Psychology*, *European Journal of Social Psychology*, and *Theory and Psychology*, are engaging with it. Growing numbers of graduate students complete discourse analytic theses while some undergraduates learn discourse analysis as a research method. 'How-to' books have even appeared (Potter and Wetherell, 1987; Parker, 1992). Feminist psychology seems less secure. Though some journals and organizations take a more or less feminist line (*Feminism & Psychology*, *Psychology of Women Quarterly*, *Sex Roles*; the BPS Psychology of Women Section and the APA Division 35, Psychology of Women; the British Alliance of Women in Psychology and the US Association of Women in Psychology); though books and book series, conferences and seminars proliferate, feminist psychology is less a field, more a perspective. It is most likely to appear in courses on the psychology of women, gender differences, or sexuality, but it may be absent even there. It remains a struggle to justify a PhD thesis or, outside selected fora, to publish a paper in which feminism plays a large part. Many psychology undergraduates reach the end of their degree thinking of feminist psychology, if it enters their minds at all, as a critique of gender-biased method and theory, a vague commitment to qualitative methods, and a short list of Great Women – Jean Baker Miller, Eleanor Maccoby and Carol Jacklin, Carol Gilligan, perhaps Juliet Mitchell.

In such circumstances, it is understandable that feminist psychologists seek to ally themselves with what they see as the greater clout of discourse analysis. My qualifications of this instrumentalist justification would be, first, that feminist psychologists overinflate the acceptability of discourse analysis; discourse analysts are, like themselves, marginal to the discipline and the objects of mainstream psychologists' scepticism. Second, and more importantly, it is difficult to maintain a dissociation between methods and theories you think are feminist, and those you adopt tactically. At the least, the latter divert you from developing your own. This objection is made not out of purism, but out of a conviction that feminist psychologists' concern to be realistic and practical should not just focus on institutions but should take on theory, too.

Shared interests

For many feminist psychologists, discourse analysis provides some help in answering questions about method and theory that block their work. Feminist psychologists share discourse analysts' dissatisfaction with cognitivism; their awareness of the ubiquity of the 'social' in psychology; their interest in structuralist and poststructuralist analyses, intensified for some by the place of psychoanalysis in poststructuralism; and their recognition of relevant work in ethnomethodology, psycho- and sociolinguistics and ordinary language philosophy. Feminists are also attracted by discourse analysis's emphasis on experience and the everyday and its qualitative yet systematized method. In addition, feminist psychologists have, like other politically interested psychologists, fastened on discourse analysis as offering hope for a radicalization of the discipline (Wetherell, 1986; Gavey, 1989; Hollway, 1989; Burman, 1991; Marshall, 1991; Gill, 1993).

These apparent convergences also provide some hints to the criticisms discursive psychology has encountered from feminists. These are: that discourse analysis does not engage fully with the social relations with which it professes to be so concerned, but retreats to language categories; that behind its apparently endless proliferations of linguistic interpretation lies the unitary, rational subject of traditional psychology, an intact and necessary part of the discourse analytic project; and that, like other psychologies affected by poststructuralism, it falls into absolute relativism, ignores its relationship to realities, and thereby avoids having to consider the power relations which help determine discourse (Burman, 1991; see also Gill, this volume). Feminist psychologists who buy the whole discourse analytic package may take on these incoherences in discourse analysis's theory and politics. Even if they adopt selected elements, the pick-and-mix approach may induce extra incoherence in their own work.

Deborah Tannen's (1991) *You Just Don't Understand*, an account of women's and men's forms of talk, is a good example both of discourse analysis's feminist and non-feminist aspects. This accessible and extremely successful book is ostensibly feminist. But despite Tannen's deliberate removal of gender conflict from the realm of the personal, her documentation of recognizable communication clashes, and her acknowledgement of social differences in communication, she reduces gender inequities to poor communication between the different communication cultures of women and men, between their 'different *but equally valid* styles' (Tannen, 1991:15; emphasis in original) (see also Troemel-Ploetz, 1991; Cameron, 1993). It could be argued that the pop-psychology genre to which *You Just Don't Understand* belongs makes simplification inevitable, and that a snobbish disdain for populism has fuelled academic feminists' criticisms of the book. But the same reductions of power relations to different communication styles appear in Tannen's more sober account of cross-cultural communication in the *Handbook of Discourse Analysis* (1985).

Pragmatic and extravagant narratives

We need an assessment of discourse analysis's possibilities and limitations for feminism that offers more than a list of each. An account focused on narratives of pragmatism and extravagance seems to provide the required framework. To give an idea of what pragmatic and extravagant narratives look like within feminist discourse analysis, I am going to look briefly at two papers. In the first paper, a 1989 discussion of feminism, poststructuralism and discourse analysis, Nicola Gavey says that since

> there is no sure way of guaranteeing our knowledges and values or of convincing others of their truth, theory and research should be assessed in terms of their utility in achieving political goals rather than their 'truth value'. (Gavey, 1989: 472)

Gavey's is a pragmatic argument, concerned, like the instrumentalist argument described above, with what is possible and effective rather than with the absolute rights or wrongs of a particular course of research, but operating with a wider notion of the political: a notion that extends into the future, and that goes beyond institutions to take in theory and subjectivity. Cornel West, in *The American Evasion of Philosophy*, describes 'good' pragmatism as 'a future-oriented instrumentalism that tries to deploy thought as a weapon to enable more effective action' (1989: 5). (I will disregard West's unnecessary rhetorical conjunction of pragmatism and militarism.) Gavey's discourse analysis of a verbal account of sexual coercion comes close to this characterization. It is an attempt to understand the complexity of discourses of sexuality, and how that complexity maintains the sexual coercion of women by men. In a woman's account of having heterosexual intercourse 'because I didn't want to hurt someone's feelings', Gavey isolates not just the discourse of female responsibility for male need, but also a discourse of sexual permissiveness – 'sex . . . [i]s just a physical activity. It's an enjoyable one' – and a third, feminist discourse of resistance to heterosexual coercion – 'I would have been better to have found the right words to say no' (Gavey, 1989: 469). She acknowledges that her categorization of discourses is an interested one. But this pragmatic partiality allows her to address significant everyday complexities in gender relations. For she uses the coexistence of the three discourses to explain how women coerced into heterosexual sex can find it impossible to perceive, let alone resist, what is happening; and how women are invested in non-feminist discourses of sexuality that are too powerful simply to dismiss as 'false consciousness'.

By contrast, in the second paper, 'Video Replay', an account of a family watching a *Rocky* video, Valerie Walkerdine says that in *her* research she wants

> to use my own fantasied positions within discursive practices as a way of engaging with their unconscious and conscious relations of desire and the plays of anxiety and meaning (Walkerdine, 1986: 191).

Walkerdine explores her fantasies as a researcher, a working-class woman, and a daughter, about the film and the family. This 'backwards movement', as Walkerdine calls it, 'traces the associations of the signifier(s) into the unconscious' (193), and ends up in what she recognizes is an exorbitant, 'impossible' place (187) – childhood feminine narcissism. Such excesses and impossibilities of interpretation and meaning are important within what I am calling the extravagant cultural narrative, a narrative marked by extremity of every kind, as Peter Wollen suggests in his account of representations of the Russian Ballet as 'both "ultra-natural" (wild, untamed, passionate, chaotic, animal) and "ultra-artificial" (fantastic, androgynous, bejewelled, decorative, decadent)' (Wollen, 1987: 27).

Narratives of pragmatism and extravagance are often present in feminist as well as discourse analytic psychology. I am going to argue that, rather than accepting or rejecting discourse analysis wholesale, feminist psychologists should frame their discourse analyses within both these narratives, thus reinforcing their own field's interests in them, rather than trying to be good discourse analysts, psychologists, or even feminists. What, then, do each of the two narratives offer to a feminist discourse analysis?

The pragmatic tradition

If feminists view discourse analysis not as a vehicle for their own theories or a surrogate solution to their problems, but as a pragmatic resistance to many of the established philosophical debates which have shaped and continue to shape much psychology, then some of the best-rehearsed criticisms of discourse analysis start to look less damning and less important.

Cornel West (1989) describes pragmatism in the USA as a twentieth-century refusal of traditional ontological and especially epistemological squabbles between idealism and materialism, rationalism and empiricism, subjectivity and objectivity, in favour of a consideration of agency, function and power: of what actually happens in the world. This characterization of pragmatism makes clear its avoidance of philosophy, its anti-philosophical nature. Pragmatic narratives have some continuity with the older, entrenched philosophical narratives of ontology, and especially epistemology, on which psychology draws. These older narratives persist alongside and within pragmatism, and since pragmatism is in any case formulated against them it can never be outside them entirely. But pragmatic narratives also resist established philosophical narratives. The means of their resistance is to privilege ordinary everyday lines of argument over abstract academic reasoning. This shifting of philosophical concerns on to the ground of everyday happenings makes them a kind of popular philosophy – the antithesis of the closed scientific narratives traditionally found in psychological texts.

The popular has a long history of being culturally identified with the female (Douglas, 1979). Through the cultural associations of the practical and quotidian with domesticity and femaleness, pragmatism becomes a soft, 'feminine' philosophy. Within the dominant cultural order, this association makes pragmatic narratives look illegitimate; but the association also brings the narratives closer to feminism. In and outside psychology, Western feminists usually *try* to be populist in the sense of representing the interests of a broad community of women; and they are in addition becoming more and more interested in the significance of popular, 'feminine' culture for women (Coward,

1984; Radway, 1985; Carr, 1989; Willis, 1991; Griffin, 1994). Populism has significance, too, for discourse analytic psychology, which is often seen within conventional psychology as a sort of popular-cultural froth around the high culture of experimentalism.

There is a large overlap between early pragmatism and psychology, in the work of William James and John Dewey especially. It could indeed be argued that the ascendancy of pragmatism is linked to the ascendancy of psychological explanation in the West in the twentieth century. Pragmatism's disavowal of the grand explanatory narratives of the Enlightenment encourages greater emphasis to fall on the only story that can still be told: that of the self (MacIntyre, 1981). But the pragmatic tradition West (1989) traces is not one of psychological explanation. It begins with Emerson and takes in not only James and Dewey but also W.E.B. DuBois and C. Wright Mills. It includes Foucault's genealogies and analyses of power. Because it is a tradition of engagement with ordinary life, it is consistently involved with social inequity, internationalism, and history, and for this reason some ahistorical philosophical pragmatists – like Rorty – are tangential to it. It exhibits a 'plebian radicalism', West says (1989: 5), directed at expanding democracy.

Discourse analysis often looks very close to the pragmatism West describes. Discourse analysis does indeed refuse to enter into many of the ontological and epistemological debates with which psychology is concerned. The first primer in the field for British psychologists, Jonathan Potter and Margaret Wetherell's *Discourse and Social Psychology* (1987), for instance, declared that it was not interested in arguing about the relationship between language and reality, subjectivity and objectivity, mind and non-mind. Discussing any such philosophical and historical construction in its own terms only leaves you 'hung on one of the contradictory poles'. For Potter and Wetherell, '[d]iscourse analysis . . . is reluctant to take any dichotomy for granted' (1987: 181). Moreover, *Discourse and Social Psychology* is not concerned to resolve inconsistencies between the different theories it draws on, for example between ethnomethodology and semiotics on the question of the subject. Compared with most conventional psychology it is not very troubled about methodological rigour; skill gained through practice and a degree of intuition are proposed as important elements of a good discourse analysis, and this procedural looseness is largely what makes it look 'soft', even 'feminine', to conventional psychologists. The emphasis on discourses as actions with discernible functions and effects is another obvious pragmatic feature of Potter and Wetherell's text. And as in the pragmatic tradition West describes, they affirm the social engagement of their work, and invoke their commitment to the everyday – in this case, to ordinary language – as the main and inescapable reason for this engagement.

Similar arguments appear in other standard discourse analytic texts, even those which have a different menu of theoretical influences. The *Handbook of Discourse Analysis* (van Dijk, 1985) also foregrounds discourse analysis's social engagement through language, and its concern with real language use rather than theoretical conundra. Even writers such as Erica Burman (1991) and Ian Parker (1990, 1992), who are more concerned about discourse analysis's theoretical status, and in particular its apparent jettisoning of reality, are proposing a kind of realism situated outside ontological and epistemological dichotomies, in a moral–political realm to whose objects they give a strategic reality. Likewise, Geneva Smitherman and Teun van Dijk (1988), in their introduction to *Discourse and Discrimination*, assert the importance of the discursive reproduction of racism by enumerating its effects. Here the pragmatic practicality of discourse analysis is justified simply by illustration. There is no need to engage the argument on a more abstract level. The text operates as if the concrete instances presented are sufficiently persuasive.

As West's (1989) characterization of pragmatism's social engagement might lead us to expect, twentieth-century feminist and other social change movements also have important pragmatist strands running through them, supporting their concerns with solving real world problems and achieving effective agency for disenfranchised groups. The atheoreticism of pragmatism, its concern with practicality, takes it out of the realm of abstract philosophy traditionally identified with male thinking and male thinkers (Grimshaw, 1986) and gives it feminist potential. Its preoccupation with everyday worlds meshes with the feminist commitment to lived experience. Moreover, within even the most apparently totalized, closed-off grand feminist narratives, stories of long-term and almost universal patriarchal oppression, pragmatism allows feminists to propose short-term tactics aimed at goals that otherwise look unattainable. Judith Butler's (1990, 1993) work on 'performativity', tactical queerings of gender and sexuality through parody and theatricality, is a recent example.

Pragmatism often emerges as a form of argument in feminist discourse analysis, as in the piece by Gavey (1989) mentioned earlier. Another example is the feminist special issue of *Discourse & Society* on 'Women Speaking from Silence' (Houston and Kramarae, 1991b) which adopted a more implicitly pragmatic strategy, focusing on particular, everyday instances of women's silencing and their resistance to it, in order to give us hope and some idea of possible oppositional steps. The editors want to remind us, they say, that though feminism seems to demand 'momentous, transformative' and thus impossible-seeming changes in communication, 'many women *have* developed such revolutionary communication methods' (Houston and Kramarae, 1991a: 398).

Contradictory, non-pragmatist narratives are also in play in feminism and in discourse analysis. Often, for instance, grand narratives of structural oppression write themselves against the more concrete and complicated pragmatic narratives. Sometimes discourse analyses use language categories merely to illustrate larger power relations, so that the discourse analysis itself comes to seem a mere support to an overarching and often rather simplistic political analysis. The autonomy and power of discourse gets lost in such accounts, subordinated to a need to show that discourse has 'real', political, meaning. For example, Hodge and Kress, in *Social Semiotics* (1988), describe how traffic lights operate in order to illustrate a structuralist analysis of symbol systems. The account concludes by interpreting traffic lights as signifiers of the rational, inhuman authority of the state, enforced through the police and the courts. In the ideology of traffic lights, Hodge and Kress say, 'faith in . . . blind impartiality, transmitted with massive redundancy by countless traffic lights day after day . . . conditions motorists to abide by their message almost unthinkingly' (39). The assertion captures well the solemn, unconsciously patronizing nature of the more simplistic political discourse analyses. It also rejects a pragmatic approach to the semiotics of traffic control in favour of an abstract homogenized analysis which has little connection with the day-to-day politics of driving.

Feminists doing discourse analysis are not immune from such simplifying politics. In *Discourse & Society*'s 'Women Speaking from Silence' issue (Houston and Kramarae, 1991b), for example, Caroline Cole's (1991) account of graffiti in women's toilets on a university campus is so directed at showing women breaking the silences imposed on them in positive and resistant ways that it ends up passing over the contradictoriness and intricacy of the material. On the representation of men in film – on whether 'women would like to start seeing men's dicks in R-rated films' – some opinions rejected the turning-the-tables strategy: 'oppression will not foster freedom'; one endorsed it as a way to change men: '. . . for men to understand the oppression women have always felt . . . they need to get a taste of their own abuse' (408); one focused on film itself: 'Only if it's totally necessary for the plot.' The analysis glosses all these opinions as women wanting an 'equal place in society', rejecting the notion that the 'taste of their own abuse' argument has anything vindictive about it and ignoring the very different relationships the comments have to feminist politics. Elsewhere, the paper analyses the graffiti in terms of the politeness rules, story chaining and serializing that characterize women's consciousness-raising groups, reducing the graffiti's structural aspects to evidence of women's resistance. The paper reverses discourse analysis's usual preoccupation with structural features at the expense of politics (Burman and Parker, 1993), but its overarching story of women's resistance leaves little space for a more particular, pragmatic analysis.

Discourse analysts also depart from the pragmatic narrative at times by trying to retain traditional notions of empiricist methodological rigour. Potter and Wetherell (1987: 168) for instance suggest that discourse analysis is not tied to conventional methods: 'there is no mechanical procedure for producing findings'. The validity criteria they invoke include the pragmatic one of participants' orientation, that is, the fit of the analysis to participants' own analyses of their discourse. But at the same time Potter and Wetherell (1987: 161) discuss the 'painstaking' empiricism required in discourse analysis, and invoke such established scientific validity criteria as coherence, the generation of new problems, and fruitfulness, or comprehensiveness of explanation, all of which depend on an equally traditional notion of good theories as testable and preferably falsifiable. Despite this persistence of conventional epistemological and ontological categories in discourse analysis, Potter and Wetherell are largely right when they say that not just their own 'turn to discourse' but discourse analysis in general usually brackets off these issues and pragmatically gets on with research.

The feminist impetus away from pragmatism and towards empiricism comes from different sources. Social change movements like feminism need to retain some semblance of grand narrative in order to provide coherent criticisms of the present and pictures of the future. Such narratives inevitably rehearse traditional philosophical positions to some extent and thus undermine the pragmatic narrative. Most notably, feminist grand narratives often assert the materiality not just of gender oppression but of gender itself, deducing different female and male subjectivities, for instance, from women's and men's different bodies. Materialism is (Lovibond, 1989) an important constant in the history of feminism. Most feminist narratives also lean heavily towards an empiricist account of knowledge about gender; 'experience', especially 'personal experience', is a founding and uncritically accepted category in much feminist analysis (Marcus, 1987). Contemporary feminists, however, use these traditional categories increasingly subtly and self-consciously (Riley, 1988; Spelman, 1990; Kitzinger, 1994; Condor, forthcoming). Feminists doing discourse analysis tend to amplify the field's general caution about discourse's relations to truth and reality. Sue Widdicombe (1993), for instance, in her study of how goths describe the relationship between their style and their subjectivities, emphasizes the important but limited access discourse, and discourse analysis, give to experience, and the restricted political value of simply giving voice to experience (see also Widdicombe, this volume). Thus, in discourse analysis, feminism's grand narratives, and their echoings of old Western philosophical debates, need not render the pragmatic narratives deployed alongside them irrelevant or powerless. Often, indeed, by counterpointing the grand narratives with accessible and achievable arguments, it is pragmatism that helps sustain them.

Extravagance
There also exists in discursive psychology, feminism and feminist-oriented discourse analysis, another more obviously disruptive narrative strand, that I shall call the narrative of extravagance. Wollen (1987) says that in the late nineteenth- and twentieth-century struggle between traditionalism and modernism in Western culture, there is also a 'liminal' third term, a tradition of 'extravagance and excess', of functionless decorative expenditure. This tradition is exemplified culturally in performances and artworks stretching from the Russian Ballet and Matisse to, at the end of this century, what Wollen rather vaguely calls 'postmodern street culture'; exemplified intellectually in psychoanalysis, Bataille, and (I would add) Nietzsche. As well as the raw – modernism – and the cooked – the official arts and culture – there is also Wollen says, the 'rotten' – extravagance (Wollen, 1987: 27).

The extravagant tradition is more overtly anti-philosophical than pragmatism. Like pragmatism, it deserts Western philosophy's established dilemmas for an account of human action and possibility. Nietzsche for instance wrote of truth not as an absolute or realizable category but as a matter of rhetoric and habit, famously calling it 'a mobile army of metaphors, metonymies, anthropomorphisms, in short, of human relationships which, rhetorically and poetically intensified, ornamented and transformed, come to be thought of after long usage by a people as fixed, binding and canonical' (Nietzsche, 1991: 180). Morality, too, for Nietzsche is a historical and political matter, not a philosophical matter (MacIntyre, 1990). Nietzsche's notion of the post-philosophical state centres on new forms of subjectivity and interpersonal relations. This psychological opposition to philosophy is common in narratives of extravagance, as it is in pragmatic narratives. Indeed, Alasdair MacIntyre (1981) suggests that the individualized, psychological solutions that have developed in Western cultures in response to the ethical impasses in Western societies are embodied in three individual 'characters' – the rich aesthete, a figure whose connection with narratives of extravagance is clear; the manager; and the therapist – characters whom MacIntyre calls utilitarian and emotivist, and who are impoverished, opportunistic exemplars of the pragmatic tradition considered above. In culture, then, if not in psychology, the narrative of extravagance is the more obvious and perhaps the more powerful form of resistance.

The extravagant narrative is much less concerned with achieving good human functioning than pragmatism is; reform and remedialism are explicitly rejected by, for instance, Nietzsche and Bataille. The tradition is often devoted, too, to the artificial, and against the natural order to which pragmatism often appeals. But, like pragmatism, this tradition has strong associations with populism, since, as Wollen points out, popular culture is itself seen as extravagant, a realm of debased taste and of unmotivated, excessive pleasures. Extravagant narratives are also associated perhaps more clearly than pragmatism with female-identified or 'feminine' characteristics of a disruptive kind. In the case of the Russian Ballet, the feminine characteristics were thought to belong to the men in the troupe, a location that was disturbing in itself. In Nietzsche, it is a mix of feminine transcendence and undecidability that disturbs. Jacques Derrida describes the Nietzschean woman as like truth, and here Derrida quotes directly from Nietzsche, '"promising, resistant, modest, mocking, sympathetic, seductive" . . . But on the other hand', Derrida continues, '. . . if woman *is* truth *she* at least knows there is no truth, that truth has no place here and that no-one has a place for truth', so 'woman is but one name for the untruth of truth' (Derrida, 1978: 51 and 53). Thus Nietzsche's project *is* this woman, the 'truth' that exists only as an untruth, yet that always presents the deferred possibility that it may be true somewhere or some time.

Narratives of extravagance also have a cultural connotation with femininity through the connections often drawn between women and popular or mass consumer culture. Women, it is supposed, are the ones who buy for everyone, who consume popular culture with the least constraint and analysis, and who have the most uncomplicated and lowest-level fun. Anne Douglas (1979) has traced the beginnings of this 'feminization' of popular culture to the feminine sentimentality of US and British Victorian religious and secular culture. Middle class women, disaffected from politics and history, gained power at this time as consumers in an elaborated capitalism newly dependent on selling unnecessary goods. Young women's narcissistic and non-productive consumption of fiction was much remarked on at the time: 'countless' of them, Douglas says, 'spent much of their middle-class girlhoods prostrate on chaise longues with their heads buried in "worthless" novels'. While Douglas abhors the depoliticization and victimology of this cultural turn she acknowledges both the energy and the utopian impulses of extravagant consumerism.

At first it may look as if contemporary psychology is the antithesis of the cultural narrative of extravagance. There are however always some extravagant elements in academic psychology, and these are most obvious in its discourse – in for instance the exciting narrative elements often present in reports of experimental investigations, or in the use of metaphor in theoretical accounts. Disruptions of this kind are perhaps easier to see in discourse analysis than in most subfields of psychology, because of its qualitative nature; its inflection by semiotics, which makes it interested in reading for what is absent as well as for what is present; and its concern with reflexivity, with examining its own processes and its practitioners' social and personal investments in them.

Discourse analysts sometimes seem to be trying to repudiate the extravagance of their field by their assertions of empiricism. Occasionally they even reject 'softness' explicitly. Derek Edwards and Jonathan Potter (1992) for example, in *Discursive Psychology*, worry that public political rhetoric might seem too easy, too much of a 'soft test' of discourse analysis since the material so obviously constructs facts and raises questions of accountability. They quiet their anxieties by arguing that political discourse is really 'a *hard* case' (Edwards and Potter, 1992: 7). Discourse analysts are also often reluctant to enter into the specificities of discourses in a way which would make their extravagance apparent. The *Handbook of Discourse Analysis* (van Dijk, 1985) looks only at speech genres. It ignores written discourses, music, and the visual discourses of (for example) art, film and clothes, all of which are highly culturally elaborated, divided up into genres and subgenres. And so the *Handbook* seems to suggest that discursive genres are natural and universal, not artificial, particular, detailed and extravagant at all. Discourse analysts also often seem to envisage reflexivity as something you have to address – but just in order to get it over with. Reflexivity is more than that: once engaged, it is difficult to finish with, and it can involve a dizzying regress to residual, difficult-to-comprehend factors like repression and desire. As Potter and Wetherell say, most discourse analysts aim to be honest about their own implication in their investigations, but also to avoid going further: they do not want 'to get either paralysed by or caught up in the infinite regresses possible' (Potter and Wetherell, 1987: 182).

Some discourse analysis, however, is less concerned with maintaining its sobriety and more interested in developing extravagant narratives. Michael Billig's *Ideology and Opinions* (1991: 31) emphasizes the value of what it calls 'wilful playfulness' in psychology – in this case, the 'wilful playfulness' of drawing on ancient Greek studies of rhetoric for contemporary rhetorical analyses. Anna Wynne's (1987) paper 'Accounting for accounts of the diagnosis of Multiple Sclerosis' is another example. This paper explores the ironies of an epistemological sceptic, as Wynne calls herself, doing empirical work: using 'real' conversations; taking extracts from them out of context; taking one extract to stand for a set of similar extracts; taking it for granted that speech documents the self; assuming an identifiable discursive object like 'traditional' or 'alternative' medicine; assuming that diagnoses of multiple sclerosis can be 'right' or 'wrong'; and implicitly making a claim to truth by producing her own account. The paper ends by saying that such ironies should be 'an occasion not for angst, but for wonder' (Wynne, 1987: 121).

Within feminism, narratives of extravagance have a stronger tradition and presence. Contemporary feminists like Judith Butler (1990, 1993), Denise Riley (1988) and Elizabeth Spelman (1990) explore a triple perspective: conventional feminist narratives, which criticize and reconstruct gender relations; pragmatic narratives, which set out do-able programmes for change; and, beyond these, extravagant narratives, that either pursue endlessly the most elusive aspects of gender – the nature of female desire, perhaps, or the hard-to-define ways in which women's and men's thinking may differ; or that affirm, equally continually and excessively, women's transcendent qualities or possibilities of body, or language, or spirituality. Explaining such extravagant narratives, Julia Kristeva (1986: 300) says that 'the sudden surge of women . . . into discourse poses insoluble questions for Reason and Right . . . because this surge is also yet another consequence of the Death of Man, with all the intolerable consequences that this entails to classical rationality and individuality'. Kristeva's account of extravagance is, like those of many feminist academics, indebted to Mikhael Bakhtin's (1968) theorization of carnival as resistance, but similar accounts can also be found among, for instance, Victorian 'free-love' feminists, experimental women writers as diverse as Dorothy Richardson, Zora Neale Hurston and Monique Wittig, and contemporary women performers like Karen Finlay and Diamanda Galas. I would not suggest that extravagant feminist narratives have quite the revolutionary effect Kristeva once postulated. The questions they raise are usually well tolerated by 'classical rationality and individuality'. But at least they do on occasion raise revolutionary questions.

Feminist-oriented discourse analysis tends to be more cautious about extravagance, contradiction and excess, more content with a didactic grand narrative. In Houston and Kramarae (1991a) for example, the story of women's resistance through lavatory graffiti (Cole, 1991) overrides not just the possibility of a more detailed, contradictory, pragmatic account but also the high carnivalesque potential of the material. In its drive to categorize all the material in consciousness-raising terms, the paper skips over erotica, snippets of 1960s hedonism ('Reality is for people who can't handle drugs') and unsisterly insults like 'Bigot' and 'Fuck off!' Most readers, however, probably remember the graffiti, rather than the interpretations. And so, in a sense, the extravagant parallel narrative that the material itself constitutes retains a place in the text. Later in the Special Issue, Gwendolyn Etter-Lewis (1991), discussing interviews with African-American women whose careers spanned the 1920s to 1940s, explores the multiple personal and social meanings of the excess, 'suppressed discourse' that appears in the women's repetitions, euphemisms and vagueness. Though the paper has an interest in how the women can and do speak out about racism it does not flatten the extravagant, excessive, contradictory aspects of their discourse into illustrations of this interest.

The conjunction of the narratives

Meaghan Morris (1988) has pointed out the banality of writing on popular culture that simply celebrates the liberatory or fantastic possibilities and pleasures of that culture. A feminist discourse analysis that concentrated on generating extravagant narratives could reach a similar banality; an example is, again, Deborah Tannen's (1991) work, which praises the communications cultures of both women and men, and, getting the best of all possible worlds, also endorses a freer flow of communication between these cultures. Tannen wants women and men to accommodate and expand their communications. 'If we recognise and understand the differences between us,' she says, 'we can take them into account, adjust to, and learn from each other's styles' (1991: 7). What is needed, though, is something less starry-eyed, an approach which limits extravagant narratives at the same time as it generates them. Valerie Walkerdine's 'Video Replay' checks its extravagant, potentially limitless interpretations by invoking a 'forwards' interpretive movement, which 'anchors and fixes the signifier within current practices, producing the regulative effectivity of the term as it operates as a relation within a regime of representation and truth' (Walkerdine, 1986: 193). What the forwards movement means in this particular case is that Walkerdine analyses the process of watching *Rocky* in terms of the class and gender dynamics of the family, and of audience research. This analysis is not just a resort to grand narratives of class and gender. Walkerdine is concerned, she says, not to idealize and naturalize, or 'essentialize', social differences. The forwards movement she tries for is explicitly placed in a 'quasi-Foucauldian' framework which does not assume that subjective identity is unified or permanent, and hence does not play identity politics with it. Instead the analysis deploys a pragmatically fixed subject in order to examine how this subject is socially positioned, 'how surveillance functions, how power works, where the buck stops' (193) at a specific time and in a specific context.

Often today within feminism, and within feminist discourse analysis, a pragmatic narrative fixes the excesses of a parallel and more extravagant narrative. Gayatri Spivak (1989) suggests the tactical use of an essentialist category of 'women' in order to anchor the networks of gendered meanings which analyses of signification produce. Lovibond (1992) argues similarly that since women are often refused a hearing 'as women' it is reasonable to critique this refusal by *using* the category 'women', even though, she says the analytic categories of 'women' and 'men' do not feature in her more utopian programme for the future. The category of women thus has a pragmatic place in her politics, as 'a practical application of discursive democracy' (Lovibond, 1992: 73). Again, in an earlier paper, Lovibond (1989) justifies her pleas for a systematic political approach to questions of gender oppression, and more general questions of social inequality, in terms of the pragmatic effectiveness of such systems in pinning down the endless though sometimes helpful questionings she sees postmodernism as generating.

Within feminist discourse analysis, Gavey's (1989) invocation of political utility works in a tactically essentialist way, to constrain the multiplicity of meanings of gender that a poststructuralist analysis of a woman's talk about sexual coercion could give rise to. Burman's instructive analysis of children's interviews of herself operates similarly. Examining a conversation about where she parked her bicycle, she focuses on a particular, symptomatic utterance by the child, 'Sometimes it can get stolen' (Burman, 1992: 52), that opens up a wide field of inquiry about adult–child power relations, the possibility of changing them, and the usefulness of discursive indeterminacy to children – allowing, in this case, a change of topic to the child's own bicycle and how *it* got stolen. At the end of the paper Burman asks if she has overinterpreted such 'tiny fragments' (1992: 56), if her analysis is a poststructuralist overindulgence. She concludes that these concerns are unwarranted because the approach lets her explore the lack of fixity in subjectivity but is also tied down by power relations and her interest in children's 'strategies of resistance' (1992:57). Burman's account, then, lest a narrative of extravagance function alongside, and in cooperation with, a pragmatic feminism.

The relationship between pragmatic and extravagant narratives need not involve simply the anchoring of the second by the first. Pragmatism, because it is in many ways the opposite of extravagance, cannot but have an intimate relationship with it. West (1989) suggests that much pragmatism has a prophetic character, a hangover from nineteenth-century Western Protestantism and Left romanticism that he thinks makes an indispensable contribution to notions of agency and tradition. This extravagant utopian legacy within an apparently highly practical frame of thought may be what makes it possible for feminists of such diverse persuasions as Spivak, Lovibond, Gavey and Burman to set pragmatic limits around their more speculative analyses. A sort of sympathy for extravagance seems to inhabit pragmatism. Conversely, even the most extravagant narratives operate with internal restrictions that divert them from absolutism towards pragmatic goals. Extravagant narratives have to start somewhere, they cannot be endless, and so they encompass a finite content; the shape of this finite extravagance is determined by practical circumstances. When Walkerdine (1986) pursues the fantasies of class and gender which her research on *Rocky* generates, for instance, the categories of fantasy she chooses, and her reflexivity, result from an interest in the neglect, on the part of film studies, of the intersections between class and gender, and of the place of the researcher. Increasingly, commentators on postmodernism, the narrative currently most indicted for extravagance, are pointing out how such restrictions shape even the most allegedly free textual play (Hirst, 1990; Norris, 1991; Cornell, 1992).

Sometimes the anchoring relationship of pragmatism to extravagance is reversed. The kind of feminism that has a privileged place in Richard Rorty's work is a Mary Daly-type discourse of excess. Rorty's insouciant liberal pragmatism is guided here by an extravagant utopianism towards a more precisely feminist position (Lovibond, 1992). Within feminist discursive psychology, Deborah Marks's (1991) discourse analysis of an education case conference, set up to ratify a boy's transfer back from a mainstream to a special school, displays a similar relationship. A narrative of the pragmatic exercise of institutional power – teachers and educational psychologists silencing parents, especially mothers, and usurping paternal and maternal authority – dominates this paper. This pragmatic narrative threatens to get extravagantly, fantastically, out of hand. Describing institutional regulation, the paper goes into overdrive and seems to have no place to stop: the pragmatic functioning of educational and psychological professional practices colonizes its analysis. What pins the analysis down are some of the small pieces of conversation it quotes, like a teacher saying with patronizing, easy familiarity that she will 'explain the situation to mum' (Marks, 1991:15); or the mother claiming that not she but Jeremy, her child, will refuse the transfer to the special school; or the teacher erasing this resistance with the comment, 'Jeremy says a lot of things' (1991:19). These symptomatic statements could be subjected to endless extravagant analyses, but in this paper they work to substantiate and concretize the account, giving particularity and reality to the pragmatic narrative of institutional power.

A mutually limiting interaction between the two populist discourses of pragmatism and extravagance is, then, often at play in feminist discourse analysis, involving each in a kind of ironic masquerade of itself to the other. Grand narratives still make appearances in such analyses, but they are coming to have a modified, less insistent place. I would argue that the interplay between the two narratives I have talked about is helpful for feminists doing discourse analysis, and that it should be an aim rather than an accidental by-product. Of course, feminists using other psychological approaches can and do deploy interlinked narratives of pragmatism and extravagance. Within discourse analysis, though, the interplay offers a specially productive 'evasion', to use West's (1989) term, of some of the going-nowhere debates in which feminist psychologists arguing 'for' or 'against' discourse analysis can get immersed. Moreover, the 'feminine', populist associations of discourse analysis, and its current attraction for many feminist psychologists, make it an apt field for developing this narrative conjunction.

References

Bakhtin, M. (1968) *Rabelais and his World*. Cambridge, MA: MIT Press.
Billig, M. (1991) *Ideology and Opinions*. London: Sage.
Burman, E. (1991) What discourse is not. *Philosophical Psychology* 4, 325–42.
Burman, E. (1992) Feminism and discourse in developmental psychology. *Feminism & Psychology* 2, 45–59.
Burman, E. and Parker, I. (eds) (1993) *Discourse Analytic Research*. London: Routledge.
Butler, J. (1990) *Gender Trouble*. New York: Routledge.
Butler, J. (1993) *Bodies that Matter*. New York: Routledge.
Cameron, D. (1993) Review of *You Just Don't Understand* by Deborah Tannen. *Feminism & Psychology* 2(3), 465–8.
Carr, H. (1989) *From My Guy to Sci-Fi*. London: Pandora.
Cole, C. (1991) Oh wise women of the stalls. . . . *Discourse & Society* 2, 401–12.
Condor, S. (forthcoming) Hearing voices? Questions of authority in feminist social

psychology. In S. Wilkinson (ed.), *Feminist Social Psychologies: International Perspectives*. Buckingham: Open University Press.

Cornell, D. (1992) *The Philosophy of the Limit*. London: Routledge.

Coward, R. (1984) *Female Desire*. London: Pandora.

Derrida, J. (1978) *Spurs: Nietzsche's Styles*. Chicago: University of Chicago Press.

Douglas, A. (1979) *The Feminization of American Culture*. New York: Knopf.

Edwards, D. and Potter, J. (1992) *Discursive Psychology*. London: Sage.

Etter-Lewis, G. (1991) Standing up and speaking out: African American women's narrative legacy. *Discourse & Society* 2, 425–38.

Gavey, N. (1989) Feminism, poststructuralism and discourse analysis: contributions to a feminist psychology. *Psychology of Women Quarterly* 13, 439–76.

Gill, R. (1993) Justifying injustice. In E. Burman and I. Parker (eds), *Discourse Analytic Research*. London: Routledge.

Griffin, C. (1994) *Representations of Youth*. Oxford: Blackwell.

Grimshaw, J. (1986) *Feminist Philosophers*. Hemel Hempstead: Wheatsheaf Press.

Hirst, P. (1990) The limits of relativism. *New Formations* 4.

Hodge, R. and Kress, G. (1988) *Social Semiotics*. London: Polity Press.

Hollway, W. (1989) *Subjectivity and Method in Psychology*. London: Sage.

Houston, M. and Kramarae, C. (1991a) Speaking from silence: methods of silence and resistance. In 'Women Speaking from Silence', Special Issue of *Discourse & Society* 2(4), 387–440.

Houston, M. and Kramarae, C. (eds) (1991b) *Women Speaking from Silence*, Special Issue of *Discourse & Society* 2(4).

Kitzinger, C. (1994) Experiential authority and heterosexuality. In G. Griffin (ed.), *Changing Our Lives: Women in/to Women's Studies*. London: Pluto Press.

Kristeva, J. (1986) A new type of intellectual: the dissident. In *The Kristeva Reader*. Oxford: Blackwell [first published 1977].

Lovibond, S. (1989) Feminism and postmodernism. *New Left Review* 178, 5–28.

Lovibond, S. (1992) Feminism and pragmatism: a reply to Richard Rorty. *New Left Review* 193: 56–74.

MacIntyre, A. (1981) *After Virtue*. London: Duckworth.

MacIntyre, A. (1990) *Three Rival Versions of Moral Inquiry*. Notre Dame IN: University of Notre Dame Press.

Marcus, L. (1987) 'Enough about you, let's talk about me': recent autobiographical writing. *New Formations* 1, 77–94.

Marks, D. (1991) Talking to mothers: rhetoric and practice within education case conferences. *British Psychological Society Psychology of Women Section Newsletter* 8, 13–21.

Marshall, H. (1991) The social construction of motherhood: an analysis of childcare and parenting manuals. In A. Phoenix, A. Woollett and E. Lloyd (eds), *Motherhood: Meanings, Practices and Ideologies*. London: Sage.

Morawski, J. (1992) Review of *Gender and Thought: Psychological Perspectives* edited by M. Crawford and M. Gentry. *Psychology of Women Quarterly* 16, 261–71.

Morris, M. (1988) Banality in cultural studies. *Block* 14, 15–26.

Nietzsche, F. (1991) On truth and falsity in their ultramoral sense. In *Complete Works*. Edinburgh: Foulis [first published 1873].

Norris, C. (1991) *What's Wrong with Postmodernism?* Hemel Hempstead: Harvester Wheatsheaf.

Parker, I. (1990) Real things: discourse, context and practice. *Philosophical Psychology* 4, 227–333.

Parker, I. (1992) *Discourse Dynamics*. London: Routledge.

Potter, J. and Wetherell, M. (1987) *Discourse and Social Psychology*. London: Sage.

Potter, J., Wetherell, M., Gill, R. and Edwards, D. (1990) Discourse: noun, verb or social practice. *Philosophical Psychology* 3(2), 205–18.

Radway, J. (1985) *Reading the Romance*. Chapel Hill: University of North Carolina Press.

Riley, D. (1988) *'Am I that Name?' Feminism and the Category of 'Women'*. Minneapolis: University of Minnesota Press.

Smitherman, G. and van Dijk, T. (1988) Introduction. In G. Smitherman and T. an Dijk (eds), *Discourse and Discrimination*. Detroit, MI: Wayne State University Press.

Spelman, E. (1990) *Inessential Woman*. London: Women's Press.

Spivak, G. (1989) In a Word. Interview with Ellen Rooney. *Differences* 1(2), 124–56.

Squire, C. (1989) *Significant Differences: Feminism in Psychology*. London: Routledge.

Tannen, D. (1985) Cross-cultural communication. In T. van Dijk (ed.), *Handbook of Discourse Analysis*. New York: Academic Press.

Tannen, D. (1991) *You Just Don't Understand*. London: Virago.

Troemel-Ploetz, S. (1991) Review essay: selling the apolitical. *Discourse & Society* 2, 489–502.

van Dijk, T. (ed.) (1985) *Handbook of Discourse Analysis*. New York: Academic Press.

Walkerdine, V. (1986) Video replay: families, films and fantasy. In V. Burgin, J. Donald and C. Kaplan (eds), *Formations of Fantasy*. London: Methuen.

West, C. (1989) *The American Evasion of Philosophy*. Basingstoke: Macmillan.

Wetherell, M. (1986) Linguistic repertoires and literary criticism: new directions for a social psychology of gender. In S. Wilkinson (ed.), *Feminist Social Psychology*. Milton Keynes: Open University Press.

Widdicombe, S. (1993) Autobiography and change. In E. Burman and I. Parker (eds), *Discourse Analytic Research*. London: Routledge.

Willis, S. (1991) *A Primer for Everyday Life*. New York: Routledge.

Wollen, P. (1987) Fashion/orientalism/the body. *New Formations* 1, 5–33.

Wynne, A. (1987) Accounting for accounts of the diagnosis multiple sclerosis. In S. Woolgar (ed.), *Knowledge and Reflexivity*. London: Sage.

9

Relativism, Reflexivity and Politics: Interrogating Discourse Analysis from a Feminist Perspective

Rosalind Gill

Postmodernism, in its infinitely skeptical and subversive attitude toward normative claims, institutional justice and political struggles, is certainly refreshing. Yet, it is also debilitating. (Seyla Benhabib, 1992)

This chapter is concerned with the relationship between discourse analysis and politics. It explores a number of theoretical assumptions which inform discourse analysis and asks whether they are compatible with feminism as an emancipatory project. It argues that although feminist engagements with discourse analysis have produced work of great interest and value, there are a number of unresolved *theoretical* tensions within the discursive tradition which make it, if not incompatible, then certainly problematic for feminists and others concerned with radical social transformation.[1] In particular, there are dilemmas raised by the conceptions of subjectivity and power which underpin discourse analysis, and with the notion of reflexivity it advocates (which has little in common with feminist conceptions). These problems have their origins in part in the particular understanding of relativism adopted by some discourse analysts, which leaves questions of politics unacknowledged – but not absent. It is this which is the focus of this chapter.

This chapter is neither an attack on discourse analysis (a tradition I am very much located *within*), nor a repudiation of relativism per se. Rather, it is an interrogation of discourse analysis from a feminist perspective; part of a growing chorus of voices, both within and outside the discursive position, stressing the need – in these 'post' times – to reinvent a new vocabulary of *value* (Soper, 1991; Squires, 1993), with which we can make political interventions – and without which we will be left theoretically and politically paralysed in the face of enduring inequalities, injustice and oppression.

The chapter is divided into four parts. In the first part I start by outlining a number of the different traditions which together constitute the 'turn to language' in the social sciences. I go on to look in more detail at one discourse analytic approach which has achieved a kind of hegemony within social psychology, and argue that it can be understood as representing a strand of postmodernist thought. Although it has produced important and illuminating analyses, it remains problematic for feminists because of its theoretical commitment to relativism. The second part of the chapter explores in detail the problems with the relativist foundations of some discourse analysis. In the third section I propose an alternative theoretical underpinning for discourse analysis; one which has political concerns at its heart. Finally, in the fourth part of the chapter, I look at the implications of this new theoretical commitment for reflexivity, which has been central to the discourse analytic tradition. I argue that some of the types of reflexivity practised by discourse analysts have served to reinforce the power of the researcher, and have been antithetical to feminist concerns. Against this, I argue for a reflexivity which stresses the accountability of the analyst, and the necessity to make the justifications for one's readings and interpretations as transparent as possible.

Feminism and 'the turn to language'

Feminists have always been interested in the connection between language and oppression. We have known for a long time that language is not a neutral, descriptive medium but is deeply implicated in the maintenance of power relations. Research over the last two decades has drawn attention to a wide variety of ways in which domination is sustained through language, highlighting phenomena such as the assumption of 'male as norm' (Spender, 1985), the existence of lexical gaps which leave women without the words to describe their experiences, and the notion that women occupy negative semantic space within language – what Julia Stanley calls the 'plus male, minus female' rule (Stanley, 1977). In recent years this work by feminist linguists and sociologists has been eclipsed by the 'turn to language' which has occurred throughout the social sciences and humanities.[2] Suddenly it is no longer just linguists who are interested in language, but sociologists, geographers, philosophers, literary critics, historians and social psychologists too. Language is no longer simply a sub-disciplinary area or topic, but a central concern of researchers across disciplines.

This shift was brought about by the prodigious influence of poststructuralist ideas, which stressed the thoroughly discursive, textual nature of social life. There are many profound differences of interest between writers whose work is designated (mostly by others) as poststructuralist; as a label it may be misleading, and creates a false unity between the ideas of thinkers as diverse as Derrida, Foucault, Kristeva, and Laclau and Mouffe. What it signals, then, is less a position in the conventional sense, than an interrogation of many of the notions which operate as 'foundations' for us – subjectivity, meaning, reality, ethics, etc. It is 'a field of critical practices' (Butler and Scott, 1992: xiii).

The main indication of the importance of poststructuralist ideas within psychology can be seen in the development of a variety of different forms of discourse analysis. As Sue Wilkinson and Celia Kitzinger point out in their introduction, these draw variously upon the historical work of Michel Foucault, psychoanalytic ideas, semiotics, and a number of Anglo-American traditions which emphasize the study of ordinary talk. Discourse analysis, then, is a complex and heterogeneous field, but perhaps the approach which has done most to popularize it within psychology is that of Jonathan Potter and Margaret Wetherell (Potter and Wetherell, 1987; Edwards and Potter, 1992; Wetherell and Potter, 1992), and the associated work of others within the so-called 'Loughborough School' – which is itself made up of a diversity of different perspectives.[3]

It seems to me that discourse analysis has an enormous amount to offer feminists. It represents a principled and coherent means by which feminists can study talk and texts of all kinds – shedding light on old questions and provoking new ones. It has the potential to revitalize feminist studies of language which have become polarized around a few key issues (see, for example, Cameron, 1985; Graddol and Swann, 1989). With its dual stress on discourse as *constructive* and as a *social practice*, discourse analysis is able to cut through old divisions such as that between feminists who see language as simply reflecting inequalities which reside elsewhere, and those who see language as playing a constructive role in the maintenance and shaping of power relations. Discourse analysts are interested in the content and organization of discourse and what it is used to *do* in particular interpretative contexts. Feminists have been able to use discourse analysis to explore a range of questions concerning the reproduction of gender power relations. These are often sensitive and sophisticated analyses which highlight features of the practice of sexism (or whatever their object of study) which would not have been noticed – or, indeed, would have been actively precluded – by other approaches. A good example is Margaret Wetherell's study of talk about employment opportunities (Wetherell et al., 1987). This showed that ostensibly positive attitudes towards equal opportunities can be effectively undermined by different discursive moves – such as the invocation of 'practical considerations' – in such a way as to restore inequality. The simultaneous use of 'equal opportunities' and 'practical considerations' talk allowed the students interviewed effectively to deny equal opportunities to women, whilst still maintaining the positive identity associated with support for them. Other studies have addressed a variety of issues (see Introduction), and this book testifies to the energy and excitement which surrounds the use of discourse analysis for feminists. Indeed, as Erica Burman (1991b) points out, discourse analysis has become almost synonymous with critical and (sometimes) feminist research.

However, following Burman (1992), I want to argue that there is no *necessary* connection between discourse analysis and a progressive or critical politics; we need, as she says, to distinguish between the *applications* of discourse analysis and the theory itself. Precisely those features of discourse analysis's theoretical commitments which make it so productive for feminists – its problematizing of truth claims, its stress on the socially constructed nature of all knowledge, its rejection of the idea of the unified, coherent subject, and its attention to power as a local practice – also make it problematic. The stress on difference, so valuable *within*, as well as outside, feminism for highlighting the exclusion of Black, lesbian and working-class women (among others, hooks, 1985; Segal, 1987) threatens to mask the fact that there are also differences of *power* (Burman, 1992); the notion that subject positions are multiple and fragmented can lead to the denial of any identity around which we can collectively mobilize; the emphasis upon looking at the micro-politics of power – how it is practised in particular discursive contexts – can serve to make structural inequalities invisible and lead to a neglect of the institutional bases of power (Gill, forthcoming b); and the discourse analytic commitment to relativism – which has led some commentators to identify it as postmodern (for example, Parker, 1989) – means that the grounds for feminist politics are disavowed. It is this last issue which I want to deal with in the rest of this chapter. In so doing, my aim is not to attack discourse analysis, but to contribute to the debate which is already going on within the 'discourse community' about the implications of relativism (Billig, 1991; Burman 1991b, 1992; Parker, 1992; Wetherell and Potter, 1992; Burman and Parker, 1993).

Discourse analysis, relativism and politics

Whilst feminist critiques of Western philosophy have centred on showing the partiality of the knowledge it produces, postmodern critiques have been less concerned with social criticism than with epistemological questions (Fraser and Nicholson, 1988). Discourse analysis is underpinned at a theoretical level by a thoroughgoing relativism or epistemological scepticism. For discourse analysts, knowledge constructs rather than reflects reality, and there are no versions of the world which are not provisional, 'susceptible to deconstruction or doubt, disproof or cancellation' (Edwards et al., 1995). All knowledge claims are treated with scepticism, and all truth claims as being in principle undecidable, since there is no transcendent standpoint from which 'the Real' can be directly apprehended.

Some feminists have argued that this commitment to relativism makes discourse analysis and other postmodern approaches incompatible with feminism. Stevi Jackson (1992) argues that relativism leaves us without the means to assert the existence of even the starkest material realities. If no one set of meanings is more valid than any other, she asks, then what basis is there for distinguishing between the rape victim's account of forced sexual intercourse and the rapist's version of it as pleasurable seduction? Similarly, Kirkup and Smith-Keller (1992) argue that feminism has at its core a concern with the realities of women's oppression; as such it has more in common with the goals of science than with those who would challenge its very claims to produce knowledge. Relativists are accused of 'moral quietism' and of defending positions which freeze power relations in their existing forms, making the weak stay weak and shoring up the power of the strong. I want to argue that this polarization is not the only way to think about feminism's relationship to relativism, and that the terms of the debate are not exhausted by, on the one hand, a commitment to science and objectivism, and, on the other, a celebration of relativism. But first, it is necessary to explore in some more detail the way in which this 'debate' is being conducted.

In order to do so, I am going to draw upon two published papers which offer explicit defences of relativism or epistemological scepticism: Edwards et al.'s (1995) 'Death and furniture: the rhetoric, politics and theology of bottom line arguments against relativism', and Grint and Woolgar's (1994) 'On some failures of nerve in constructivist and feminist analyses of technology'. It is important to note that these do not represent the only epistemological foundations for discourse analysis. As I have noted, work by a number of discourse analysts has recently addressed the relationship of relativism and political engagements (Billig, 1991; Burman, 1991b, 1992; Parker, 1992; Wetherell and Potter, 1992), and there are a variety of different theoretical positions taken. Nevertheless, the ideas under discussion do represent an identifiable position, and one which is

worth taking seriously, and interrogating for its political implications.

Relativist theology

One of the interesting things about the way discourse analysis's
defence of relativism is couched is the evangelical quality of much of
the rhetoric used. Relativism is treated as an ethical, or, indeed,
moral requirement for discourse analysts. Their position is described
as 'principled' and as occupying 'the moral high-ground' (Edwards et
al., 1995). But their morality appears to have *no content*; relativism is
treated as an unquestionable good in and of itself. Scepticism is
presented (ironically, of course) as the true inheritor of the Enlightenment project, where inquiry is a goal in its own right:

> We, the 'amoral' relativists, are the ones who insist upon the right to
> inquire and who are thus (arguably) the true keepers of the flame of the
> ethic of science. (Edwards et al., 1995)

Defences of relativism have recently been given a political inflection.
No longer is epistemological scepticism – or, as Grint and Woolgar
(1994) call it, post-essentialism – only a tool for academic inquiry;
now it is also held to play a role in political struggle:

> The recognition that the truth is socially constructed facilitates rather than
> debilitates those who are relatively weak in society. (Grint and Woolgar,
> 1994)

Clearly, some relativists feel defensive to accusations of political
indifference – and they never said that they would not use any
rhetorical strategy in the book to defend their position! Before
looking at this in more detail, I will examine their critique of the kind
of realism often espoused by feminists.

'Death' and 'furniture'

The central plank of relativists' criticism of realists is that they are
inconsistent. The realist position, it is argued, is a straw position; in
fact, there are only 'weak' relativists and 'strong' or 'true' relativists
(read: the authors of such critiques). All academics use 'the tools of
relativist–constructionist analysis', but realists use them selectively:

> only against *opponents*; and only *against*. Conceived exclusively as a
> method of criticism, Analysis (whether as sociology of knowledge,
> psychoanalysis, rhetorical critique . . .) is used to *undermine* that to which
> it is applied. Relativists insist on the *general* applicability of Analysis. In
> particular, no self-serving exception can be made on one's own behalf: it

has to apply to one's own position too – relativists are reflexive. (Edwards et al., 1995; emphasis and capitalization in original)

Realists or weak constructivists are accused of speaking 'with forked tongue' (Edwards et al., 1995) and of 'ontological gerrymandering' (Woolgar and Pawluch, 1985) – that is, of using a variety of (often subtle) means (such as selective use of inverted commas) to maintain distinctions between that which they wish to analyse as constructed and that which they hold to be real.

> Realist discourse dichotomises everything; and it does so *prior* to Analysis. It knows *already* what to relativise (criticise, undermine) and what to leave untouched, preferably unspoken of, the privileged site of certainty being buried in the brain as 'intuition', 'tacit knowledge' or a similarly sacred and inexplicable faculty. (Edwards et al., 1995)

Mostly, relativists point out, realists' assumptions remain hidden. But they *are* brought out occasionally – for use in what Edwards et al. call 'bottom line arguments'. They are interested in these arguments and have identified two common types of rhetorical device which realists use to assert the bedrock of reality which may not be treated as epistemologically constructed (and therefore deconstructible). These are 'furniture' moves – involving the hitting of tables, walls, rocks and assorted hard objects, to demonstrate the reality that *cannot* be denied, and 'death' moves which invoke torture, genocide and human misery – the reality that *should not* be denied.

Both these moves are used routinely in arguments against relativists – as when people thump the table to show conclusively that it has a 'reality' that cannot be denied, or refer to the Holocaust to indicate the horror, danger and absurdity of holding a position which 'allows' one to deny such a terrible, historical reality. Edwards et al. demonstrate brilliantly that realist arguments are themselves a form of rhetoric, and they show that neither of the 'undeniability devices' they discuss ('death' and 'furniture') is effective as a refutation of relativism. However, both, they argue, take a fair amount of work to rebut – and they discuss ways in which these moves may be persuasively deconstructed, and shown up for the rhetorical moves they are.

As I will argue later, I have considerable sympathy with this critique of realism, but what worries me about the position of these and other relativists is that it offers no principled alternative to realism by means of which we might make *political interventions*.[4] They deconstruct realism's claim to offer ontological guarantees, and highlight the duplicity of 'weak' relativist arguments, but do not have anything to substitute with which we could challenge oppression in all its monotony and all its variety.[5]

Innocent knowledge

Against realism, relativism is presented as the Truly Radical path to liberation – but *whose* liberation and what constitutes it are not made clear; their radical project appears to have no goals other than scepticism itself.[6] Paradoxically, they seem to have reasserted the very notion of Enlightenment thought that postmodernism set out to undermine – namely the idea that there can be 'innocent knowledge' (Flax, 1992). For scepticism is treated simultaneously as neutral *and* as socially beneficial – just as Reason was for Enlightenment philosophers. Like overzealous deconstructionists, relativists appear to have no aims but relentlessly to interrogate and dissolve every last claim, highlighting its status as construction and deconstructing, with surgical precision, each last shred of meaning. As Terry Eagleton has written in relation to literary theory, such deconstruction is 'a power-game, a mirror-image of orthodox academic competition' (1983: 147) which is devoid of progressive impulses.

Epistemological correctness

Part of what angers some feminists – myself included – about defences of relativism (by a variety of writers, not just discourse analysts) is the rather self-righteous and dismissive tone in which they are often argued. Attempts by feminists and others to raise as issues oppression or injustice – whether it be domestic violence, poverty, racist attacks or the Gulf War – are dismissed as rhetorical or discursive moves, as 'predictable devices', and those who would treat such things as material realities lay themselves open to accusations of crudeness or inconsistency (Cameron, 1989). This has the effect of silencing many feminist voices, and, I would argue, contributes – at an intellectual level – to the backlash against feminism and other progressive movements which is a feature of contemporary social life; it is especially clear in the attack on 'political correctness' (Gill, forthcoming a). This is undoubtedly not the intention of the epistemological sceptics, but it is one of its effects. Whilst they (rightly) point out that saying something is a construction is not the same as saying it is a lie (Grint and Woolgar, 1994), it is not clear what the implications of this are for attempts, say, to challenge domestic violence. In practice what the emphasis on the constructed nature of all our social categories has done is allowed the Right and the anti-feminist lobbies considerable leverage to deny or redefine many of the categories for which we have struggled to gain acceptance.

Meanwhile, critical voices have often been suppressed – paralysed by the fear that to invoke in an undeconstructed way the idea (say) that many women routinely get beaten up by their male partners will lead to their being viewed as theoretically naive and unsophisticated. There is a growing climate of 'epistemological correctness'[7] which operates in subtle ways to silence feminist (and other critical) voices. Indeed, part of its project has been the redefinition of what counts as criticism, such that it is now synonymous with epistemological scepticism (whilst analyses by realists of various kinds – including some feminists and Marxists – are treated as uncritical).

It is important to be clear that I am not accusing relativists of somehow orchestrating a backlash against feminism; I am simply attempting to highlight some of the unintended consequences of intellectual trends which go far beyond discourse analysis. As I argued earlier, poststructuralist and postmodernist thought, liberating in many ways, has served to problematize the very language that we use to intervene politically, without yet offering us new and alternative languages with which to engage. The effects of this are (presently) debilitating.

It is illuminating to examine how 'traditional' critics such as feminists and Marxists are treated by relativists. In their paper, 'Death and furniture', Edwards et al. (1995) respond to an article written just after the American attack on Libya, in which the author, reviewing a text from the relativist canon, asserts that the people killed in Tripoli were neither killed by words, nor are they dead 'because the rest of the world decides to call them dead' (Craib, 1986, quoted in Edwards et al., 1995). The writer concludes with the assertion that if we see this as 'just another story, then we too deserve to fall victim to it'. Edwards et al. (1995) have three different kinds of retorts to this. Firstly they point out that 'Real Human Suffering is not obviously ameliorated by writing designed to display concern, anger and fellow-feeling.' This is a common relativist move, and is linked to the claim that there is no *necessary* relationship between the quest for truth and the end of social inequality. I will discuss this later. The second and third responses are related, and concern the way in which relativists see the connection between personal life, political struggles and their academic work.

The personal, the political and the academic
The way in which relativists theorize the relationship between politics, personal life and their academic research is antithetical to feminist concerns. We can see this in the second response of Edwards et al. to Craib's assertion that those who would treat the murder of the people of Tripoli as 'just another story . . . deserve to fall victim'. They comment: '[this is] a brutal nemesis, it has to be said, for writers

of texts to wish upon one another' (Edwards et al., 1995). What is striking about this is its disingenuousness: here are people who have doggedly asserted the thoroughly textual nature of social life, who have refused to recognize any uninterpreted reality, suddenly claiming to be mere innocents, 'writers of texts' who do not deserve such harsh attack. As if the texts they write were devoid of implications, were not involved in social practices. Texts may be everything, but relativists' texts, it seems, occupy a privileged position. They are positioned in a sealed and protected realm where they can avoid being subject to precisely the kinds of analysis that make discourse analysis so valuable – namely examinations of the discursive or ideological work they accomplish. The academy is treated as a separate realm, divorced from the political and personal. This stands in stark contrast to feminist research which sees the personal as inevitably political, and academic research as a part of, or a form of, political practice, designed to empower women and to generate new and non-oppressive knowledge – quintessentially involved with feminism as an emancipatory project.

The sense, in relativist arguments, that academic work is entirely separate from political struggle or from one's personal life, means, as I have argued, that their own texts are not looked at for what they do in particular discursive contexts (despite claims to reflexiveness); they are not treated as political. It also means that one's position as a relativist academic need seemingly have few (if any) implications for one's life outside the academy. For this is Edwards et al.'s third retort to Craib: that he is mistaken to assume that rejecting realism means rejecting all the things realists think are real. There is no contradiction, they argue, between being a relativist and being a fully paid-up member of a particular culture with commitments and a commonsense notion of reality. Indeed, since realism is primarily a type of rhetoric, why let the devil have all the best tunes, and why not employ realist rhetoric oneself? There is no need to feel uncomfortable about it. Being a relativist, it seems, means never having to say you are sorry about your contradictions.

But contradictions there are. For whilst realists have a coherent and principled basis for their arguments, grounding them in ontological discourse, relativists do not. They offer no principled basis for choosing between any number of competing versions of events or phenomena, since they have neither ontological commitments nor explicit political commitments which inform their work.

Discourse analysts' devices

In practice, discourse analysts generally fail to live up to their programmatic relativism. In fact, they are not immune from 'ontological gerrymandering' (Woolgar and Pawluch, 1985), and routinely employ various means to maintain distinctions between that which they are investigating as constructed and that which they hold to be real. As I have argued elsewhere (Gill, 1991), discourse analysts (myself included) have a number of subtle (and not so subtle) devices for privileging particular versions of the world – including straightforward assertion, smuggling in particular (unproblematized) accounts via other sources, and being selective about the injunction to focus on participants' orientations. In making this point I am not (merely) being mischievous and claiming that discourse analysts have been hoist by their own petard, but am also making a serious point: namely, that discursive analyses (like all research) are not – and cannot be – value-free. This is a point made long ago by feminist critics of science. When values are not made explicit, as in some discursive analyses, it is not because they are not present, but simply that they have gone underground.

Paradoxically, epistemological sceptics seem to have reinstated, rather than challenged, the notion of value-freedom in research. Disinterested inquiry is their regulative ideal – not dissimilar from that of positivist researchers. All discussion of values, as Barbara Herrnstein Smith (1988) has argued, has been evaded and exiled. In the context of Government attacks on the social sciences in Britain and the USA, it is not difficult to suggest 'materialist' explanations for this trend (Connor, 1993). But the question is, where does it leave feminists who are drawn to discourse analysis as an approach?

I have argued that as an epistemological position relativism is extremely problematic for feminists and anyone else interested in social transformation. Its conception of scepticism as both a good in its own right and the true path to (some unspecified) social justice is contradictory. The way in which relativists theorize the relationship between politics, personal life and academic research is antithetical to feminism. They explicitly proscribe political commitments in their research, whilst surreptitiously importing values of all kinds. And the dismissive way in which those who try to raise questions about oppression are treated has had the effect of silencing many feminists, and has contributed to a backlash against feminism.

Does this mean, then, that we should abandon relativism? Should we, as feminists, be committed to realism, to the idea that there is a clear rupture between language and being, and that it is possible to obtain more or less accurate knowledge about the (social) world? I want to suggest that our choice is not confined to the polarization between relativism and realism. I believe that it is possible to fashion a type of 'passionately interested inquiry' which would represent a principled foundation for discourse analysis. In the next section, I will draw on ideas from feminist postmodernists to argue for such a position.

Principled positions: towards a vocabulary of values

Kate Soper (1991), discussing the impasse between postmodernist thought and the realist and materialist positions with which many feminists would identify, has produced a witty, yet very acute, caricature of the conflict:

> The caricature presents us on the one side with the dogged metaphysicians, a fierce and burly crew, stalwartly defending various bedrocks and foundations by means of an assortment of trusty but clankingly mechanical concepts such as 'class', 'materialism', 'humanism', 'literary merit', 'transcendence' and so forth. Obsolete as these weapons are, they have a distinct advantage in that in all the dust thrown up by their being flailed around, their wielders do not recognise how seldom they connect with their opponents. On the other side stands the opposition, the feline ironists and revellers in relativism, dancing lightheartedly upon the waters of *différance*, deflecting all foundationalist blows with an adroitly directed ludic laser beam. Masters of situationist strategy they side-step the heavy military engagement by refusing to do anything but play. (Soper, 1991: 122)

As Soper argues, the struggle is, in part, an *emotional* one, with the 'burly crew of metaphysicians' asking us to keep a grip on the horrors, injustice and oppression in the world and to analyse all practices in terms of how much they contribute to greater equality, justice, democracy, etc., and the 'feline ironists' telling us that we may as well give up our feminist commitments and just accept the end of Enlightenment values. There are, as I have argued, good reasons for misgivings about relativism. As feminists we should feel cynical about attempts to persuade us to abandon the 'emancipatory metanarratives' (Lovibond, 1989). Those who ask us to bid farewell to such modern ideas do so from a position of privilege unimaginable to 'the African peasant, the street child in Rio de Janeiro or the Iraqi political prisoner' (Soper, 1991). Indeed, in many respects they do so *on the backs* of victims of oppression across the world (Gill, 1991). But does this critique lead us inevitably back to 'the burly crew of metaphysicians'?

It need not. There is another way out of the impasse; a way of articulating poststructuralist and postmodernist ideas to an emancipatory political project. It involves constructing a position from precisely what is attractive about postmodernism and poststructuralism: namely the way in which they deconstruct and interrogate the nature of Enlightenment thought – its false universality, the partiality of its knowledge, the notion of the white Western male which constitutes its unified subject. We need to ask of relativists:

> Why lend ourselves to the politics of 'difference' if not in virtue of its enlightenment – what it permits in the way of releasing subjects from the conflations of imperialising discourse and the constructed identities of binary oppositions? Why lend ourselves to the deconstruction of liberal humanist rhetoric if not to expose the class or racial or gender identities it occludes? Why challenge truth if not in the interests of revealing the potentially manipulative powers of the discourses that have achieved the status of knowledge? (Soper, 1991)

Relativists are quite right to point out that 'the truth' has often been very oppressive to women (Grint and Woolgar, 1994). They are also correct to highlight the fact that there is no *necessary* relationship between an objectivist commitment to the truth and the advancement of social justice (Edwards et al., 1995). They rightly criticize realists for collapsing moral conviction into ontological realism, suggesting that realists' convictions often come not from careful study of 'the facts' but from somewhere more 'irrational' (Edwards et al., 1995). However, they have not moved on from this critique to any positive position in which concerns about social justice, political concerns, are given any space in their theoretical work. It is as if they have only achieved half the purpose off critique. In their concern to repudiate ontological guarantees they have also exiled discussion of values. Instead of values being central – which seems to me the only principled position for a relativist – they are disavowed completely. Indeed, for some relativists, feminist standpoint research is described as being analogous to having to read out one's 'police record' before one is allowed to speak (Mol and Hirschauer, 1995).

Feminist postmodernism

Relativists' refusal to engage with questions of value has led to political paralysis. There is no principled way in which they can intervene, choose one version over another, argue for anything. Against this, feminists who have engaged with postmodernism and poststructuralism have taken a rather different position. There is a growing awareness that questions of value are inescapable and must be addressed (Soper, 1991; Butler and Scott, 1992; Squires, 1993). In the absence of ontological guarantees, then, values, commitments, politics must be at the heart of analyses.

Feminist writers such as Jane Flax (1992) and Judith Butler (1992) share the view of relativists that a belief in the connection between truth and emancipation is mistaken, and are thus critical of realist feminists who sustain the hope of achieving 'better' knowledge.

> Just because false knowledge can be used to justify or support domination, it does not follow that true knowledge will diminish it or that the possessor of 'less false' knowledge will be free from complicity in the domination of others. (Flax, 1992: 458)

Political action, it is argued, may not be best served by asserting truth. There is no evidence that appeals to reason or truth are uniquely effective as strategies for bringing about change; in fact, the impetus for social transformation may call equally upon empathy, anger or disgust, and to suggest that seeking truth is the answer to domination is to encourage a 'dangerously blind innocence' (Flax, 1992). What we – as feminists – want is not truth but *justice*.[8] Claims about domination are claims about injustice, and as such they belong on the terrain of politics and in the realm of persuasive speech and action. What we need is a perspective which frees us from 'transcendental guarantees' and 'illusions of innocence' (Flax, 1992) but does not deny us a political vocabulary, a vocabulary of values. Elsewhere I have characterized this position as one of 'politically informed relativism' (Gill, 1991), but it bears many similarities to other writers' positions – for example, Judith Butler's (1992) notion of 'contingent foundationalism', Stuart Hall's (1988) notion of Marxism 'without guarantees'; and Fraser and Nicholson's (1988) notion of 'feminist postmodernism'. It also shares similarities with positions adopted by some discourse analysts (such as Billig, 1991; Wetherell and Potter, 1992). Billig (1991), for example, argues:

> In offering an account, the analyst is also producing an argument. Because of this, and not despite it, there is the possibility of critique. . . . In the last analysis, or rather in the first analysis, critique depends upon the argument produced by the analyst. (Billig, 1991)

Butler argues that we need *permanent contestation* over those things which seek to pass themselves off as self-evident: 'this is . . . in my view, at the heart of any radical political project' (Butler, 1992: 8). What this move means is that we can no longer hide behind notions like 'truth' or 'objectivity' as guarantees for our knowledge production. But nor do we go down the route of the 'theory boyz'[9] in simply eschewing questions of value (whilst allowing them to enter through the back door). Rather, we make social transformation an *explicit* concern of our work, acknowledge the values which inform it, and situate all interpretations and readings in a realm in which they can be *interrogated* and *argued* about. In short, the political realm.

Discourse analysis and reflexivity

This critique has a number of implications for the way in which discourse analysts theorize power, subjectivity and the role of the analyst. There is not space to discuss all of these issues (but see Gill, forthcoming b). Instead I am going to focus on the issue of reflexivity which, as we have seen, occupies a special place in the relativist's heart. Reflexivity is, as I hope has been clear, an essential part of the theoretical position I am proposing, which requires analysts to make explicit the position from which they are theorizing, and to reflect critically upon their own role – not simply becoming the 'certified deconstructors' (Jackson, 1992) of other people's discourse. As such, the reflexivity proposed is clearly recognizable as a *feminist* reflexivity (see Wilkinson, 1988) based on the notion that the researcher's values should be 'acknowledged, revealed and labelled' (Reinharz, 1983: 172) and that the researcher is '*accountable* for her interpretations' (Henwood and Pidgeon, 1995).

This view of reflexivity contrasts starkly with that which is practised by some relativists. This has been less concerned with accountability and acknowledging their own position, than with rhetorically accomplishing themselves as cognizant of the fact that their own texts are constructions and thus differentiating themselves from those 'self-serving' critics who treat only their opponents' discourse with scepticism. Some critics have described the reflexive strategies of relativist discourse analysts as self-referential and elitist, facilitating nothing but a 'wallowing in the researcher's interpretative assumptions' (Parker and Burman, 1993: 168). The target of my critique is slightly different: I want to argue that an apparent reflexivity has become a powerful way of protecting one's argument from cricitism.

Reflexivity, as it is 'done' by relativists, has become virtually synonymous with the use of 'new literary forms' – these can include plays, poetry, performance art and 'happenings', but the most favoured appears to be the dialogue. The purpose of new literary forms include drawing attention to the artificiality of conventions for academic writing, highlighting the fact that *all* texts are constructions, which can be subjected to discursive analysis, and (thus) challenging the authorial power of the writer. These are all concerns which relativists share with feminists. Sometimes (especially in performance) these texts can be dramatic, and they also can be moving and exhilarating in a way unimaginable in a traditional text. The project to produce new ways of writing is an immensely important one. It is something with which feminists have long been concerned, and new literary forms are being used increasingly by writers in a variety of traditions, from Donna Haraway's (1991) experiments with 'cyborg manifestos' to Michael Billig's (1994a, 1994b) attempts to 'repopulate' the dehumanized pages of psychology texts. Both these examples show the political and theoretical value of new forms of writing. What I want to challenge is the idea that new literary forms in and of themselves *necessarily* serve to question the authority of the writer.

It seems to me that sometimes, far from challenging authorial authority, they actually reinforce it. Using dialogues or the conventions of the play, authors may script in 'critical' voices, which may raise objections to their argument, or highlight its status as construction. But rather than undermining the author's argument, these voices make it *more* difficult to rebut. It is not the fact that the author has constructed characters which is the problem – all texts are constructions – it is the discursive work that particular characters are doing that can sometimes be problematic. Critics who wish to mount an argument against a particular piece of research or reading have to attend to the fact that the author *seems already* to have acknowledged that point; in Barthes' sense the writer has provided an 'inoculation' against critique. She or he has rhetorically defended him/herself against attack.

By way of an example, we can examine the 'Reflexive Box' which appears in *Discursive Psychology* (Edwards and Potter, 1992). This takes the form of a dialogue between the two authors of the book, Derek Edwards and Jonathan Potter, in which they talk about how they are going to deal with the issue of reflexivity. It 'works', then, as both an example of reflexivity and also as a meta-comment on the process of being reflexive, or, rather, doing reflexivity – for this is definitely performance. Reflexivity becomes a tokenistic, ritualistic exercise, here (ironically? symbolically?) boxed off from the rest of the text. Rather than raising issues of politics or accountability, it works as a means for the authors *not* to have to expose their own position(s). Instead they are able to script in a range of different positions, thus heading off potential criticisms. As this particular exercise in reflexivity is itself about the practice of reflexivity, I find myself in the position of reading precisely the criticisms of reflexivity that I would want to make:

> *Derek*: I suppose we could do a multi-voice thing; you know, the usual slightly embarrassing fake conversation like Mike's stuff and the Woolgar book
>
> (. . .)

Jonathan: (interrupting) Also, I don't know about these fake
   dialogues. I know they are meant to show the informal negotiation
   that lies behind the polished final text; and highlight the way
   descriptions are sited in rhetorical contexts; and I know they remind
   readers that formal scientific texts are a particular literary
   convention, and all that, but they can come over as pretty stilted and
   artificial.
Derek: (stifling a yawn) Yeah.

My point exactly! Not only have they 'covered' the artificiality of
these dialogues, but they are so familiar with the predictable line of
argument that 'Derek' can barely keep himself awake to continue the
conversation. My criticisms have been undermined, by being (super-
ficially) acknowledged. And yet, they still have a 'Reflexive Box'.
Nothing has changed.

Another way in which this sort of exercise in reflexivity can
undercut the necessity of researchers having to address the way in
which political concerns enter the research process is by allowing
'credentialling' (Hewitt and Stokes, 1975). To put it crudely,
reflexive boxes (and their ilk) allow the researcher to present him or
herself in a particular (desirable) way, so that issues about the
conduct of the research are effaced. In another part of Edwards and
Potter's Reflexive Box, one of the crucial identities being creden-
tialled is that of left-wing, politically committed guys. This is
signalled by jokey references made in the dialogue to being thought
'soft on the Tories'. I am not arguing that the authors are not indeed
concerned and politically committed, but what the credentialling
does is to establish this identity *independently* of the research being
discussed, so that there is no need to actually work through the
implications of this position *in the research itself*.

Perhaps the most pernicious aspect of the elision of reflexivity in
research with the use of new literary forms in writing is that the
multivocality it produces is fake (as 'Jonathan' and 'Derek' are aware).
The injunction to take *difference* seriously has been cynically sold back
to us as *pseudo-multivocality*, in which all the 'different' voices are not,
genuinely, those of different people, but are, in fact, *all* the
construction of the author. In this way, new literary accounts pretend a
pluralism which they just do not have; the 'Others', in a new twist of
colonialism, are all inventions of the author. He or she simply debates
with himself or herself in a parody of genuine intellectual exchange. I
can only speculate about the reasons for this, but it seems significant
that the growth of interest in this type of writing is occurring at a time of
unprecedented attacks on higher education and on the 'relative
autonomy' of intellectuals. As opportunities for real debate are

eroded and it becomes more and more difficult to do collective work, this represents a pessimistic scenario for the future of intellectual exchange. But it is just one possible future.

Conclusion

In this chapter, I have argued that the theoretical 'foundation' of some discourse analysis in a relativist epistemology is problematic for feminists. I hope to have shown that there are a number of good reasons for feminists to reject some form of relativism. Principal among these is the refusal of some relativists to engage (explicitly) with questions of value, which has led to political paralysis – an inability for relativists to intervene, to choose one version rather than another, to argue for anything. Against this, I have also argued that epistemological scepticism has a lot to offer feminists – most obviously in the way in which it interrogates every claim which tries to pass itself off as self-evident, and highlights the partiality and contingency of Enlightenment knowledge, showing its groundedness in the assumption of the white, male, Western subject – and also in its emphasis that there is no necessary connection between truth and justice.

What is needed is a kind of relativism or epistemological scepticism which does not eschew or efface the question of values. I have argued that a new, principled theoretical underpinning for discourse analysis would be one in which values come to the fore, are made explicit, placed in a realm where they can be *argued* about. That is, we need a relativism which is unashamedly political, in which we, as feminists, can make social transformation an explicit concern of our work. This is something that feminists have always done, but which is at present ruled out by the relativist commitments of some discourse analysts. One implication of this argument is that discourse analysts should rethink their understanding of reflexivity.[10] Currently, discourse analytic adventures into reflexivity have often served to reinforce, rather than to challenge, the authority of the analyst, and have been used as a vehicle for disavowing explicit commitments, whilst pretending to give voice to other positions. Against this, I have argued that discourse analysts should adopt a notion of reflexivity which stresses the need for the analysts to acknowledge their own commitments and to reflect critically upon them. By seeking to explain and justify the basis for their readings or analyses, discourse analysts become accountable for their interpretations and the social and political consequences of these interpretations (Henwood and Pidgeon, 1995). In this endeavour they (*we*) have a lot to learn from feminist research.

Notes

I am extremely grateful to Mick Billig, Keith Grint, Ann Phoenix and Margaret Wetherell for their helpful comments on an earlier draft of this chapter. I have benefited enormously from discussions with them, but am still struggling with the difficult issues raised by relativism, and responsibility for all the problems within these arguments is my own.

1 I write as someone whose feminist commitments are indivisible from my other political commitments concerning class domination and racial oppression. My critique of discourse analysis is thus not 'simply' a feminist critique, but has equal relevance for all emancipatory struggles.

2 As Erica Burman (1990) has pointed out, male poststructuralist writers rarely acknowledge any debt to feminism. Similarly, few discourse analysts mention feminist research on language when charting the trajectories of their intellectual histories.

3 I am hesitant about reproducing the idea that there is a 'Loughborough School' of discourse analysis, since work at Loughborough is heterogeneous and represents no single tradition. It seems to me that there are at least as many differences within Loughborough Discourse and Rhetoric Group as between the group and other analysts.

4 This is not to suggest that various writers committed to relativism do not, on a private basis, have political commitments. The point is that these are not made explicit in their analyses.

5 There is little in Edwards et al.'s (1995) argument which gives me hope as a feminist, and certain things which concern me greatly. One of these is the use of a quote from Barbara Herrnstein Smith which argues that 'wife-beating, bride burning and clitoridectomy' are frequently cited in 'death' arguments. She goes on: 'The added piquancy of examples in which the victims are female can hardly be missed' (Smith, 1988, quoted in Edwards et al., 1995). It took me some time to figure out exactly why this quote bothered me so much. I think I have it now. It is the kind of construction which discourse analysts (myself included) use a lot: it states that the implications of something are clear, that the significance of something else could barely be greater, that the piquancy of yet another thing can hardly be missed – but then it does not go on to make explicit precisely what the nature of that significance is; the reader is left to fill it in. In the present example the 'piquancy' refers, in one sense, to the invocation of women's stereotypical status as both innocent and vulnerable – viz. news reports of war in which 'women and children' come bracketed together as icons of innocence, who are undeserving of their terrible fate in a way not true of men. But it also has another sense in the context of a discussion of 'death' devices as rhetoric: it seems to me to signal the *illegitimacy* of claiming that women are victims. Since *all* 'death' arguments have been ruled out *tout court* as effective refutations of relativism, the singling out of one particular subset for comment is unnecessary, and must have a more particular purpose. I want to suggest that – albeit perhaps unwittingly – the endorsement of this quote serves to support the current trend for denying that even victims are victims – particularly when they happen to be women. Hungry for something to attack feminism with, the media have seized greedily on quotes from American women like Camille Paglia and Katie Roiphe who dismiss the last three decades of feminist struggle as 'victim culture' (yet still describe themselves as feminists). The words 'bleating' and 'whingeing' can be heard ever more

frequently on the British media whenever date rape, sexual harassment, or any number of other 'feminist' topics are discussed. Being the victim of oppression is definitely not fashionable – unless, of course, you happen to be a divorced father or a member of one of the other new categories of 'victims of feminism' (Gill, forthcoming a). It is not that this can be laid at the door of relativists, but that, as I shall argue, being a relativist means that one should be more, not less, concerned about the effects of one's constructions.

6   However, Grint and Woolgar (1994) claim that epistemological scepticism is unlikely to be utopian or revolutionary, and 'is more likely to encourage liberalism than fascism or communism'.

7   This term was coined by Christine Hine, and suggested to me in a personal communication.

8   There is an interesting question about whether the notion of justice itself depends upon an implicit realism – that is, whether we can have commitments to justice without being implicitly committed to some view of how the world 'really' is. See Gill, 1995, for a discussion of this.

9   I am quoting from a leaflet which introduces the 'Foucault: Tenth Anniversary Conference'.

10   The notion of feminist reflexiveness has several other dimensions, including ethical ones, which are not discussed here, but see Wilkinson (1988).

References

Barrett, M. (1991) *The Politics of Truth: From Marx to Foucault.* Cambridge: Polity Press.

Benhabib, S. (1992) *Situating the Self.* Cambridge: Cambridge University Press.

Billig, M. (1987) *Arguing and Thinking: A Rhetorical Approach to Social Psychology.* Cambridge: Cambridge University Press.

Billig, M. (1991) *Ideology and Opinions: Studies in Rhetorical Psychology.* London: Sage.

Billig, M. (1994a) Repopulating the depopulated pages of social psychology. *Theory and Psychology* 45, 307–35.

Billig, M. (1994b) Sod Baudrillard! or ideology critique in Disney World. In H. Simons and M. Billig (eds), *After Postmodernism.* London: Sage.

Burman, E. (1990) Differing with deconstruction: a feminist critique. In I. Parker and J. Shotter (eds), *Deconstructing Social Psychology.* London: Routledge.

Burman, E. (1991a) Power, gender and developmental psychology. *Feminism & Psychology* 1(1), 141–53.

Burman, E. (1991b) What discourse is not. *Philosophical Psychology* 4(3), 325–43.

Burman, E. (1992) Feminism and discourse in developmental psychology: power, subjectivity and interpretation. *Feminism & Psychology* 2(1), 45–59.

Burman, E. and Parker, I. (1993) *Discourse Analytic Research.* London: Routledge.

Butler, J. and Scott, J.W. (eds) (1992) *Feminists Theorise the Political.* London: Routledge.

Butler, J. (1992) Contingent foundations: feminism and the question of 'postmodernism'. In J. Butler and J.W. Scott (eds), *Feminists Theorise the Political.* London: Routledge.

Cameron, D. (1985) *Feminism and Linguistic Theory.* London: Macmillan.

Cameron, D. (1989) Conversation, discourse, conflict: a reply to Torode. *Network* 45.

Connor, S. (1993) The necessity of value. In J. Squires (ed.), *Principled Positions: Postmodernism and the Rediscovery of Value*. London: Lawrence and Wishart.

Eagleton, T. (1983) *Literary Theory: An Introduction*. Oxford: Blackwell.

Edwards, D. and Potter, J. (1992) *Discursive Psychology*. London: Sage.

Edwards, D., Ashmore, M. and Potter, J. (1995) Death and furniture: the rhetoric, politics and theology of bottom line arguments against relativism. *History of the Human Sciences* (in press).

Flax, J. (1992) The end of innocence. In J. Butler and J.W. Scott (eds), *Feminists Theorise the Political*. London: Routledge.

Fraser, N. and Nicholson, L. (1988) Social criticism without philosophy: an encounter between feminism and postmodernism. In A. Ross (ed.), *Universal Abandon? The Politics of Postmodernism*. Edinburgh: Edinburgh University Press.

Gill, R. (1991) Ideology and Popular Radio: A Discourse Analytic Examination of Disc Jockeys' Talk. Unpublished PhD Thesis, Loughborough University.

Gill, R. (1995) Theorising the Gender–Technology Relation. A CRICT discussion paper.

Gill, R. (forthcoming a) *Gender, Media and Culture*. Cambridge: Polity Press.

Gill, R. (forthcoming b) Power and empowerment in poststructuralist and feminist standpoint research. In C. Griffin, K. Henwood, and A. Phoenix (eds), *Standpoints and Differences: Essays in the Practice of Feminist Psychology*. London: Sage.

Graddol, D. and Swann, J. (1989) *Gender Voices*. Oxford: Blackwell.

Grint, K. and Woolgar, S. (1994) On some failures of nerve in constructivist and feminist analyses of technology. *Science, Technology and Human Values*. London: Taylor and Francis.

Hall, S. (1988) The toad in the garden: Thatcherism among the theorists. In C. Nelson and L. Grossberg (eds), *Marxism and the Interpretation of Culture*. London: Macmillan.

Haraway, D. (1991) *Simians, Cyborgs and Women: The Reinvention of Nature*. London: Routledge.

Henwood, K. and Pidgeon, N. (1995) Remaking the link: qualitative research and feminist standpoint theory. *Feminism & Psychology* 5(1), 7–30.

Herrnstein Smith, B. (1988) *Contingencies of Value: Alternative Perspectives for Critical Theory*. Cambridge, MA: Harvard University Press.

Hewitt, J.P. and Stokes, R. (1975) Disclaimers. *American Sociological Review* 40, 1–11.

hooks, b. (1985) *Feminist Theory from Margin to Center*. Boston, MA: South End Press.

Jackson, S. (1992) The amazing deconstructing woman. *Trouble and Strife* 25, 25–31.

Kirkup, G. and Smith-Keller, L. (1992) *Inventing Women: Science, Technology and Gender*. Cambridge: Polity Press.

Lovibond, S. (1989) Feminism and postmodernism. *New Left Review* 178, 5–28.

Mol, A.-M. and Hirschauer, S. (1995) Beyond embrace: multiple sexes at multiple sites. *Science, Technology and Human Values*.

Oakley, A. (1979) *Becoming a Mother*. Oxford: Martin Robertson.

Parker, I. (1989) *The Crisis in Modern Social Psychology and How to End it*. London: Routledge.

Parker, I. (1992) *Discourse Dynamics*. London: Routledge.

Parker, I. and Burman, E. (1993) Against discursive imperialism, empiricism and constructionism: thirty-two problems with discourse analysis. In E. Burman and I. Parker (eds), *Discourse Analytic Research: Repertoires and Readings of Texts in Action*. London: Routledge.

Potter, J., Wetherell, M., Gill, R. and Edwards, D. (1990) Discourse: noun, verb or social practice? *Philosophical Psychology* 3, 205–17.

Reinharz, S. (1983) Experiential analysis: a contribution to feminist research. In G. Bowles and R. Duelli-Klein (eds), *Theories of Women's Studies*. London: Routledge and Kegan Paul.

Segal, L. (1987) *Is the Future Female? Troubled Thoughts on Contemporary Feminism*. London: Virago.

Soper, K. (1991) Postmodernism, subjectivity and the question of value. *New Left Review* 186, 120–8.

Spender, D. (1985) *Man Made Language*. London: Routledge and Kegan Paul.

Squires, J. (ed.) (1993) *Principled Positions: Postmodernism and the Rediscovery of Value*. London: Lawrence and Wishart.

Stanley, J. (1977) Gender marking in American English. In A.P. Neilson (ed.), *Sexism and Language*. Urbana, IL.

Weedon, C. (1987) *Feminist Practice and Poststructuralist Theory*. Oxford: Blackwell.

Wetherell, M., Stiven, H. and Potter, J. (1987) Unequal egalitarianism: a preliminary study of discourses concerning gender and employment opportunities. *British Journal of Social Psychology* 26, 25–41.

Wetherell, M. and Potter, J. (1992) *Mapping the Language of Racism: Discourse and the Legitimation of Exploitation*. Hemel Hempstead: Harvester Wheatsheaf.

Wilkinson, S. (1988) The role of reflexivity in feminist psychology. *Women's Studies International Forum* 11(5), 493–502.

Woolgar, S. and Pawluch, H. (1985) Ontological gerrymandering: the anatomy of social problems explanations. *Social Problems* 32, 214–27.

Index

Note:
The letter n following a page number indicates a reference in the notes.